HJ1080
ae H9977

DATE DUE FOR RETURN

NEW ACCESSION
CANCELLED

15 JUN 1977

15. NOV. 1977

20 FEB 1978

-9. JUN. 1978

-5. DEC. 1980

-11 MAY 1981

-8 DEC. 1981

1 5 DEC 1994

4 DEC 1996

WITHDRAWN
FROM STOCK
QMUL LIBRARY

D1355902

QMW Library

23 0957677 6

CRISIS IN FINANCE: CROWN, FINANCIERS AND SOCIETY IN SEVENTEENTH-CENTURY FRANCE

CRISIS IN FINANCE: CROWN, FINANCIERS AND SOCIETY IN SEVENTEENTH-CENTURY FRANCE

Julian Dent

DAVID & CHARLES
NEWTON ABBOT

173628
DC (b) 121

0 7153 5979 7

QUEEN MARY
COLLEGE
LIBRARY

© Julian Dent 1973
All rights reserved. No part of this
publication may be reproduced, stored
in a retrieval system, or transmitted,
in any form or by any means, electronic,
mechanical, photocopying, recording or
otherwise, without the prior permission
of David & Charles (Holdings) Limited

Set in 11 on 12 point Monotype Imprint
and printed in Great Britain
by Latimer Trend & Company Ltd Plymouth
for David & Charles (Holdings) Limited
South Devon House   Newton Abbot   Devon

Contents

Introduction

FINANCIERS LOOMED very large in the society of seventeenth-century France. The tax-paying public hated them with a primeval and unremitting ferocity which expressed itself in violence ranging from isolated lynchings of financiers to bloody revolts of whole provinces. The largely inarticulate anger of the masses was translated on to the printed page by pamphleteers and other social critics. Their testimony has a quality that did not change appreciably over the century. It was composed of a series of charges: financiers were men of low origins who made a great deal of money out of the state's financial system; they bought expensive official posts, built mansions, acquired estates, and gave large marriage portions to their children; the financiers formed a conspiracy of thieves united in their aim of destroying the state; they corrupted the rest of society by the scandalous example they gave of high living, which caused less wealthy men to ruin themselves by attempts at emulation. In short, France would be better off without them.

The most severe criticism of the financiers was written by men who had personal knowledge of the financial system. Jean Bourgoin, who wrote in the early seventeenth century, had been the clerk of a financier, while Jean de La Bruyère, who wrote towards the end of the century, was the son of a *contrôleur-général des rentes sur l'Hôtel de Ville*, and himself owned a post of *trésorier-général de France* of Caen. Bourgoin brought a baroque flurry to his attack on financiers. He started off by saying that they should all be hanged, and he continued:

Les financiers sont dénaturés, inhumains et enclins à la ruine de l'état.[1]

La Bruyère, as befitted a man of classical interests, was more moderate. The financier is, he said, a bear whom no one knows how to tame. He was as much puzzled as angry about the moral failings of financiers:

> *Champagne*, au sortir d'un long dîner qui lui enfle l'estomac, et dans les douces fumées d'un vin d'Avenay ou de Sillery, signe un ordre qu'on lui présente, qui ôterait le pain à toute une province si l'on n'y remédiait. Il est excusable: quel moyen de comprendre dans la première heure de la digestion, qu'on puisse quelque part mourir de faim?

La Bruyère was rather remarkable in the seventeenth century in that he possessed a social conscience. He was genuinely distressed by the suffering of the lower orders. But he was also aware of the charge that most members of polite society would have considered the most serious that could be made against financiers:

> Si certains morts revenaient au monde, et s'ils voyaient leurs grands noms portés, et leurs terres les mieux titrées avec leurs châteaux et leurs maisons antiques, possédées par des gens dont les pères étaient peut-être leurs métayers, quelle opinion pourraient-ils avoir de notre siècle?

But at the same time, he points out how ambivalent polite society was towards financiers:

> Si le financier manque son coup, les courtisans disent de lui: C'est un bourgeois, un homme de rien, un malotru; s'il réussit, ils lui demandent sa fille.[2]

There was in fact a dilemma in the collective consciousness of seventeenth-century society about financiers. They were hated on the one hand, but accepted on the other. What made things even more difficult was the fact that, philosophically speaking, they should not have existed. If France was composed, as people from Charles Loyseau to Bishop Bossuet insisted, of a neatly defined and divinely inspired hierarchy in which everyone had his place, the financiers, who were socially mobile, had no fixed position and were simply not part of France. Furthermore, even if one abandoned the certitudes of philosophy for the contingencies of history, there was no clear reason why financiers should exist. On the face of it there was no need for them in France. While in England Elizabeth I was driven to distraction by her parliament's unwillingness to defray the cost of wars which parliament, not she, had wanted, in France Henri IV and the Duc de Sully claimed that they had salted away millions of livres in the Bastille.[3] On the one hand, in the great sequence of legislation of 1640–2 the English Long Parliament buried the ignoble tricks by which Charles I had sought to evade the firm but kindly hand of his legislature. Meanwhile, on the other hand, Cardinal Richelieu and his creatures raised the level of French taxation to unprecedented heights by the use of expedients that made the activities of the English administration of the 1630s seem pure and rather innocent.[4] The fiscal situation that confronted Charles II was, it is true, rather better than that which had confronted his predecessors, but even so he was chronically poor. And while he wrestled with his recalcitrant Parliament, his cousin the king of France had the resources to wage war of an agreeably landed and gentlemanly kind, build an appropriately magnificent residence at Versailles, and make his Stuart poor relation his pensioner.

One thing, observers agreed, was abundantly clear: the French Crown had a large income, which grew prodigiously over time. In the early eighteenth century, it was calculated that royal resources had increased in the following way. In 1514 Louis XII commanded an annual revenue of 7,650,000 livres. In 1547 François I raised over 14 million livres. By 1574 the annual figure was some 21 million livres. By 1581, it was getting on for 32 million livres. Thereafter the situation was fairly static until 1610, when revenues were calculated to stand at 32,589,659 livres. But under Richelieu, a series of satisfying upward leaps occurred. By 1643, the income of the French Crown had risen to some 79 million livres. Another lull ensued. By 1661, the total had risen merely to 84 million livres. But, taken over the long view, this last figure was dramatic enough. In 1661, the revenues of the French Crown were nearly eleven times bigger than they had been in 1514.[5]

And yet, for all the jealous glances shot across the Channel, and for all the apparently effortless increases of French taxation, the French fiscal system staggered from one crisis to another, barely performing the complicated feat of standing upright under two centuries of buffeting. Though the amount of money that was supposed to accrue annually to the Crown might double and double again, the monarchy was able only at the very best of times, and for short and infrequent periods, to break even. It had to run faster and faster to stay at best balanced on a knife-edge between bankruptcy and solvency. The situation would have seemed normal enough to the Red Queen, but it was a continuing nightmare to men brought up in a psychological and philosophical frame of reference where fixity and clarity, subordination and order, were deemed natural, reflecting the laws of God.

One of the major causes of this insufficiency of royal income in the sixteenth century was, obviously, the price revolution. But this was already weakening in France as the second third of the seventeenth century began. As the tide of inflation ebbed, the falling level revealed an aged causal chain whose effect in raising royal expenditure had been temporarily hidden. The monarchy, as it had done since the time of Hugues Capet, spent too much money. Its normal methods of extracting money were excessively inefficient. To make money to compensate for the deficiencies of normal methods, the Crown had recourse to expedients which periodically—and not surprisingly—brought it to financial ruin. And what is more, it never learned. It could not understand that a man can be in desperate financial straits even though from time to time large sums pass through his hands. Nor could it ever resist short-term profit at the expense of long-term and solid investment.

The problem was discussed in general terms and at length by eighteenth-century fiscal theorists like Forbonnais and Moreau de Beaumont.[6] But neither of them was able to explain why the situation should have persisted. The answer to this question is complex. On the one hand, it involves examination of the structure of administrative institutions, to explain the inability of the financial machine to provide adequate support for the government despite the enormous increases in the taxes paid by primary taxpayers. But inefficiency on its own, complicated, devious and wide-ranging though it was, is not enough to explain the continuing financial crisis. The point is that everybody knew something, albeit nothing very precise, about the flamboyant corruption of tax-collecting agencies, and there was a spate of comment on the gravity of the situation, together with sugges-

tions on what should be done about it. Further than this, royal
ministers like Effiat and Colbert worked with enormous energy
and high intelligence to put things right. It seems probable that
the vast bulk of the population, the peasants, divided though
they might be into various strata by economic and social factors,
were united at least in their hostility to *Taille, Taillon, Etape,
Subsistance* and *Gabelle.*

With such leadership and such support, it would appear that
something could have been done. Yet it was not. To find out
why not involves first an examination of the kind of people recruited to the financial administration. This would explain both
the corruption of institutions and hostility to their reform. But
there is more yet that needs to be examined. Had corrupt
members of the financial administration been genuinely un-
popular in governmental circles; had there been, for example, a
substantial body of opinion hostile to financial administrators
amongst the men who were made *intendants de justice, police et
finances* and secretaries of state, something might yet have been
done. It becomes necessary to examine why such opinion did not
exist, or if it did exist, why it was not effective. This involves an
analysis of various key groups in French government and the
relationships of such groups with the financial world. In short,
then, this study must deal first with institutions, and then with
men. The way in which this dual task is undertaken demands
some explanation.

Contrary to what one might have expected, relatively little has
been written by modern historians on the form and operation of
the financial system in the seventeenth century. It is true that
research has illuminated vital aspects of the system as it existed
during the century—one thinks immediately of Mousnier on the
venality of offices under Henry IV and Louis XIII, and of
Esmonin on the Taille under Colbert.[7] But it is important to
realise that the conditions described in a study limited to a particular period may not apply to another period. For example, the
Crown could not rely on income from the sale of offices under
Mazarin to anything like the extent of its reliance on such a
resource under Richelieu. This decline in the value of venality
was not permanent, and by the end of the century, the Crown
was once more creating and selling offices. From an examination

of the two high points of selling, the gap in the middle, which lasted for the best part of two decades, could hardly have been deduced. Yet it was there, and made its presence felt throughout the length and breadth of France as the government turned to more desperate expedients and ever more savage methods of extracting the income from such expedients. Or take the Taille: the normal conditions of its levy as they are described by Esmonin were virtually in abeyance throughout the period of Mazarin's ministry. To ignore such variation in some resources, and deviation in the extraction of others, is to miss an essential quality of French financial administration in the seventeenth century. What is more, to this phenomenon of kaleidoscopic change in operation one must add the fact that no one has attempted to relate the elements of royal income together in a systematic way for the seventeenth century. It would be quite wrong to assume that the excellent works of MM Doucet and Zeller dealing with the sixteenth century, and of M Marion and Professor Bosher dealing with the eighteenth century, have much relevance for the century between—which stands as a curiously ill-defined halfway house.[8] There are enormous gaps in the knowledge of quite basic elements in the structure of French finance in the seventeenth century. The first part of this book is therefore devoted to filling the worst of these gaps, and, more important, to showing as precisely as possible what the structure was of financial institutions, how they fitted together, and how they brought in the money that kept the monarchy alive.

It rapidly became apparent during the undertaking of this task that an administrative approach was not enough. If one relies purely on government pronouncements, one can produce a nicely articulated picture of the French finances as in theory they should have operated. But such a picture is always inadequate, and often basically wrong. Take, for example, Marion's article on the post of *contrôleur-général des finances*, in which it is stated that, before Colbert's reorganisation of the royal finances in the 1660s, the contrôleur-général exercised a purely passive role as a certifier and authenticator of other officials' administrative acts.[9] This is an accurate reflection of reiterated *règlements* describing the duties of the contrôleur. But since nobody outside the *cours souveraines* paid attention to such règlements, it is unwise to accept their authority. In fact Particelli d'Emery was anything but passive while he was contrôleur-général from 1643 until 1647. He ran the whole financial system as though he was *surintendant des finances*.

The formal structure of institutions *was* important, if only because it provided a framework behind which technically illegal operations could be undertaken in safety, and because bodies like the *Chambre des Comptes* of Paris made such a fuss if they found out how large the gap was between legal form and day-to-day operation of institutions. But at the same time, if one wants to find out exactly what went on, one has to come to terms with a basic fact about seventeenth-century French financial institutions. The people who ran the institutions defined the way in which those institutions worked. This is not to say that administrators sat down and thought out in a formal way just what it was that they were doing, but rather that individual administrators ran their own part of the administrative system in individual and particular ways, and that when a post changed hands it was very likely to change almost out of recognition. But this is only the most obvious element of the individualism and particularity of French finance. That is to say, it deals only with people who held formally constituted posts. There was a whole miasma of people around the nexus of defined posts. These persons did not have any post in the royal finances. Yet they were vitally involved in expedients like treaties, *Rentes sur l'Hôtel de Ville* and loans.

Given the extreme importance of such expedients, known formally as Extraordinary Affairs, which produced money over and above that produced by the Ordinary Financial Machine with its formally constituted posts and defined and limited sources of income, and given the vague and ill-defined body of people who were involved in such expedients, it becomes apparent that some new approach must be found to deal with the problem of understanding and elucidating French finance in the seventeenth century. Since the structures involved had little to do with formally defined institutions, it is necessary to search for structures, or at least common patterns of behaviour, amongst all those involved in any way in finance. The only way to undertake such a study is by looking for as many financiers as one can find, and subjecting their careers to as detailed and minute an analysis as can be achieved.

The best conceptual framework for such an examination of the financiers is a series of questions. The first of these is this: What was a financier? It can be answered here and now. A financier, under the *ancien régime*, was a man who handled 'the finances, that is to say, the King's money. In general this name is given to all those known to be involved in the farms, *régies*, undertakings or enterprises which concern the revenues of the King.' This definition from the *Encyclopédie méthodique* was written on the eve of the French Revolution, but it holds good for the seventeenth century.[10] The other questions can be rapidly stated. They are these: What were the origins of the financiers geographically and socially? How did financiers succeed in the finances? How did they fail? To what use did they put such money as they made? What points of contact were there between financiers and other groups in French society? What were the families of financiers like? Were financiers in fact socially mobile? Lastly, by way of conclusion, comes the question: What sort of people were financiers?

Data were found on 744 people who had some involvement in the royal finances, most of whom were active during the period 1600–90. Data were also found on 810 people who were related to such financiers by either blood, marriage, or business interest. Working on the data that had been found revealed that the big questions of origin, ascent, and so on, while they remained important, had to be broken down into components before useful analysis could be undertaken. For example, a financier's origin is composed of a number of factors: his family's place of origin, his own place of birth, his father's occupation and quality, his mother's quality, and the financier's first known occupation. Analysing a man's career in the royal finances involved placing him in the structure of financial administration, which was composed of at least forty-eight *categories* of post. Each category might be composed of twenty-five distinct *sets* of offices or commissions. And this concerns merely official position. Analysis of a man's conduct as a financier involved dealing with sixty-six major factors. But this was not all. Since many financiers and members of financiers' extended families held posts outside the finances, it was necessary to consider aspects of the non-financial governance of France, which was composed of tens of thousands of posts. Even to analyse the magistrates of the more important cours souveraines, from *Parlement* to *Chambre aux Deniers*, involved twenty-nine grades of officer spread over thirty-nine separate institutions. There were similar problems of enumeration and size with central non-financial administration (which I call modern administrative machine); local judicial institutions; military posts connected with regular army, navy and militia; the Church; the royal court; and so on. In the end analysis of all the data on all the people involved the asking of some 750,000 separate questions.

It need hardly be said that it was necessary to use a computer to handle the body of data and questions. Within their limits, which become clearly understood after working with them, computers are the only way to handle problems of mass or group history with accuracy and speed. As all researchers do, the social historian frames hypotheses, in this case about the nature of the group or society that he is studying. Given the structure of the human mind, the judgements that are made are usually, at least in part and often very largely, intuitive. And they are based for the most part on data derived from a relatively small number of cases that spring to mind. But such judgements are really no more than speculation unless they can be checked exhaustively, and verified or discarded. Without this process of checking, one can make serious errors. The point is that the computer makes such checking very easy, and, which is more important, very quick.

Nor is this all, for the data that the computer prints out, even the basic data statistics produced before more specific analyses are undertaken, suggest all sorts of possibilities that would not have been considered had the computer not been used. These possibilities can be fed back into the computer, and tested. And so a process is begun that ends up with a refinement of hypotheses and a more acute sense of the structure and convoluteness of the population that one is studying. It becomes apparent what is truly typical and what atypical. The limitations of the data become clear. For example, it is quite impossible to say much in a general way about the size of financiers' fortunes. But even more important is the fact that quantitative methods have a way of forcing one to reject interpretations that previously would have been accepted without question. The origins of financiers proved to be an example of this. At the beginning it seemed probable that the financiers were drawn from the upper levels of the middle class. The data contradicted this idea. Financiers could not be tied to any particular class, and it was very clear that they had little to do with what one might call 'bourgeois capital accumulation'. Furthermore, the world of the financiers existed apart from the world of production and trade. Though a few members of the latter might enter the former, they found themselves in the company of men who were central administrators, lawyers, soldiers, clerics, or courtiers, or else professional financiers sprung from the dragon's teeth of war itself.

What, in general terms, does this study show about French government and society in the seventeenth century? There was much that seemed new about government. Looking back from the year 1680, it would have been clear that the ambit of government had increased enormously since the accession of Louis XI in 1461. New institutions had been created, like the secretary-ships of state and the various *intendances*. Old institutions had been refurbished and extended. At the centre there was the powerful *Conseil du Roi*, and in the provinces a continually proliferating system of *bailliages*, *sénéchaussées*, *présidiaux*, *généralités*, and so on. Old representative bodies, which might have maintained a constitutionalist opposition to the Crown, either were permitted to fall into desuetude, like the Estates-General of the kingdom and some of the provincial Estates, or else were browbeaten until they exhaustedly agreed to do what the Crown wanted. The cours souveraines of France were slowly stifled, until in 1673 their power of remonstrance was so drastically reduced that it ceased to hamper the monarchy.

Roman law, which saw an extraordinary vogue in the sixteenth and seventeenth centuries, gave a powerful theoretical justification for and provided a necessary co-ordination of the activities of successive monarchs and their advisers. So powerful was the Roman stress on centralisation and order, discipline and subordination, that constitutionalist thought did not re-emerge in any considerable form until the early eighteenth century, when it was to become the ideological force which bound Robe and Sword together in an alliance of inestimable significance.[11] For the moment, however, the tide of history seemed to be flowing with the absolute monarchy of Louis XIV, before whose majesty the once mighty nobility now trembled, grateful that their last major indulgence in the heady joys of insurrection—the Fronde —should be conditionally forgiven. The Ludovician monarchy at the zenith of its power and reputation was to serve monarchs in lesser and less favoured lands throughout Europe during the later seventeenth and eighteenth centuries as a pattern for modern, efficient, reliable, absolute government. Historians, in their turn, have rightly stressed the newness and the efficiency of the absolute monarchy in France, and it has been said with a good deal of force that the late seventeenth century saw the creation of the first genuinely bureaucratic government of the modern age, perhaps even the first in the history of the world.[12]

But, at the same time, it is important to point out that there was a great deal about the French monarchy in the last two centuries of its pre-revolutionary existence that dated from long before the rise of what some historians still call the New Monarchy. More than anything else, this study shows that France was far more closely bound to the medieval world than historians might have thought. Much of the local administration of the country derived from the Capetian period, particularly the reign of Louis IX (1226–70). Roman law had been neither unknown to nor unused by monarchs in the twelfth century. The intendants could trace their institutional ancestry back to the *missi dominici* of the Carolingian age. The Crown itself, pinnacle of the absolutist state, was conferred in a ceremony whose origins were lost in the far off mists of Merovingian France. Nor was the medieval legacy of the French monarchy limited to factors which kings would have been pleased to consider positive elements of their absolute power. Even in the seventeenth century, power itself remained dangerously personal. There was little conception of an impersonal state to which citizens were bound in allegiance. Just as his predecessors had been over the centuries, the king *was* France—sworn protector of the people, fount of authority and law. Were he weak, or should he succeed to the throne as a minor, should he in fact be unable to provide a personal focus to the loyalty of the people of France, then all manner of age-old forces would once more begin to make themselves felt: nobles, magistrates of cours souveraines, the populations of large towns and cities, all would disport themselves in ways reminiscent of the bad old days of the early fifteenth century.

There were, then, many things about the absolute monarchy of the seventeenth and eighteenth centuries that were very old, yet which had important roles to play, some positive, some negative, in the disparate congeries of institutions which are commonly lumped together as the *ancien régime*. And there is a second point that should be stressed: the development of the monarchy was by no means a uniform linear progression towards a more or less fully bureaucratised absolutist state. There were phases of great development: the reign of François I, the administration of Richelieu (particularly the years 1624–35), the administration of Colbert. Equally, there were phases of stagnation, and even of regression: the civil wars of the later sixteenth century, the minorities of Louis XIII and Louis XIV, the Regency of Orléans. During such periods of regression, it seemed at times almost as if the monarchy was about to be destroyed. Certainly the governmental development of previous periods of state-building would be called into question, and occasionally even reversed. An obvious example of this is the suppression of intendances during the Fronde; another is the Polysynodie experiment that followed the death of Louis XIV. But the field in which the most serious reverses tended to take place was undoubtedly the royal finances, for these combined extreme fragility with a medieval imprint far less congruent with the particular conditions of the seventeenth and eighteenth centuries than that borne by the more radically transformed institutions of more general central government—in particular the Conseil du Roi.

It is important not to overstress the weakness of the royal finances. As was mentioned a few pages ago, the theoretical income of the Crown increased enormously in the years 1514–1661. It was to continue to increase down to the end of the reign of Louis XIV and beyond. Despite the fact that actual receipts did not equal theoretical income, nevertheless it would be otiose to pretend that Louis XIV was not vastly better off than any of his predecessors. He could hardly have kept western Europe in turmoil for forty years without the possession of considerable funds, for even kings needed to put up some kind of collateral for the loans that they so recklessly contracted. And if the ability to extract larger and larger sums from a given area—even if those sums did not always find their way into the royal coffers—is evidence of a powerful state, then France was indeed powerful. Moreover, it is necessary to concede that the activity of the apparently most modern, or, if you will, absolutist, element of the monarchy's institutional apparatus, the *Intendance de Justice, Police et Finances*, was intimately, though not exclusively, bound up with the royal desire for larger income.[13]

Nevertheless, at the centre of affairs, where one might legitimately have presumed that the tide of royal absolutism would have flowed strongest, the monarchy itself showed a critical ambivalence towards the whole subject of royal finance. Successive kings could see in the abstract the advantages of being economical, and of not imposing an unbearable load of taxation on peasants. Furthermore, there could be no question of doubting the value of making royal officials render accurate and honest account of the sums that they had received and paid out in the royal service. But at heart men like Richelieu, Mazarin and Louis XIV simply did not think such things very important. The attitude of kings and their advisers to economy, accounting and the situation of the vast bulk of the population was comparable to that of governments and business corporations in the later twentieth century towards the control of pollution of the environment: such goals may be obviously desirable, and even ultimately essential to survival, but their pursuit can never be allowed to interfere for one moment in the quest for the dual shibboleths of national security and profits. In the seventeenth century, if the French Crown or its advisers wanted money, then they would do anything, no matter how reckless, to get it. The irresponsible attitude of those in high places may have changed in the eighteenth century. Certainly the calibre of financial officials improved somewhat, and it has been argued that the fiscal reforms carried out in the early stages of the French Revolution owed a great deal to institutional developments taking place during the last few decades of the *ancien régime*, and to the further plans of the men who were the force behind such changes.

But the fact remains that it was a financial crisis which brought
the monarchy to its knees in the later 1780s. That crisis does not
seem to have been fundamentally different from those of 1715,
1661, or even 1559. The Crown had borrowed so much money
that it found even the paying of interest too great a burden. It
therefore collapsed into bankruptcy. The different political,
economic and social conditions obtaining at the time of each
bankruptcy decreed whether the results of their occurrence
should be trifling or disastrous.

To speak more specifically of the finances of the seventeenth
century and of their relationship to government as a whole, it is
clear that the advances in financial administration made in the
sixteenth and seventeenth centuries, particularly during the
reign of Henri IV (1589–1610), the surintendance of the Maréchal d'Effiat (1626–32) and the administration of Colbert (1661–
83), were immensely fragile. During the years 1635–61 and
1683–1715, financiers came to dominate the financial administration of the state, parcelling it up into private fiefs in a fragmenta-
tion of authority and power redolent more of a low species of
bastard feudalism than of an absolutist bureaucracy. All this
illustrates how weak, halting and uncertain the development of
absolutism was, and how far it was compromised by Bourbon
military activities and the consequent need for money. What
emerges more than anything else is the crippling incompleteness
of the reorganisation of the royal finances carried out in the sixteenth and seventeenth centuries. France could certainly have
supported armies and expenditures far larger than those of the
reign of Louis XIV. The example of Brandenburg-Prussia
shows what could be done on an economic base far weaker than
that of early modern France. The reason for the incompleteness
of French reorganisation has much to do with the length of
French history and the strength of old tradition. This kind of
argument could be applied to a number of fields, but it is relevant
here to discuss only the finances and that part of the social field
which had direct relationships with those finances.

The fiscal forms by which the French monarchy essentially
supported itself down to the Revolution of 1789 were laid down
by the mid-fifteenth century: they were *Taille* and *Aides*. These
were elaborated and expanded over the centuries. Other taxes

gradually emerged from them and acquired a separate existence, as the *Gabelles* differentiated themselves from their parent Aides during the sixteenth and seventeenth centuries. Other taxes were, it is true, added later. But the fact remains that the fiscal base, with its exemptions, its erratic assessment, and its sheer inefficiency, was never fundamentally altered. The only important financial devices that the Crown added after the beginning of the sixteenth century were essentially merely expedients which anticipated income extracted by means of the basic fiscal forms. There was never any serious and sustained attempt to change this situation. Privileged groups were always able to remove the teeth of royal proposals to tax a wider segment of the population by bribing the Crown to make exemptions—which came to include most of the members of the groups which had previously had exemption from older taxes. The classic examples here are the *Capitation* and the *Vingtième*.

From a financial point of view, old regime France was in itself a classic example of a phenomenon more obviously seen in the problems of the British economy in the late nineteenth century. In Britain, the first industrial revolution, based on an earlier revolution in banking and on a relatively primitive technology in which scientific principles were almost at a discount, was wildly successful, largely, one suspects, because of the relative backwardness of the rest of the world at that time. This success, so easily accomplished (from the point of view of the entrepreneur at least), bred a contempt for science and technology, for scientific and technological education, and for the possible industrial applications of new discoveries. As a result, in the second—and ultimately much more significant—industrial revolution of the later nineteenth century, Britain lagged distressingly behind countries like the United States of America, Germany and Japan, which possessed shorter industrial traditions that did not inhibit the ready acceptance of more efficient techniques and, indeed, whole new industries.

The government of old regime France suffered from a legacy comparable in certain ways to that of nineteenth-century Britain. French government in the seventeenth and eighteenth centuries was crippled by the fact that the form of public administration had become too nearly complete in the thirteenth and fourteenth centuries. The epiphenomena of absolutism—in particular the intendant system of Richelieu and Colbert, and the division of labour and specialisation of the work of the Conseil du Roi which began under Richelieu and was more or less completed towards the end of the reign of Louis XIV in what can fairly be called the bureaucratisation of French central administration—concealed the fact that a vast accretion of substrata of ancient administrative institutions and techniques continued to function. Their operatives, in parlements, chambres des comptes, bureaux des finances, and innumerable other places, might pay lip-service to the absolutist ideals of the monarchy. But in their hearts they nourished black thoughts of the revenge that they would take once the great king, whom they so much feared, was dead.

States younger than France, borrowing from the administrative ideas forged in the French monarchy's attempts to deal with its social and political difficulties at home and with its concern with military and diplomatic affairs on the international scene, could apply those ideas far more successfully to their more malleable social, administrative and economic situations. The Great Elector, Frederick William I and Frederick the Great could achieve organisational success of a kind that Colbert could conceive only as a series of ever-receding mirages, which were to achieve a brief reality only in the promising but ultimately tragic experiment of New France.

The mirage specific to Colbert's view of the royal finances was that of royal solvency, and it was glimpsed only for a fleeting decade after 1661 before it was obscured for ever by the dust of war. The sad fact is that in finance the king barely went through the motions of modernisation and rationalisation in the 1660s before he and the triumphant Louvois forced Colbert to return to the bad old days of the past. As far as the financiers were concerned, this portentous change in royal policy meant that far from being integrated into and subjected by a public system of bureaucratic administration, they were able to regain their former privileged semiprivate relationship with the Crown, while Colbert, in a desperate attempt to continue his reforms of government and society as well as meet the ever-growing demands of the military, was forced to resort after 1672 to the kinds of obfuscation and deceit in the state's finances which he had once believed could be torn out, root and branch.

The extraordinary continued vitality of old methods of financing the state had its parallel in the role played by financiers in society at large, a role which fits into what has been revealed of French society under the *ancien régime* in the works of social and demographic historians and historical sociologists. Attention has been focused on the situation of the peasantry and the rural situation generally in works by Roupnel, Bloch, Goubert, Le Roy Ladurie and others.[14] In a sense, the general crisis of the seventeenth century in its rural manifestations took France back to the great crises of disease and subsistence of the fourteenth and fifteenth centuries. What is clear, too, is that the effects of crisis were present at other levels of society. The general social mobility of the sixteenth century came more or less to an end. Only the financiers and the central administrators continued to rise while the crisis was still taking place. Their rise was indicative not of a transformation of French society, but rather of the fascination of French kings with ritualised mass violence. Financiers whipped in money from local areas. Intendants helped them, and kept the populace quiet. As a result, the monarchy could fight its wars. Complaisantly, it permitted both financiers and central administrators to prosper enormously and to use the money that they made to rise to more prestigious levels of society.

What did this rise signify? To contemporaries like La Bruyère it seemed that financiers were taking over French society. But the data do not confirm this assumption. The rise of financiers was really the rise of a series of individual families. These had no concept of collective class action, but merely of personal ambition based on family. The rise of such families had been going on for at least two centuries before 1600, and it had not destroyed the old France of king, nobility and peasantry by 1700. On the contrary, financiers strengthened the old social and governmental systems, transfusing new blood, talent and naïve enthusiasm into them at a time when the best that was left to older families like the La Rochefoucauld seemed to be an elegant, civilised and justified cynicism about French society and the monarchy it served.

Notes to the Introduction are on pages 244–5

PART 1

THE ADMINISTRATION OF FINANCE

Chapter 1 THE ORDINARY
FINANCIAL MACHINE

IF MEN in the seventeenth century ever waxed enthusiastic over financial institutions, it was not because of any drama or attraction inherent in such things, but rather because the form of such institutions reflected the desire of monarchs, and those who served them, to create an order and clarity in government which would mirror on earth the structure of the heavens themselves. The theological implications of the Cartesian system might worry both its progenitor and the ecclesiastical authorities, but its stress on common sense defined as reason struck a sympathetic note in the hearts of all manner of men, not least the solemn drudges who repeated, year after year, descriptions of the framework of French institutions in the annual, quasi-official *Etats de la France*.[1]

From the writings of such authors and from the texts of innumerable royal *règlements*, a clear and distinct idea of financial institutions can be built up. The *surintendant des finances* and the *Conseil du Roi* stood at the apex of the administrative pyramid. They performed the function of *ordonnancement des fonds*, that is to say, of ordering the disposition of royal resources. Below them came the category of *comptables*, those who were involved in actually disposing funds as the central directorate dictated. The head comptable was the *trésorier de l'Epargne*. The *Epargne* itself was where funds came in and went out, and so naturally one comes to the question of actual resources. These were divided formally into two categories, Ordinary and Extraordinary. Under the first heading came traditional and accepted taxation. Under the second came everything else, and in particular expedients, like the venality of offices, and credit, both public (*Rentes sur l'Hôtel de Ville de Paris*) and private (short-term loans). The framework was completed by the accounting systems of the state.

The trouble was that this short and clear-cut description related only to what the government thought it good that the world at large should see. The formal financial institutions were in fact quite unsuited to the inordinately heavy demands that the monarchy made of them, and so it was necessary to conduct financial administration outside the normal modes of operation of such institutions. These normal modes were written into laws that the monarchy had itself made long ago, but the monarchy was not strong enough to change those laws, even under Richelieu. Things were much worse after his death. Even after the Fronde, the absolutist state found it difficult to control institutions like the *Parlement* and *Chambre des Comptes* of Paris. It knew well that to attempt to reorganise its financial machine on more productive lines would have reversed its close-fought victory over the political aspirations of the high robe nobility and the princes. Such a reorganisation was made even less likely since it was precisely on the ground of the administration of the royal finances that the first Fronde had broken out. The constitutional demands of the Chambre Saint-Louis in 1648 had stemmed from dissatisfaction with the financial policies of Mazarin and Particelli d'Emery and, indeed, with the whole trend of royal financial devices since the reign of François I.

As a result of the Crown's failure to reorganise institutions, financial administrators resorted to certain tactics which further obscure the picture of what really happened in the royal finances. Everything that was done had to be made to look as though it were legal, and it is from the dressing-up of extra-legal devices in para-legal terms that much of the complication of the system was derived. This central problem can be resolved only by taking the elements of the financial machine, defining their legal form, showing how the government in its search for short-term credit operated outside legal form, and how it reconciled its actions with legality by means of devices like forged documents which would satisfy the vigilance of bodies like the Chambre des Comptes and thus allay, it was hoped, the hostility of the population at large. Showing how the government covered up the high price which it paid for credit, a price far above the legal interest rate of 5·55 per cent, by uttering all kinds of fictitious or fraudulent documents, is complex enough. What makes analysis of the financial machine more complex still is the fact that corruption of the legal framework operated to a second end. The state had to allow those who might be persuaded to lend to it an inducement, which took the form of allowing men with money to monopolise large sectors of the financial machine. This meant that while the formal relationship of the surintendant des finances and the *trésorier des Parties Casuelles* worked in one way, the informal relationship of Nicolas Fouquet and Claude Girardin, an important financier who bought a treasurership around 1660, worked in quite another. On one level Girardin was a subordinate officer, on another he was a large-scale royal creditor who could demand to be placated by all kinds of illegal payments. An even better example of this distinction between formal and informal, or between legal and actual, relationships can be seen in the way in which Fouquet went in mortal fear that his own clerks might plan and accomplish his downfall.

It is clear, then, that the legal form of institutions was of political importance, in that care had to be taken to make it appear that form was being observed, but that the way in which administration operated, particularly in relation to expedients and credit, cut across formal lines of demarcation. The best example of this lies in the post of *contrôleur-général des finances*. Although this was merely an accounting post, Particelli d'Emery acted, while contrôleur-général, as though he were surintendant des finances, while his successors failed even to operate as accounting officials, their work being carried out by their own *premier commis*. In considering each institution, it is imperative to consider the individual people holding office just as much as the legal definition of their function. The general conclusion to be derived from this procedure is that the state depended in its search for credit almost entirely on financiers, and indeed abandoned the control of financial administration to them. The basic theme of the first part of this book is an explanation of how and why this was so.

CENTRAL DIRECTION

The focal point of the Ordinary Machine was the *Surintendance des Finances*. This was a royal commission, the changes in whose structure during the seventeenth century reflected the recurrent dissatisfaction felt by kings, regents and their advisers concerning the central direction of financial administration. At times during the century the surintendance was exercised by a single person, at other times by a pair of officials, who might be very hostile to one another. Occasionally it was suppressed completely, its functions being carried out by a *Conseil des Finances*.

The basic function of the surintendant lay in ordering how money should be levied and spent. This process was called the ordonnancement des fonds, the surintendant being consequently known as *ordonnateur principal des fonds*. The most important instrument of policy in the levying of money was the *Etat des recettes*. There were two forms of this. One was the *Etat par estimation*, which was drawn up at the beginning of the year by the surintendant and his clerks from tables of estimated receipts provided by the officers or farmers in charge of the various sources of royal income. At the end of the year, the receipts which were supposed actually to have come in were collated to form a final *Etat au vrai*, or corrected statement of funds available. The Etat par estimation was always difficult to draw up even when the country was at peace with foreign powers and subject to less than the normal level of the endemic local revolts discussed by Professors Mousnier and Porchnev. All kinds of local difficulties unforeseen at the beginning of the year conspired to lower the level of actual receipts. Similarly, the final Etat au vrai was at best approximate. Even under Colbert, it contained a certain amount of wish-fulfilment, reflecting the need to show what ought to have happened rather than the often bleak realities of the fiscal situation. The surintendant was also responsible for drawing up the statements of estimated and actual expenditure. Here again, the documents had an important political loading. Tenure of the surintendance depended to some degree at least on putting up a bold front. Expenditure of a particular year, especially during war, was habitually deferred or kept secret, and thus did not appear in the year's accounts.

There was, therefore, no way of knowing precisely what was happening to the royal finances at any given point. There was no credible French budget in the seventeenth century because the political dispositions of the administration militated against it, and because, even without the intrusion of politics, the cumbersomeness of that administration and the ineffectiveness of its accounting techniques would have made the drawing up of a budget impossible. It was possible only in time of peace and economy to use the various statements as rough guides for the conduct of policy. Henri IV and Sully were able, or so the latter said, on the basis of the broad relation of income to expenditure, to balance the royal accounts and even to save an average of 700,000 livres a year. But, given a monarch less concerned with economy than Henri IV, the patiently constructed edifice of financial stability crumbled into confusion, and it became necessary to live from hand to mouth, using disastrous expedients. During most of the seventeenth century the monarchy found itself in such a situation. In the middle of the century it was at times impossible to draw up the Etat au vrai, so confused had things become. In these circumstances the surintendant tended, if he were an effective figure, to become a sort of state banker. Thus is to be explained the role of both Particelli d'Emery and Fouquet. The conduct of both men in this field is discussed below in the section on loans.[2]

The surintendant was in theory assisted in his deliberations and administration by three elements of the nexus of administrative bodies known as the Conseil du Roi. These were the *Conseil Secret*, the *Conseil d'en Haut*, and the *Conseil des Finances*. The first two of these were responsible for general policy matters on the highest level. They were not particularly concerned with finance, but merely approved or disapproved matters sent to them by the Conseil des Finances. This last, though admittedly the most professional of all the elements of the Conseil du Roi, was really dependent during much of the century on the work of a small inner group of administrators, composed of the surintendant, directeurs, contrôleur-général, and intendants des finances, and the various central trésoriers. The group was called the *Petite Direction*. Its role was, originally, simply to sort out any difficulties that might slow down the conduct of business in the full Conseil des Finances. Such a mandate was so vague that it was possible to expand it until the Petite Direction took most of the important decisions itself, leaving to the Conseil des Finances the undemanding function of a rubber stamp. Early in the century, the Petite Direction had encountered opposition. In 1614 it was suppressed because the nobility felt that its existence excluded them from any say in financial affairs. By 1616, however, it was again in operation. It met at least twice a week, often at the house of the surintendant, occasionally in the apartments of the King or Queen Mother. By 1647 it was so well established that Particelli d'Emery was able to administer the royal finances using the Petite Direction without summoning the full Conseil des Finances. It was said, rather unkindly, that he felt better able to tackle administrative difficulties in his own way with so small a body. In it, opponents to his ideas were fewer and there were, therefore, fewer people to bribe. This method of administration was far less inefficient than the conventional picture of Particelli d'Emery would lead one to assume. Nicolas Fouquet had his own way of short-circuiting the full Conseil des Finances by 1661. As the Abbé de Choisy put it:

> The Conseil was . . . composed of two contrôleurs-généraux, two directeurs, two intendants (des finances), and the surintendant, who ran everything according to his own fancy. He was content to pay good salaries to the other members.[3]

The Crown promulgated many règlements which stated in great detail on which days of the week the Conseil des Finances should meet, and at what time, what business should be discussed and how decisions should be taken. These rules were designed to tie the surintendant des finances down to a precise pattern of behaviour which a relatively large number of royal councillors would know about and be able to correct if necessary. In fact the surintendant was able to ignore such regulations and to run things as he wished, aided only by a handful of eminently bribable cronies. It was not a situation that boded well for the purity of financial administration.

THE ORDINARY RESOURCES OF THE CROWN

The surintendant and the Conseil des Finances performed the function of ordonnancement. In theory they were not allowed to handle public money. The elements of the financial administration which did handle money were known as comptables—that is to say, they were obliged to render account to the Chambre des Comptes. The heads of the comptable administration were the trésoriers de l'Epargne. The Epargne, or central treasury, had been set up by François I in 1523. It was originally run by a single treasurer. The number was increased to two under Henri II, and to three under Louis XIII. Each treasurer served for one year at a time. To him were paid, in theory at least, all elements of royal income during that year.[4] Income was divided into two basic categories: Ordinary and Extraordinary Receipts. Ordinary Receipts were the income from those taxes which were imposed by the Ordinary Financial Machine. They comprised: Direct taxes (*Domaines, Tailles,* and other taxes, all of which were grouped together as the *Recettes-générales*); Indirect taxes (*Aides, Gabelles* and *Traites*); and Occasional taxes (*Dons gratuits* and other sums granted by provincial Estates and the Assemblies of the Clergy). Together they formed the traditional taxes imposed by the monarchy.

The only taxes that accrued to the Crown by absolute right were the direct taxes which derived from the king's position as feudal landlord. These dated from the days when the kingdom of France could be administered as a series of fiefs, when the state barely existed except as an idea. By the seventeenth century, most of these taxes, the so-called *Droits de Domaine*, were farmed out. The most important rights were the *Censives*, derived from dues and services paid by the king's own peasants. Next in importance were the *Péages*, which were tolls imposed on roads and rivers, originally to pay for their upkeep. From the time of Charlemagne onwards their existence was a burden to economic activity. Worse still, efficient royal supervision was impossible. Then there were the *Quint* and *Requint*, feudal rights levied by the king on the sale of fiefs belonging to the Domaine.[5] But these and the lesser domanial rights were of small importance compared to the next category of royal income, the *Taille*.

B

The tax known to the *ancien régime* as Taille derived from a grant by the Three Estates of the nation, and never entirely lost some element of justification by particular necessity, that of providing money for the royal armies.[6] But it became ordinary and perpetual by the middle of the fifteenth century. By the sixteenth century, it had achieved the general forms in which it was to persist down to the end of the *ancien régime*. The Taille corresponded to modern taxes on land, on the individual (income tax), and on movable effects. There were two types. *Taille réelle* was levied on landed property alone. Its value, once assessed, was fixed. In the seventeenth century it was levied in the five *généralités* of Grenoble, Aix, Montpellier, Toulouse and Montauban, and in the *Elections* of Agen and Condom, which were parts of the généralité of Bordeaux. It was an equitable tax compared with *Taille personnelle*, which was levied on all the assets of those who contributed, the so-called *Taillables*. Taille personnelle was current in the remaining eighteen généralités of Alençon, Amiens, Bordeaux, Bourges, Caen, Châlons, Dijon, Limoges, Lyons, Moulins, Orléans, Paris, Poitiers, Rennes, Riom, Rouen, Soissons, and Tours.[7]

Certain other taxes were grouped with the Taille. Henri II imposed the *Taillon* as an augmentation of the basic tax. This was supposed to correspond to the increased cost of upkeep of an army on active service. About the same time, the *Subsistance* was added. This was paid by townspeople to exempt them from having to accommodate soldiers in winter quarters, although few could protest if soldiers demanded billets of them. The case of the *Etape* was similar. Its nominal purpose was to ensure that soldiers did not lay waste the countryside through which they moved. In fact its institution was no more than a fiscal manoeuvre. Its lack of practical effect can be seen in the engravings of Jacques Callot, and in the harrowing documents quoted by Feillet and M Jacquart. Apart from these additions to the Taille, there were also the *Fonds des Maréchaussées*, the *Fonds des Ponts-et-Chaussées*, and the *Ustensile*, which was supposed to pay for troops in winter quarters.[8]

The levying of the Taille had two basic forms. The *Pays d'Etats*, specifically the areas of Burgundy, Languedoc, Brittany, Provence and Dauphiné, and smaller areas like the counties of

Pau and Foix, had retained the medieval right to an assembly, the provincial Estates, which met at the order of the king to conduct the affairs of the province and to vote contributions for the needs of the state. The provincial assembly drew up the assessment for the sums it voted. The tax was then levied by its local agents. The *Pays d'Elections* levied the Taille in a different way. Here assessment was organised through the *trésoriers-généraux de France* of the various généralités and their subordinate *élus* in Elections down to the actual contributors in the local parishes. By the middle of the seventeenth century there were twenty-three généralités: five (Aix, Dijon, Montpellier, Rennes and Toulouse) lay in the Pays d'Etats; eighteen (Alençon, Amiens, Bordeaux, Bourges, Caen, Châlons, Grenoble, Limoges, Lyons, Montauban, Moulins, Orléans, Paris, Poitiers, Riom, Rouen, Soissons and Tours) lay in the Pays d'Elections.[9]

It is impossible to state with precision the yield of the Taille in any given year. Financial administrators gave precise figures, but these are extremely unreliable as a basis for discussing money levied. Under Henry IV, the Taille provided a theoretical sum of about 20 million livres a year. By 1661, the total, according to Forbonnais, had risen to 57 million livres a year. Despite this almost threefold increase, the sum that the Crown actually received in the latter year was less than what had been received in the time of Henri IV. The successive increases in the Taille had been absorbed partly through fraud among tax-collecting officials, and partly through the alienation of Taille in the form of Rentes. But the major cause of the shortfall, according to Forbonnais, was simply that the basic contributors could not or would not pay the sums demanded of them.[10]

The other elements of the Ordinary taxes were indirect. The most important were *Aides*, *Gabelles* and *Traites*.

The Aides derived initially from a grant made in the fourteenth century by the Estates-General to the king giving him the temporary right to levy twelve deniers per livre value on all merchandise and goods sold within his realm. They soon became permanent, and by the seventeenth century had achieved considerable diversity. The *Pancarte*, or general table, of Aides published in 1687 enumerated 148 articles on which Aides were levied. The most important categories were those which affected

towns. These were the *Octrois* and *Droits d'entrée*. They were
difficult to levy, and were subject to a level of endemic fraud
which struck men of the seventeenth century, inured though they
were to such things, as rather high. Nevertheless, despite all the
trouble they caused, the Aides brought in little money. In 1640
the total income was said to be only 5,553,000 livres. In 1648, the
total was higher at 6,069,712 livres, of which 4,049,416 livres was
consumed in permanent charges like the payment of Rentes. The
permanent charges rose to 5,759,000 livres when half the Octrois
of the towns of France were alienated in 1657 by Fouquet
and Mazarin. This alienation was not permanent, but even
so in 1661, out of a total of 8,140,000 livres of Aides, the
Crown could hope to receive at best only just over 2,700,000
livres.[11]

The second element of the indirect taxes were those on salt,
the Gabelles. By the seventeenth century, the administration of
the Gabelles had formalised itself into three parts: the *Grandes
Gabelles*, *Petites Gabelles*, and *Pays rédimés des Gabelles*. The area
of the Grandes Gabelles took in the northern and central regions
of France made up of the généralités of Paris, Soissons, Amiens,
Châlons, Orléans, Tours, Bourges, Moulins, Dijon, Rouen,
Caen and Alençon. Salt was brought in from the salt marshes
around Nantes and sold from the 229 *Greniers à sel*, or magazines,
which were contained in the area in the mid-seventeenth century.
The salt taxes functioned not only as indirect taxes (*Perceptions*)
but also as direct taxes (*Impositions*). The customer was not only
forced to purchase his salt at a high monopoly price, but also
compelled to buy a minimum quantity of salt annually. The
price which the individual paid for his salt varied widely from
place to place even within the limits of the Grandes Gabelles.[12]
Outside the Grandes Gabelles lay two areas. The first, the Petites
Gabelles, included the provinces of Lyonnais, Languedoc and
Dauphiné. The laws of this area were largely uncodified, and the
size of the sums exacted varied wildly. In the areas adjoining the
Spanish frontier the tax was under one-sixth what it was in
Maconnais, which adjoined the Grandes Gabelles. Each Grenier
was almost completely independent, operating under its own
rules. The second area, the Pays rédimés, was one in which no
Gabelle was paid at all. In the valleys of the Charente, Dordogne,

Garonne and Gironde, the provinces purchased their freedom from the tax in 1549. In lieu of it, salt in the area paid high import duties called *Droits de convoi* and *Traites de Charente*. [13]

The Gabelles provided one of the biggest elements of royal income. But the state never drew any large direct profit from them. They grew continuously from the reign of François I down to 1648, but the growth was almost entirely absorbed by the payment of the wages of newly created officers and by the payment of Rentes. In 1661, the Grandes Gabelles produced 14,750,000 livres, of which fixed charges consumed 13,351,000 livres. To get some idea of the total weight of the Gabelles overall, one has to add to this sum the 4,998,000 livres produced by the Gabelles of Languedoc, Lyonnais, Provence and Dauphiné, to come to a total of 19,738,000 livres for the kingdom of France apart from the Pays rédimés des Gabelles. Against this have to be allowed charges of 16,315,714 livres. The remnant that was supposed to come into the Epargne was a mere 3,422,286 livres. [14]

The third large form of indirect taxation was the Traites. These were, broadly speaking, customs duties levied on goods entering or leaving the realm, and also those moving into or from certain regions and provinces within the kingdom. The most important region was that comprising Normandy, Ile-de-France, Maine, Anjou, Poitou, Aunis, Perche, Berry, Nivernais, Burgundy, Bresse, Bourbonnais, Beaujolais, Touraine, Champagne and Picardy. These provinces were enveloped in a common perimeter of customs posts. The area was known as that of the *Cinq Grosses Fermes*, because the Traites had formerly been farmed out to five companies of farmers. Some Traites were levied either at entry or at exit of goods, others were levied at both. Some had been established for the protection of industry, others were purely fiscal. Some were levied on all types of merchandise, others merely on selected goods. Outside what was called the *Etendue*, or extent, of the Cinq Grosses Fermes, lay the provinces *réputées étrangères*, which had their own particular customs systems, like the *Douane de Valence* which affected Lyonnais, Languedoc, Provence and Dauphiné. Guienne and Gascony had a similar institution called the *Convoi et Comptablie de Bordeaux*. In 1661, according to Forbonnais, the income of the most important Traites came to 8,416,000 livres, of which

charges consumed 4,039,672 livres. This left a theoretical sum of
4,376,328 livres for the Crown.[15]

Almost all the indirect taxes were extracted not by the state
itself but through the use of tax-farmers. The initial impulse
towards the institution of tax-farming was the wish of the
government to ease its administrative load. It seemed impossible
for the state to levy each of the myriad droits economically. The
central administration found it easier to permit private individuals
to assume the right to collect indirect taxes, the state taking in
return a previously fixed series of payments. During the later
sixteenth century there was a clear tendency for the state to
encourage the concentration of farms into larger units, or general
farms. With larger farms, the state found that it had to negotiate
with fewer people. Moreover, the responsibility for failure to
fulfil the terms of a farm could be more easily apportioned, and
redress more effectively achieved. The process of concentration
continued until 1610, but despite the efforts of Sully, there were
at least forty large farms outside the general farms of Aides,
Gabelles and Traites. Beside these there was an uncounted
number of lesser farms which evaded the ambit of centralisation.
The limits of rationalisation of the tax-farming system were made
even more apparent by the freedom of larger tax-farmers to sublet elements of their farms to smaller farmers.

During the half-century between the fall of Sully and that of
Fouquet, the development of general farms tended to lapse. The
Cinq Grosses Fermes, being the simplest to administer and the
longest established, did not disintegrate, but equally did not expand beyond the boundaries of the Etendue. The organisation of
the general farm of the Grandes Gabelles suffered when, occasionally, its farmers failed to provide the advances demanded by
the state. But it was the general farm of the Aides which achieved
the highest level of confusion. Many of its most valuable elements
were farmed separately during the regency of Marie de Medici.
Nevertheless after the Fronde, in a climate more congenial to the
tax-farmer though not to the financial health of the state, a certain degree of stability was achieved. The general farms and the
larger farms outside their ambit tended to be administered by
relatively constant groups of men forming companies which,
though by no means as stable and accepted as those of the later

seventeenth and eighteenth centuries, had begun to acquire a recognised existence. The position of the farmers was, like so many of the institutions of the *ancien régime*, ill-defined. In so far as farmers had been successful in securing a farm at auction, they were speculative businessmen. In so far as they were involved in the collection of state taxes according to certain defined, though often ignored, procedures, they were royal functionaries. In so far as by law their companies had no collective personality, but had to operate behind the façade of a man of straw known as an *adjudicataire-général* or *prête-nom*, they were in danger from the rigorous interpretation of obsolete statute. In so far as the Crown itself connived with them and accepted loans and bribes, they were recognised.[16]

In theory the overall amount of taxation deriving from royal farms increased by over 60 per cent in the period 1630–61. At the time of the fall of Fouquet, it stood at 36,858,000 livres. Yet the maximum that the state could hope to receive from farms in 1661 was a mere 11,066,188 livres. The charges on the farms resulting from the alienation of sums for the payment of the wages of venal officers, Rentes sur l'Hôtel de Ville and pensions for important personages consumed the balance of 25,791,812 livres.[17]

The last category of income from the Ordinary Financial Machine may be described as occasional taxation granted from time to time by representative assemblies. In its desperate search for money, the monarchy attempted to use for fiscal purposes the old representative institutions which survived from the medieval world into that of the *ancien régime*. Sometimes such attempts misfired. For example, the assembly of the Estates-General of 1614–15 provided cold comfort for the monarchy, confining its activities in fiscal matters to attacks on royal financial expedients and the financiers who operated them. Nevertheless, a well handled assembly could often be persuaded to grant lump sums disguised under the euphemism of the term *Dons gratuits*.

The monarchy would occasionally summon special assemblies like that of the Notables of 1626, which the then surintendant des finances, Effiat, attempted to persuade to grant gifts. But it had more success with the Estates of the various provinces, in particular those of Brittany, Burgundy and Languedoc. In 1626 the Estates of Britanny were browbeaten into granting the King a subsidy of 500,000 livres to assist him in a planned campaign against La Rochelle. Such persuasion depended very largely on the personal influence of the king. During a royal minority, provincial assemblies showed a pronounced lack of generosity. In the 1650s in particular, the amount provided by provincial Dons gratuits was small compared to the support exacted during the later period of the reign of the Sun King, when repeated giving came near to destroying the economic life of the towns of the Pays d'Etats.[18]

A more reliable source of Dons gratuits was the French clergy. Here again, royal control during the age of the Fronde was far less effective than that exercised by the king at the height of his power. Nevertheless a certain level of support from the clergy had been expected as early as 1561 when, with the approval of the Crown, the Second and Third Estates of the Estates-General demanded that the First Estate, the clergy, contribute to the expenses of the kingdom. The clergy agreed to make an annual contribution of 1,600,000 livres for six years to underwrite the emission of royal Rentes. This annual payment, which came to be known as the *Décimes*, was renewed successively as it expired. The clergy's liability to give support having to some degree been accepted, it was but a short step to inveigling them into providing Dons gratuits.[19]

Such then were the Ordinary receipts. The income from them was supposed to be over 92 million livres in 1649, while Colbert claimed that the income of the Crown from such resources in 1662 was 87 million livres. Whether the Crown ever really received these enormous sums is, of course, another matter. Forbonnais reproduces the whole Etat au vrai for 1649, which comes to the figure just cited. But since the Fronde raged throughout 1649, and since the local intendants had been suppressed the previous year at the insistence of the cours souveraines, there was not the slightest chance that more than a tiny part of the theoretical income would be collected. Even Colbert's figures for 1662 fail to take account of the recalcitrance, incompetence and ingrained fraudulence of the financial machine. Comptables lied as a matter of course, almost as a way of life. It was rarely possible to catch an individual officer out, and never possible to reform the system as a whole. The weakness of accounting institutions is discussed below in Chapter 4. Suffice it to say here that this weakness destroys any credence that might be given to figures, except in the purest Panglossian sense.

One clear statement can, however, be made about the Crown's ordinary income: it was never enough. This can be seen from even the most cursory glance at the expenditures that had to be made.

There were two categories of royal expenditure. One was made more or less automatically, the other had to be made from year to year. The borderline between the two categories is not easy to draw, but it seems that automatic recurrent expenditure was usually paid locally as a relatively fixed charge on income, whereas other expenditure was paid, in theory at least, in money which had actually come into the Epargne as *deniers revenants bons*. Despite the lack of reliable figures, it is possible to establish the rough proportions of these two elements of expenditure. Forbonnais believed that in 1661 the fixed charges on income accounted for about five-eighths of the theoretical income of the Crown, and that this proportion fell to about one-half in 1662. But this should not leave one with the impression that three-eighths or one-half of the royal income *did* come in to the Epargne. In fact almost all royal expenditure was made by royal warrants, each of which allowed the bearer to collect what the Crown owed him from a specific part of the financial machine.[20] No more than a fraction of a percentage point of the royal income was handled in specie at the Epargne.

It is impossible to say where the category of fixed charges ends and where that of more floating expenditure begins. Payment of the wages of royal officials in institutions like the royal court and the various parlements and chambres des comptes was made by fixed charges, and so was that of Rentes sur l'Hôtel de Ville. But the most pressing royal expenditure, that on military affairs, admits of no clear and simple categorisation. The basic financial organisation of the army at this period distinguished two groups: the *Ordinaire des Guerres* included the more permanent elements of *Ban* and *Arrière-ban*, *Compagnies d'ordonnance*, *Francs-archers* and *Prévôté*, while the *Extraordinare des Guerres* included mercenary formations both French and foreign. Both divisions had their own treasurers, who were responsible to the trésorier de l'Epargne, as also were the treasurers of various specialist services like artillery and fortifications.[21] In theory, a certain number of taxes, the Taille, Taillon, Subsistance and Etapes, were supposed to be paid to support the Ordinaire des Guerres, while the Extraordinaire des Guerres depended on a less definite series of sources of income. But it is clear that by the seventeenth century the definite appropriation of the Taille had ceased to apply, and that the army as a whole depended on flexible arrangements. The provisioning of troops had for long been arranged by more or less private companies of *Munitionnaires* led in the seventeenth century by profiteers like François Jacquier and Claude de Boislève, while payment of the wages of troops depended very largely on loans contracted by the Crown. All this makes it impossible to say exactly how much the military cost. Some attempts were made, but these are no more than inaccurate guesses. For example, Richelieu estimated in 1642 that annual expenditure on war ran at the rate of 36 million livres. But this took account of what the various contractors *said* they had charged, not what their services to the Crown had actually cost.[22]

Richelieu's optimism is not hard to understand, for royal officials habitually claimed that expenditure ran very close to, but miraculously did not quite exceed, royal income. Like the balance sheet of a public company about to collapse in bankruptcy, the documents put out by the administration lied manfully in the attempt to conceal the real situation. It would be unkind to say that royal officials knew how badly things were going at any given time—even treasury officials of our own day have trouble with that kind of perception. And further, it is impossible to say in retrospect how large the shortfall was. But one can speak in relative terms of a worsening situation during the seventeenth century. The French monarchy perhaps balanced its books under Henri IV and Sully, though it is highly unlikely that it did as well as the old Duc de Sully, writing in sustained fury at his enforced resignation, said that it had done. Under Louis XIII the situation deteriorated rapidly. In the 1620s, while the kingdom was not engaged in foreign war, there was a small deficit which was estimated by the Maréchal d'Effiat to run at an annual 5 million livres. But when France went to war, the deficit was multiplied by a factor of ten or more. By 1661, according to Colbert's private calculation, the total indebtedness of the Crown amounted to just over 451 million livres.[23] To put it another way, according to Colbert's figures, if the Crown had collected every sou of its theoretical income, and if that income had been entirely devoted to paying off royal debts, it would have taken the Crown over five years to return to solvency.

The Ordinary Receipts were, it is clear, too small to pay for the needs of Bourbon monarchs even in peacetime. In war, those receipts became totally inadequate. This much was understood by royal officials, and so they had recourse to other sources of income, that is to say, to the second major division of the finances, the *Affaires Extraordinaires*. And having had recourse to such things, officials came first to have a dependence on them, and then to be dominated by them. A body of men emerged who handled Extraordinary Affairs, and these men came to be of greater importance than the men who ran the Ordinary Machine. In the end, the new men simply took over the Ordinary Machine. Officially that machine still ran the finances of the state. But essentially the official structure of the machine came to be little more than useful cover behind which the real decisions about French finance were taken. Those decisions were extraordinary in several senses, as the following two chapters show.

Notes to this chapter are on pages 245–6

Chapter 2 THE EXTRAORDINARY FINANCIAL MACHINE: Rentes and Treaties

THE SECOND broad division of the administration of the French financial system was that of the Extraordinary Machine. *Affaires Extraordinaires* logically succeed *Affaires Ordinaires*. But the simple division of ordinary and extraordinary perhaps hides more than it reveals. It may be accepted that regular sources of income like the *Taille* and the *Gabelle* can be distinguished from expedients which were often quite ephemeral. This was the distinction made by contemporary analysts. But if one penetrates rather deeper than such men into the nature of the finances as a whole, the distinction tends to lose the hopeful simplicity with which it was originally endowed.

Things were called extraordinary until they had become so generally accepted by law and custom that they became ordinary. The example of the Taille was mentioned in the previous chapter. That of the venality of offices is perhaps less obvious. Venality, which is discussed in this chapter, was still technically extraordinary in the seventeenth century, but during the middle years of the century it underwent a series of complicated changes. While it seems unlikely that the creation of offices and the manipulation of their wage rates ever came to be accepted as ordinary, a number of the elements of income which the venal system provided, like the *Droit annuel*, were rapidly assimilated into the normal pattern of ordinary resources. The distinction of ordinary from extraordinary was not absolute. Elements of the latter were transferred to the former as time went by. But this is by no means the whole story. A bland picture of the transfer of sources of income from one category to another fails to reveal the essence of what was happening to French public finance in the seventeenth century. In fact, the absolute monarchy went through a financial crisis whose significance can be evaluated only in the context of a process of development in French finance which lasted for the best part of eight centuries.

There were five big phases in that development down to the middle of the seventeenth century. The first was the rise of the royal *Domaine*, whose origins dated from the foundation of the Capetian monarchy. The second phase, the creation of the *Recettes-générales*, formally began in the mid-fourteenth century, and was complete in all its essentials by the middle of the sixteenth century. The third phase, the creation of the farms of the indirect taxes, was more complex in that a plateau was reached about 1610 and lasted until Colbert's reorganisation of farms into the general farms of 1681. But the form of the taxes extracted by farms had certainly been established by the end of the sixteenth century. All these sources of income were designated as ordinary by the middle of the seventeenth century. The sources utilised in the fourth and fifth phases were still termed extraordinary. The fourth phase, the use of Rentes and Treaties, had a fairly long gestation in the sixteenth century, but it achieved its greatest sway in the relatively short period of the ministry of Richelieu, when the *premier ministre* rode both sets of devices if not to death then at least to a state of exhaustion virtually indistinguishable from that final condition. The fifth phase, reliance on short-term loans, had an even longer pre-history than Rentes and Treaties had—monarchs had borrowed from time immemorial. But, on the other hand, the period of dominance of the fifth phase was shorter than that of the fourth had been. Effectively the fifth held sway only over the years 1643-8 and 1653-61. These five phases point towards a conclusion: there was a long-term deterioration in the Crown's financial position, which can be deduced from its recourse to devices that were more and more desperate. What was worse was that each successive phase brought progressively shorter relief to the monarchy. But even this was not the whole story.

During the seventeenth century, the fourth and fifth phases

were not merely dominant: they took over control of mechanisms dating from preceding phases. The Extraordinary Machine (that is to say, the set of mechanisms by which, and the people by whom, Affaires Extraordinaires were administered) existed as a parasite on the body of the Ordinary Machine. Even within the Extraordinary Machine, important changes were under way. As Rentes and Treaties reached temporary exhaustion, they came to be used as the Ordinary Machine had long been used, as a background for a newer range of expedients connected with short-term loans. By 1661 all other elements of the finances of France were subject to the overriding influence of loans, in that everything else was used as a means of providing the excessive interest rates which the financiers extracted from the state. The way in which this happened is the subject of the present chapter, which is concerned with Rentes and Treaties, and of the chapter which follows, which is about short-term loans and fraud connected with interest rates.

1. RENTES SUR L'HOTEL DE VILLE

Of the fourth phase in the development of the royal finances, it seems that Rentes were the older phenomenon.[1] Their origins lay far back in the medieval period, for they were once fairly closely related to the *Censives* derived from feudal tenure of land. By the sixteenth century, Rentes had come to mean the right to levy annual contributions known as *Arrérages*, which may be roughly translated as 'interest'. The evolution of Rentes as instruments of credit was closely related to the doctrine of the Church prohibiting the lending of money at interest. The Church would permit lending at interest by merchants one to another on the theory that the debtor in some way caused a loss of earning power to the creditor through the latter's lending some of his liquid assets to the former, and that therefore the debtor should pay so-called 'damage-interest' to his creditor. Nevertheless, loans at interest between private individuals were rigorously forbidden, and it was only to the merchant, the banker, and the sovereign that the Church permitted such loans. There were certain breaches in this attitude. Lending at interest was authorised by some provincial *parlements* under certain conditions. Areas like Lorraine which were joined to France at a late date practised such lending openly. Apart from these exceptions, lending at interest remained officially forbidden in France until the Revolution of 1789.

If a private individual wished to obtain credit there were only two legal ways open to him. One was for him to contract free loans, which seems to have been possible in the later medieval and early modern periods more often than one might have expected. The other was for him to constitute a Rente. For the person who wished to invest his money for profit in credit operations, the only way in which this could be legally done was by buying such a Rente. Thus emerged the set form of the *Rente à prix d'argent*, which the Church felt able to accept as the partial sale of the revenues of a fixed asset.[2]

Constitution of Rentes by individuals and their sale to other individuals was common in the seventeenth century. The general form of such transactions can be seen from the constitution of a Rente on 16 August 1660 by a collection of Nicolas Fouquet's friends and relations. They constituted at the rate of the eighteenth denier to Françoise Tuffier an annual Rente of 1,111 livres 2 sols 2 deniers, payable every quarter and assigned on various specified lands belonging to the constitutors. In language more straightforward than the original text, the constituting parties had alienated a Rente of 1,111 livres 2 sous 2 deniers of income from their lands for a sum eighteen times the total of that Rente, a sum which happens to come to 20,000 livres. They bought back the alienated Rente from the descendants of the contracting party, or *Rentier*, on 11 April 1672. The nature of the device, the flimsiness of the pretext of such early modern Rentes, is obvious. To all intents and purposes, the sellers of the Rente had simply contracted a loan at an annual interest of one-eighteenth of the principal (5 5/9 per cent). Interest on this loan was paid for twelve years, and ceased only when the loan itself was repaid.[3]

Public Rentes were by no means unknown before the sixteenth century. Certain big towns, in particular Paris, constituted Rentes in much the same way as that used by private individuals. The central authority of the state had for a long time done the same. The only difference was that whereas the private constitutor of Rentes and the public corporation could be forced to honour their obligations in the way of interest by due process of law, the king was himself the fountainhead of law and could not be compelled to pay up. This was one reason—though by no means the only one—why the Crown's credit was extremely bad. It did not matter particularly so long as the demands on the normal financial resources of the monarchy were not too far ahead of royal income. But with the development of the grandiose foreign policy of François I in the earlier years of the sixteenth century, the Crown's financial advisers found it necessary to increase royal credit by creating new forms of Rentes.[4]

This was done in 1522 by establishing a two-stage instrument of credit as a means of providing more solid guarantees that their interest would be paid for the persons purchasing Rentes emanating from the king. The first stage was the constitution and alienation of Rentes assigned on royal income by the king in favour of the *prévôt des marchands et échevins* of the *Hôtel de Ville* of Paris. These were royal Rentes. The second stage was the constitution and alienation by the Hôtel de Ville of municipal Rentes equivalent in value to the primary royal Rentes. The Hôtel de Ville thus acted as guarantor, or *caution*, for the Crown. The theory was that the Hôtel de Ville could itself be forced by the individual Rentier to honour its obligations in the matter of interest and that it was a body powerful enough to make the king think twice about failing to pay his debts to it. In fact the vigilance of the Hôtel de Ville was made even stronger because many members of the municipal administration were themselves buyers of the new so-called *Rentes sur l'Hôtel de Ville*. Many buyers were also members of the Parlement of Paris and were thus capable of using a body which considered itself the highest judicial authority in the kingdom to protect the Rentier.

The new mechanism was not widely used until the second half of the sixteenth century because, although Rentes sur l'Hôtel de Ville represented a rate of interest on loans far lower than that habitually demanded on loans by financiers to the Crown, the alienation of revenue represented by the Rentes permanently decreased royal income from more usual sources. Although in theory the Crown intended to buy back the alienated revenue, in practice it was very rarely, if ever, able to do so. This

led it to constitute Rentes sur l'Hôtel de Ville only as a last resort. Nevertheless, as the Italian wars dragged on, and were
succeeded by the internecine strife of the second half of the
century, extreme financial exhaustion made the constitution of
new Rentes more common. Elements of the income of the
Domaines, Tailles, Aides, Gabelles and Traites (*Cinq Grosses
Fermes*) were all alienated by means of Rentes. More than this, by
the Contract of Poissy of 1561, the Crown, having played on
ecclesiastical fears of the spread of Protestantism, secured an
undertaking from the French clergy to underwrite the payment
of Rentes sur l'Hôtel de Ville.[5]

As the Rentes increased in size, so a bureaucracy grew up to
deal with them, a bureaucracy ominously, as it was to prove in
the future, dependent on the monarchy rather than on the Hôtel
de Ville. In the early part of the century, the king had allowed the
Hôtel de Ville to arrange with farmers of its own choice the collection of the interest on the Rentes from the particular elements
of royal income to which they had been assigned. This permission
soon lapsed as the Crown found that it was possible, by appointing its own farmers, to benefit from the rise in prices of the
century by increasing the price of each farm as it came up for
renewal, and even to constitute new Rentes on the increase. Even
within the Hôtel de Ville the intrusion of the state was felt. Originally the money destined for the payment of Rentes had been
centralised in the hands of a *receveur de la ville*, an official of the
city, but by an edict of April 1594 posts of *receveurs-payeurs des
Rentes* were created for sale by the Crown. These officers came to
have considerable freedom in the administration of the sums
entrusted to them. Their independence contributed in no small
measure to the crisis of confidence in Rentes in the middle of the
seventeenth century.[6]

The level of Rentes sur l'Hôtel de Ville created during the
period 1522–1610 was relatively low. In the years 1522–50, the
total was about 1,350,000 livres. Between 1550 and 1610 the
figure was a little over 2 million livres. On the other hand, the
reign of Louis XIII saw the creation of 16,327,000 livres, making
a total creation in the years 1522–1643 of 19,755,000 livres.
Some of these Rentes were bought back, or reconstituted, so that
the sum which had to be found to pay the interest on the Rentes

stood in 1643 at 18,028,000 livres. The creations of the reign of Louis XIII were so heavy that by 1643 the market was flooded. Despite this, the royal administration continued to create and to try to sell Rentes. By 1648 the total of outstanding Rentes came to 19,919,800 livres. During the years 1653–9 there were at least ten important constitutions of Rentes, which together came to 9,722,436 livres. The amount of capital that the Crown ought to have received from the constitutions of 1653–9 at the legal rate of 5 5/9 per cent was 175,003,848 livres. In fact, the amount of money received was probably just over 20 million livres. The smallness of the sums which the Crown received from Rentes demands some explanation.[7]

In the beginning, Rentes sur l'Hôtel de Ville had been a good source of credit for the Crown, but this was purely because they had been reliably administered by a body relatively independent of the Crown. Long before the end of the sixteenth century, the Crown had begun to interfere in their independent administration, which soon came under royal control. The inevitable followed. As early as 1574, interest on the Rentes was paid only irregularly, so that big arrears built up. After 1583 it was rare for interest to be paid at all, although it seems likely that with the return of peace in the 1590s contracts with the Rentiers were once more honoured. Nevertheless, the problem of interest persisted and inevitably became much more serious after the vast new creations of the reign of Louis XIII. Disaster could be staved off for a time by creating new Rentes and other resources, whose proceeds were used to pay the interest on existing Rentes. But this merely compounded the gravity of the Crown's position, and made the eventual collapse more far-reaching.[8]

There were, however, certain other ways of dealing with the problem of interest payments, ways which were less tainted with the bizarre financial insanity by which the royal administration was possessed. Thus the receveurs-payeurs of the Rentes assigned on the clergy, finding themselves unable to provide their quarterly payments of interest, hit on the happy idea of lengthening the quarter-year from three months to five. Consequently, for example, it was not until 1710 that the clergy got around to paying the Rentes of 1679. Particelli d'Emery's solution in 1648 to the problem of interest was even simpler. He announced that the Crown could not pay interest for the moment. Despite the furore that this created, the most that the government would promise was to pay two-and-a-half of the four quarterly instalments. Another drastic manoeuvre was to reduce the size of specific Rentes. Alienations which had produced capital at a particular rate of capitalisation, perhaps fourteen times, were reduced so that they corresponded to the same capitalisation at a better rate of eighteen times.* Fouquet carried out such an operation in the spring of 1660, and by it reduced the Crown's expenditure on Rentes by 2 million livres a year.[9]

These methods of direct and obvious interference on the part of the Crown were politically dangerous. The prévôts des marchands and échevins of the Hôtel de Ville tended not to be docile men, as the Fronde showed. For example, in 1650 the clergy proved remiss in providing the sums destined for the payment of the Rentes assigned on them, and attempted to reduce their official weekly contribution. The Hôtel de Ville retaliated with an ordinance insisting that the clergy's debt be paid, and stating that if the receiver of the clergy did not produce the sum owed, his worldly possessions would be seized.[10] By failing to meet obligations in the Rentes, the Crown also risked the hostility of the parlement. Whatever the Fronde afterwards became, it began partly as a revolt of the Rentiers seeking payment of their Rentes. This revolt became serious partly because, as was mentioned above, many parlementaire magistrates were the owners of Rentes, and partly because the parlement considered itself responsible for the protection of property against the encroachments of the monarchy. What the parlement could describe as one more attack on property in the long centralising revolution carried on by the French Crown served as a pretext for the four years of disorder which followed. As late as August 1652, the parlement threatened death to any person involved in the

---

* For example: to elicit a capital sum of 100,000 livres at denier 14 required the constitution of a Rente of 7,142 livres 17 sols 1 denier. If the government later reconstituted its debt of 100,000 livres as a Rente at denier 18 of 5,555 livres 11 sols 1 denier, it could make a reduction of 1,587 livres 6 sols. This was no more than a reduction of the interest rate.

collection of sums destined for the payment of Rentes who hindered the arrival of those sums at the Hôtel de Ville.[11]

The events of the Fronde, in particular the rebellious activities of the Rentiers and their defenders, tend to obscure the reasons why the Crown behaved as it did towards the Rentes sur l'Hôtel de Ville, and why ministers like Mazarin and Colbert were so implacably hostile to their owners. Colbert attacked the presumed idleness of owners of Rentes, and spoke of their wickedness in living off what he felt was unearned income. The fundamental reason for this hostility lay in the intervention of the financiers in the Rentes. At the same time, if the Rentes had become a ruinous expedient, it was largely through the shortsightedness and even the connivance of the government itself.

One form of intervention by financiers was that by which they undertook the farming of those taxes on which the payment of Rentes had been assigned. Fraud in this department was regrettable from a moral point of view, but could be of advantage to the state in the short term. Money which the financiers failed to pay to the Rentiers might be used for loans to the Crown.[12] Another more serious form of intervention was the purchase of Rentes as speculative investment by financiers. The financiers had subscribed Rentes issued on the Hôtel de Ville long before the middle of the seventeenth century. From 1572 onwards almost all new Rentes were first taken up at a discount by financiers. The Rentes were only then sold off to the ordinary Rentier, at a significant profit to the financier. This process was still going on in the 1650s. In April 1659, the Crown alienated the enormous sum in Rentes of 4,335,000 livres (for a nominal capital value of 78,390,000 livres). The archives of the Parisian notary Jérôme Cousinet contain a list of all those who initially purchased these Rentes. It is dominated by the names of financiers like Jacques Tubeuf and Jean Hérault de Gourville, and of other men known from other contexts to have operated as proxies for financiers.[13] The reason why the state allowed the financiers to monopolise the Rentes was quite simple. Financiers advanced money to the Crown in return for the right to sell Rentes for an enormous personal profit.

The price paid by the Crown in falling off from the high

aspirations of 1522 was catastrophic. By 1634 Rentes created at
the fourteenth denier could be sold to the financiers at only the
third or second denier.* This represents a rate of interest of from
33⅓ per cent to 50 per cent. Occasionally things could come to an
even more serious pass. The *Chambre de Justice* stated in March
1662 that of one alienation of 1 million livres of Rentes on the
Taille made in 1659, from which the king should technically have
received 18 million livres, the money which actually accrued to
the Crown came to less than 100,000 livres. This represents an
interest rate of something over 1,000 per cent.[14] However, such a
colossal interest rate was more hypothetical than actual. One of
the reasons for the lowness of the price paid by financiers for the
Rentes which they bought was undoubtedly the failure of the
Crown to fulfil its obligations in interest payments, which inevitably decreased the value of alienations of revenue. This element of the fall in price must have been operative right across the
market, for it affected the final owner of a Rente just as much as
if not more than the middleman financier. Another reason for the
depth to which prices fell was the need to give the financiers a
satisfactory rate on their private loans to the monarchy. The way
in which this need was fulfilled is discussed in Chapter 3. As far
as Rentes were concerned, the taking up of such things had become a highly speculative investment in the hope of capital gains.
Those who bought Rentes did so because they could buy them
cheaply and hoped to be able to sell them back to the Crown at
something nearer the full nominal value. Income from interest
payments, when these were made at all, was insignificant compared with the profits to be made from fraudulent capitalisation.
The Crown connived at this. Its need for short-term loans was so
pressing, the involvement of its agents in the desperate struggle
to keep the state afloat from day to day so close, that it would take
greatly reduced payments for the sale of a given body of Rentes

---

* An example of how this was worked out may be of some value. A
Rente of 1,000 livres created at the nominal rate of denier 14 should have
been sold for 14,000 livres. But if the government insisted on payment
of the full price, the Rente would not have found a buyer. The government had therefore to recognise that the highest price paid for a Rente
of 1,000 livres would be in the region of 2,000–3,000 livres, or, as the
seventeenth-century phrase ran, at the second or third denier.

knowing well that the amortisation of those Rentes might be made eventually at their full face value.

From the 25,532,000 livres of Rentes which, Colbert calculated in 1661, had been created since 1631, the Crown received nothing but the most paltry and transitory benefit. It was Colbert who finally did what was necessary by revoking most of the Rentes. Particular financiers who had acquired Rentes were called on to produce the documents relating to such acquisition. Private individuals who had bought Rentes in good faith, and who could prove it, were repaid the money they had put up for their Rentes. Woe betide those who could not produce a valid title to Rentes created after 1656, for all such Rentes, amounting to 8,240,436 livres of annual value, were abolished in April 1664. Nor did Colbert stop there. By the time of his death in 1683, only 8 million livres of Rentes remained outstanding.[15]

The principal behind Rentes sur l'Hôtel de Ville, the alienation of royal capital assets, was not, it must be admitted, a particularly sound one. But at least in the beginning the intention to administer them honestly, to make them in fact the basis of a reliable system of public credit, had a certain dim sense to it. Indeed, several authorities have claimed that the scheme could have given the French monarchy a financial strength and resilience comparable to what the English were to acquire in the later seventeenth century. Be that as it may, it is clear that Rentes were soon administered so corruptly that their original value, a low rate of interest, disappeared. Nor was this all. By the 1650s, Rentes had been to all intents and purposes subsumed in the mechanisms of mobilising short-term loans.

2. TREATIES

The second Extraordinary device was the treaty. Treaties seem to have been considerably less old than Rentes. It was commonly alleged that France had not known of treaties until they were introduced in the later sixteenth century by the Italian financial advisers of Catherine de Medici. This may have been no more than the patriotic reluctance of the French to admit that such things could have been invented at home, for though the treaty was not perhaps the most corrupt device in French public finance, it was certainly the mechanism by which the most visible harm was done to the population at large.

The treaty was used to extract sums of money from groups of luckless individuals on whom the eyes of the Crown's financial agents happened to fall.[16] The basic form of the device was a contract between the king and a financier, who in this context was known as a *Traitant*. As in the case of the tax-farm, the treaty did not mention the name of the real *adjudicataire*, but cited the man of straw or *prête-nom* as the person with whom the treaty had been made. The particular expedient to be adopted was described in as much detail as was considered necessary. The postulated income from the treaty was then stated. This was the nominal *Forfait* or price which the Traitant ought to have paid on the treaty. It was never paid in full because written into the treaty was a clause allowing the Traitant a *Remise*, or reduction, of a certain proportion of the basic price of the treaty. The Remise was intended as an inducement to members of the financial world to take on treaties. The maximum legal rate was one-sixth ($16\frac{2}{3}$ per cent) of the Forfait, but in practice far larger Remises had to be granted before the financiers would co-operate.

The factors behind this reluctance were numerous. Three stand out in importance. First, it was unusual for a treaty to be completely successful. For example, the Forfait of a treaty creating offices for sale was calculated on the value of all the offices, yet it was rare for all the offices of a particular creation to be sold promptly, if at all. Although the Traitant could, during the operative period of his treaty, claim allowances for what were called *non-valeurs* if he were unable to make his estimated profit, it was more encouraging for him to be indemnified at the start for a basic level of probable failure. Second, the Traitant often underwent considerable personal risk in undertaking a treaty, particularly if that treaty involved extracting sums of money from persons in the depths of rural France far from the comparative safety of Paris. Third, if, as was often the case, the state wished to avail itself of the credit of the Traitant, it had to make the affair worth his while. Once the Remise had been calculated, the mode of paying the adjusted price of the treaty, that is to say the net income to the Crown, was set out. The Traitant would agree to make an advance to the Crown, and to pay the balance of the price of the treaty at fixed intervals during the course of the treaty. The intervals varied between one month and three months.

Having signed the treaty, the Traitant had to raise enough capital to pay the advance and the instalments. Often he took others into association with him. For example, in a treaty made by François Jacquier with the Crown in 1654, the financier took Charles Fleuriau and Adrien Bance as his partners. They had proportional interests in the treaty of eight-twentieths (Jacquier), seven-twentieths (Fleuriau) and five-twentieths (Bance). Other treaties contained secret partners. One of the more interesting documents found by the officers of the Chambre de Justice of 1661 in their investigation of another treaty made by Jacquier with the king in August 1657 was an engagement, sealed with the financier's private seal, recognising an interest of three-twentieths in the treaty held by a person whose name had been left blank. Such a document preserved the anonymity of the individual who wished to dabble in such affairs so long as there was no need for him to insist on his rights. Only if Jacquier tried to cheat him would he need to declare himself. The *procureur-général* of the Chambre de Justice tried to show the responsibility of men like the former *surintendant des finances* or the *trésoriers de l'Epargne* for this sort of thing. But the secret partner could have been anyone of means, not least Jacquier's colleague in the war-contracting field, the understandably reticent cardinal-minister of state.[17] There had, of course, to be more than a series of partners if a treaty were to work. It was necessary to employ a whole team of subordinates to carry out the terms of a treaty, whose application to the suffering body of France might parallel the size and mode of operation of a tax-farm. Like the tax-farmer, the central Traitant had his own *commis* and *huissiers* in the provinces, and the expenses of these men were allowed for in the calculation of the Forfait of the treaty. Similarly, the Traitant was allowed to enter into engagements with *Sous-Traitants* of his own choice.

The most productive use ever made of treaties was undoubtedly in the sale of offices by the Crown. The practice of selling offices had been carried on by the Crown for centuries. The first relatively large-scale operation seems to have been the sale of the offices of *prévôtés* in the thirteenth century. Certainly the habit was already strong in the fourteenth and fifteenth centuries. Nevertheless it was not until the sixteenth and seventeenth centuries that the expedients comprised under the heading of venality became systematised. It was only then that the Crown, sensing the impossibility of destroying the phenomenon, came to terms with it and sought to make it more productive. In 1523 François I instituted the post of *trésorier des Parties Casuelles*, to whom royal receipts in this field were to be directed on their way to the Epargne and by whom the wages of the large number of venal officers were to be paid. Thus he consecrated a system which was to be a limiting factor on all other administrative systems. The proliferation of offices for the sake of gain was one of the fundamental causes of that universal *dérèglement* deplored by Richelieu. With the institution of the Droit annuel or *Paulette* by Henri IV and Sully in 1604, the final blessing, that of security of tenure and succession, was given to the officers, who became a major stumbling block in the way of administrative reform.[18]

During the first fifty years of the sixteenth century, only financial offices were bought and sold freely, but it was perhaps inevitable in the confusion of the civil wars of the second half of the century that the state would seek to sell its judicial offices as well. By the time of Louis XIII almost all offices of local administration except that of *premier président* of provincial parlements were bought and sold, subject to only minor restrictions. On the central government, however, venality appeared to have not quite so firm a grasp. The various treasurers might be the holders of venal office, as in the case of the three trésoriers de l'Epargne. Yet the Crown had maintained the theoretical distinction between the *office*, which might be venal, and the *commission*, which could not. Loyalty might be expected from *commissaires* like the surintendant des finances and the contrôleur-général des finances, in that they had no security of tenure beyond the royal document appointing them. But by the middle of the seventeenth century even this distinction had in practice disappeared. Commissions of contrôleur-général were bought and sold during the ministry of Mazarin as though they were simple offices.[19]

The disadvantages of the system of venality seem to have been overwhelming. For one thing, the officers had to be paid.

Although the Crown fulfilled its obligations to them only hap-hazardly, often paying them only part of their wages, nevertheless the amount of revenue consumed by them was substantial. Richelieu calculated that the full bill for the wages of the officers of the royal household and of the judicial and financial machines stood at 34 million livres in 1639. In 1664 the figures probably stood at nearly 42 million livres for the officers of justice and finance alone. The state solved the problem of wages at this period by paying merely one-quarter or three-eighths of what it owed. The figure which, Forbonnais states, was paid out in 1664 was a mere 8,346,847 livres.[20]

But the system was too firmly entrenched to be removed. All that successive ministers could do was to try to make it as produc-tive as possible. There were five elements in its income. Three were relatively stable. The Droit annuel was paid by the officers to permit them to pass on their offices to their heirs or assigns. It was periodically revalued, as in 1655, but the agreement of docu-ments of 1649 and 1664 implies a relatively constant level of some 2 million livres during the middle years of the seventeenth century. The *Marc d'or* was paid by the buyer of an office to be permitted to swear an oath of allegiance to the king. Its level vis-à-vis the individual office remained fixed despite the rise in price of offices during the sixteenth and seventeenth centuries, so that by the reign of Louis XIII it had fallen to about one or two per cent of the value of the office. Apart from these, there was the *Droit de confirmation* exacted by the king on his accession from all officers together with other persons. All three of these elements were farmed.[21]

Of much greater importance was the fourth element of income, the actual creation and sale of office. Initiative for the creation tended to come not from the state but from *donneurs d'avis*, which might be translated as 'projectors', and defined as finan-ciers who, having thought up a new set of offices, hoped to be allowed to sell them. If a particular idea was initiated by a man of substance, he might be allowed to sell his brainchild. If the idea belonged to a poor man, he might be paid no more than a com-mission for it. At all events, having accepted the viability of a proposal, the surintendant des finances and his close personal assistants worked out a general plan of procedure which was submitted to the *premier ministre* for his approval. The financial specialists of the *Petite Direction* then worked out the details of an edict creating the particular offices. The draft was then submitted to the *Conseil des Finances* and the *Conseil d'en Haut* for their approval. It was not, however, until the edict had been published in the *Grande Chancellerie* and registered in the parlements, *chambres des comptes, cours des Aides* and *bureaux des finances* affected by the particular creation, that the new offices had legal existence.

The initiative in the processes of publication and registration was usually taken by the financiers who would be responsible for selling the offices.[22] Delays in registration were commonplace, for there was a great deal of hostility towards the creation of offices from within the *cours souveraines*. These institutions had the power to delay the execution of a treaty, and they might even succeed in modifying it out of existence. In these circumstances the Traitant would agree to undertake his treaty on the express condition that the cours souveraines did not modify his contract. As for the evaluation of the offices for the purposes of sale, the Traitant was usually responsible for this, because he tended to know better than the state how to relate the commodity on sale to the precise nature of what was often a limited and local market. This done, title deeds to the offices, sealed by the chancellor, with the name of the prospective buyer left blank, were given to the Traitant by the trésorier des parties casuelles in return for the usual written promises to pay made by the Traitant. After that it was up to the Traitant to sell the offices as best he could. The only concern of the Crown was to make sure that he paid his instalments on time.[23]

The basic creation and sale of offices were not the only ways in which the Crown extracted money from the administrative system by the use of treaties. Another method was by imposing so-called *suppléments de finance*. When the Crown created offices at too high a rate, their value tended to fall to well below what it would have been in more normal circumstances. Therefore, offices might have to be sold at a figure representing six times their annual wage instead of eight times. When the Crown felt strong enough or desperate enough, it would insist that the sum originally paid, the *finance*, be made up to the regulation figure.

A slightly less direct way of extracting money lay in forced payments in return for compulsory wage increases. Here the officer would be accorded an *augmentation*, and forced to pay a sum perhaps ten times as large in return. Similarly, the Crown might award increased income to local officers by augmenting the sums they were allowed to take as surcharges on taxation. In return, the local officers would have to make capital payments to the Crown. The Crown could also decrease wages in such a way that officers could be forced to pay capital sums. This was done by making the decrease retrospective, so that the officers had to pay *taxes* in respect of wages received over a period of time. Even the threat of such exactions was used in the 1650s to extract money from officers. It need hardly be pointed out that all these disagreeable tricks, even those based merely on threats, were made by means of treaties.[24]

But such secondary methods of making money were far less productive than the creation and sale of offices. And it is clear that the market for such sale had simply been swamped by 1642. Consequently the proportion of the income of the Crown provided by the Parties Casuelles, that is to say from all elements deriving from the system of venality, fell from 38 per cent in 1638 to 10·5 per cent in 1642. This decline continued until the end of the Fronde, during which the number of treaties on all subjects (which had been seventy-nine in 1639) fell to one in 1652, according to a list in the Bibliothèque nationale.[25] Figures for the period 1653–61 are not available, but there are indications that the sale of offices did not pick up again after the Fronde. The only important creation mentioned by Forbonnais as having occurred during the surintendance of Fouquet is that of forty-six posts of *secrétaires du roi* in 1654. There were other creations, it is true, but their significance is exemplified by a treaty of 1655, which took

> the form of a tax-farm lasting twelve years [the income from which will come] from those who carry out by commission the functions of officers hiring out horses, until the offices have been sold and established properly, within the jurisdiction of the Cour des Aides of Paris.

The income from such ludicrous affairs was tiny. Forbonnais

included in his statement of royal income in 1661 a figure of 800,000 livres under the heading *Revenus Casuels*. If this heading may be identified with income from the actual sale of offices in the year 1661, it would imply that the sale of offices played little part in the desperate task of supplying the Crown during the last years of the ministry of Mazarin.[26]

But the damage that had been done did not disappear with the rapidity that so distressingly marked the exhausting of the profits that the Crown had taken from venality. Those who purchased venal offices were not uniformly corrupt. Indeed, by some strange accident there were some venal officials who were honest —like Olivier Lefebvre d'Ormesson and Gabriel Nicolas de la Reynie. But they were exceptions, and the general level of men recruited by this bizarre system seems to have been low. Ironically, the best example of the worst that might happen lay in the administration of the venal system itself. Pierre and Nicolas Monnerot and Claude Girardin were powerful men who in 1655 captured the most important tax-farm of all, that of the *Grandes Gabelles*, and, not content with this coup, went on to take over the posts of trésoriers des Parties Casuelles. They were all in office by 1660, and using their posts to put pressure on important figures at the heart of the financial administration. The Chambre de Justice of 1661 was set up before the new dispensation at the Parties Casuelles had time to make the most of its opportunities. Judging from the fines of 4 million livres and 5 million livres at which the Chambre respectively assessed Girardin and Nicolas Monnerot, primarily for their activities as *Munitionnaires*, *Gabelleurs* and Traitants, to have allowed such men to become entrenched in the Parties Casuelles would no doubt have been an unmitigated disaster.[27]

Despite the decline in the sale of offices, the method of disposal, the treaty, continued to attract the Crown. The advantages of the device were, at least in the short term, obvious. The Crown gained an immediate cash advance and a series of regular payments, while it left to others the odium of enforcing the expedients which gave rise to the treaty. So the Crown applied treaties to supplementary fields. The most important of these was the Recettes-générales. It is not clear how far the Traitants took over functions formerly the preserve of the usual officers of the Taille. Contemporary documents refer to direct action by financiers in levying the Taille. They tell further of the use of companies of fusiliers as auxiliaries of the tax-collectors, of the seizing of goods and animals by the troops and of the consequent impossibility of cultivating the land properly. Such violence was condoned by the government, despite the fact that the Traitants were almost certainly more corrupt than the regular officers formerly responsible for the Recettes-générales. The government's tolerance can be explained only by the attraction of the cash advances offered by the Traitants. These last, on the other hand, undertook the levying of the Taille because it was one of the easiest ways of making a fortune.[28] What worked well with the Taille was applied on a smaller scale to other elements of the ordinary financial machine, and in particular to the income of the Crown from the feudal system. For example, in December 1658 the Crown passed a treaty with one Anne de Chambré for the recovery of sums of money from those who bought land which had been sold by persons both clerical and lay who had originally held such land in mortmain. Assets which were held by mortmain were free of all royal domanial taxes. It would be logical, if they were disposed of by their owners, the so-called *mainmortables*, for the new owner to pay something for their return to normal ownership.[29]

These were not the only uses of treaties in matters relating to the Ordinary Machine. When it was found that even the use of Traitants failed to extract the entire amount of a given tax for a given year, the government sought to solve the problem neither by improving the efficiency of its local administration nor by asking itself whether there was something wrong with the taxes and their incidence. It simply arranged more treaties, like one passed on 24 October 1658 for the

> recovery of sums which are due to the King for outstanding accounts, ordinary debts, remnants of the Tailles from 1647 up to and including 1656, and such sums as remain to be collected from treaties and loans made from 1653 until 1659, together with other moneys due and supposed to be paid in cash to His Majesty.[30]

Despite the evident inability of more usual modes to extract taxes at the already enhanced level at which they stood, the Crown strove ceaselessly to raise the nominal rate of taxation. The increases were on the whole levied by treaty.[31] And if such increases did not alleviate the financial hunger of the monarchy, royal ministers might proceed to the direct sale of elements of taxation to private individuals, as in 1657 when half the *Octrois* of the towns of France were alienated. Needless to say, the operation was conducted by means of a treaty.[32]

Finally, one should mention a type of treaty which has an ironical sound. The seventeenth century railed against the financiers in terms which were cited at the beginning of this book. Periodically, financiers were fined for the misdemeanours for which, it was claimed with some justice, they were responsible. These fines were extracted by means of further treaties with financiers. For example, one of the biggest treaties of the seventeenth century was that by which the fines imposed by the Chambre de Justice of 1661 were to be extracted. The irony of such treaties was the more compelling in this instance because, despite Colbert's stand upon the need for rectitude in public affairs if the state were to survive, the treaty was adjudged to a man by no means above suspicion of financial impropriety.[33]

What positive value had treaties for the Crown? Probably it would be correct to say that their value in the 1630s, at the high tide of the creation and sale of offices, was great. And it is clear that the income fell off dramatically in the years that followed. Figures were added up by solemn royal officials which indicate that tens of millions of livres accrued every year from treaties. For example, on paper the Crown received 57,230,699 livres from treaties in 1657.[34] But such a figure means no more than that in 1657 the Crown was involved in a lot of treaties. The figure includes all sorts of sums which also appeared elsewhere in government statements of sums received. Thus it was with the product of the Taille, which would appear in the total for the income from treaties and also in the income from the Ordinary Machine. There was an even more potent factor destroying the significance of such a figure. This was the mounting level of fraud in the 1640s and 1650s. Treaties might be passed with the Crown for Forfaits of up to 10 million livres, yet the Crown might see none of the money which it should have received. The reason for the spiriting away of such sums and the means by which it was done are dealt with in the next chapter, where it is shown that treaties, like Rentes sur l'Hôtel de Ville, were used as part of the mechanism which allowed financiers to draw large sums in unofficial payments of interest on their short-term loans.

Notes to this chapter are on pages 247–8

Chapter 3 THE EXTRAORDINARY FINANCIAL MACHINE:
Short-term Loans and Frauds

THE WEAKNESS of the monarchy's private credit forced the government in the sixteenth century to invent *Rentes sur l'Hôtel de Ville*, but these, as was shown in the previous chapter, had become useless save as a vehicle of corruption by the 1630s. The Crown was forced to rely once more on its own direct private credit. This credit was no better than it had been in the sixteenth century, for there was still no automatic method of ensuring the repayment of principal, nor was there any legal way of paying interest at a level high enough to persuade capital holders to lend. There was, however, a way out. Just as the Crown had sought the intermediary of the Hôtel de Ville in the matter of constituting Rentes, so did it encourage the growth of intermediary powers in the contracting of loans.

Whereas the private lender would not lend directly to the state, he was prepared to lend to individual financiers, sometimes by legal private Rentes but usually by technically illegal and usurious loans at interest known as *Promesses* and *Obligations*. So desperate was the Crown's need that there was never a thought of prosecuting for such breaches of the law, despite the collective hostility of the *cours souveraines* to such things. The financiers thus became centralising agents for speculative investment in the financial machine of the state. The records of the *Chambre de Justice* of 1661 contain numerous references to primary capital holders who lent to the financiers (ie those who had some direct formal or informal connection with the financial machine). An analysis of the group formed by primary lenders

is to be found below in Chapter 6. A single example here shows
what went on: in 1657, one Claude Bavot, *Banquier Bourgeois de
Paris*, agreed to lend some 50,000 livres to the financier Baron on
the strict written condition that Baron would lend the money to
the Crown.[1]

The taking of precautions did not end there, however, for the
big financiers were as reluctant as were primary lenders to lend
directly to the Crown. They in their turn tended to lend only
against the guarantees of a further set of intermediaries. For
example, when financiers made advances on a treaty where repayment should have been more or less automatic as the income
began to come in from the treaty, they secured the written personal word of the *trésorier de l'Epargne* that they would be repaid.
They did not make direct unsecured loans to the Crown at all,
but insisted on making such loans to highly placed officials of the
state. These loans would not have been made if the individual
officials had not been in positions of power from which they
might exercise influence to ensure their own repayment from the
state's income, and thus the repayment of their creditors. But
equally, such loans were made to them formally not as officials
but as private individuals against whom redress might be had at
law in the event of failure to repay. The chief of such officials was
the *surintendant des finances*. During the years 1610–61 it seemed
that the arrangement of credit was the most important role that
the surintendant could be called to fill, and that his direction
(described in Chapter 1) and his control (described in Chapter 4)
of the financial machine were of relatively minor importance.

Surintendants des finances who were appointed because there
was some hope of their being competent administrators were rare
in the seventeenth century. Only Sully and the Maréchal
d'Effiat can be said to have done anything to stabilise the financial position of the French monarchy.[2] As for the others, the
main reasons behind their selection were either their relationship
with the world of the financiers or their native ability to woo
loans from it. Thus Charles Coskaer duc de la Vieuville (1582–
1653) was appointed surintendant in 1623 because it was thought
(erroneously, as it turned out) that, as son-in-law of the financier
Beaumarchais, he would be able to contact sources of money
normally not available to the state.[3] Particelli d'Emery's position

was somewhat more complex than that of La Vieuville. He certainly did have close relationships with the financial world, indeed he had served as a financier since the second decade of the seventeenth century. What was more, he was the son-in-law of Nicolas I Le Camus, one of the most important financiers of the period. His twelve years as *intendant des finances* (1631–43) gave him wide experience of the complicated operation of the state financial machine, so that to appoint him *contrôleur-général des finances* in 1643 was natural and obvious. The only strange thing about his career from 1643 is that he was not made surintendant before 1647. The probable reason for this is discussed below in Chapter 4. Certainly, as contrôleur-général and surintendant, Particelli utilised to the full his considerable talent for soliciting loans.[4]

Nicolas Fouquet's position as surintendant was different from Particelli's. He was not connected closely with the financial world in that curious way which gave seventeenth-century family alliances the status of business associations. His early career was spent as an intendant first with the army, and later in Dauphiné and the Ile-de-France. He was conspicuously loyal to Mazarin during the early years of the Fronde, and as a reward for this was allowed to purchase the post of *procureur-général* of the *Parlement* of Paris in 1650. By 1652 he had acquired enough influence over the magistrates of the Parlement to persuade those who were basically loyal to the Crown but intimidated by their Frondeur colleagues to go to Pontoise to set up a royalist Parlement of Paris far from the squabbles of the capital. Those who remained in Paris were easily branded as members of a factious opposition to the Crown. Mazarin, whose ability to select able subordinates was one of the secrets of his power, could not fail to be impressed by Fouquet's initiative.[5]

Therefore, when the *Surintendance des Finances* fell vacant in January 1653, Mazarin considered appointing Fouquet to the post. The choice was not an easy one, for a large number of candidates made haste to inform the cardinal of their qualifications. At the same time, doubts were expressed of Fouquet's capability. Mazarin took little notice of the warnings. Fouquet possessed what were for the cardinal two supreme advantages: he was good at persuading people to do things, and he was

Mazarin's creature. The only concession that was made to administrative rectitude was that Mazarin appointed Fouquet joint surintendant on 3 February 1653. His new colleague was Abel Servien, an aged diplomat who had all the advantages of a primeval megalith—he had an imposing presence, which would overawe critics, but lacked the agility and perception that would have been necessary to bring a halt to Mazarin's profiting from financial maladministration. In fact, the cardinal had miscalculated, for Servien was more spry than his appearance suggested. For a time, as senior surintendant, he tried to limit Fouquet's activities. This distressing situation came to an end in December 1654, when Servien was confined to the control of royal expenditure, while Fouquet was given the much more difficult task of procuring funds. In the straitened circumstances of the 1650s this came down essentially to the mobilisation of short-term loans.[6]

There were two bases from which Fouquet operated to mobilise credit. One involved the use of his own property as security for loans intended directly or indirectly for the Crown. The other involved loans contracted by the surintendant on the security of state resources. References to specific transactions involving Fouquet's own resources are rare, although when he fell seriously ill in June 1658 he drew up a statement of his financial position which gives an idea of what went on. In the statement, the surintendant referred to his having alienated 2 million livres of his wife's possessions and used the money for loans to the king. In the same personal crisis he was too ill to bargain with the financiers for money to pay the *Etapes* due to the army. In desperation he raised the money by selling his wife's estate of Belle-Assize.[7]

The range of such transactions can be inferred from accounts preserved in the Ormesson archive, which were rendered to Fouquet by his clerk Charles Bernard and others during a period which corresponds to the period of Fouquet's tenure of the surintendance.[8] The total of the receipts mentioned is 35,916,168 livres 13 sols. The total expenditure came to 33,672,916 livres 10 sols. Of the expenditure various items represent sums disbursed for matters not relating to the credit of the state. These form a total of 10,333,437 livres to be deducted, thus producing a figure of 23,339,479 livres, which represent the major part of Fouquet's personal expenditure on credit for the state during his surintendance. This can be broken down into various categories: 5,674,297 livres were spent on repayment of loans and on payment of interest on loans; 10,860,736 livres were spent on the orders of Fouquet and his clerk Bruant; 3,474,585 livres more were spent at Fouquet's orders but in ways that were not explained by him to the satisfaction of the Chambre de Justice, although it was accepted that such expenditure related to credit operations on behalf of the state; another 3,105,769 livres is described as money for Bruant, which is so far above any reasonable level of wages that it obviously represents repayment of advances to the surintendant; finally, there was a total of 404,092 livres spent on operations connected with *Billets de l'Epargne*.

This does not represent all the money borrowed by Fouquet. It is necessary to take into account sums borrowed and still outstanding on 5 September 1661, the day of his arrest. The names of all Fouquet's legitimate creditors at that time have survived. They formed a militant body over five hundred strong.[9] Many may be ignored as purely domestic creditors, such as cohorts of ironmongers, bricklayers and washerwomen. Others were creditors in respect of lands acquired from them by the surintendant. Of those who remain, it is obvious that not necessarily all lent to Fouquet money which was destined for the royal service. But it is interesting none the less to observe the categories of people from whom he borrowed. There were numbers of officers of the cours souveraines, including présidents, conseillers and procureurs of parlements, présidents, maîtres and auditeurs of *chambres des comptes*, and the *premier président* himself of the *Cour des Aides* of Paris. There were several *conseillers d'état* and *maîtres des requêtes*. Members of Fouquet's immediate family and of the families of his wife and mother were represented too. But pride of place must go to the financiers: treasurers of the Epargne, of various royal households, and of the *Parties Casuelles*; farmers-general; and, most important of all, war-contractors like Claude de Boislève, the brothers Gruin, and François Jacquier. Fouquet estimated that his total liabilities in September 1661 came to 12 million livres, of which some 8 million livres represented borrowing for loan to the state.[10]

Altogether, then, it appears that Fouquet's borrowing on behalf of the state came to a figure of about 30 million livres. It would not be sensible to express this as an annual average, because the level fluctuated widely. Fouquet estimated in March 1659 that his liabilities were only 5 million livres, less than half those of 1661. The relatively high level of 1661 was reached as a result of the attempts of Colbert, Le Tellier and Louis XIV during the middle of the year to persuade Fouquet to borrow so much that his credit would be exhausted and his destruction more easily achieved.[11]

While the private credit of the surintendant was at times of considerable use to the Crown, there was a second and far larger field of borrowing in which he operated. This, too, was dependent on his personal credit, but in a different way, for it is clear that in no conventional sense was the credit of the surintendant actually engaged in this second type of operation, that is to say, in advances on income.

The primary documentary instrument for securing such advances stated that the king found himself in dire need of a particular sum for the payment of various (unspecified) expenses. A specified person had presented himself to his sovereign, offering to make a loan of the sum needed and suggesting the repayment of the loan by assignment on the revenues from a particular element of the fiscal system due to be paid at some future date, usually during the following year. If this proposition was accepted, and the loan made, the trésorier de l'Epargne would give the lender a document known as a *Rescription*. This ordered those responsible for paying into the Epargne the income from the particular element of royal income to pay a sum corresponding to the amount of the original loan to the lender. The latter also received a *Remise* on his loan which was in fact a payment in advance of interest. This was given by an *ordonnance de comptant*, which declared that the *Conseil des Finances* had allotted such a sum to the specified person, and ordered the trésorier de l'Epargne to pay it in cash.[12]

Advances in this form were made on all elements of the taxation system. The *Recettes-générales* provided annually during the later 1650s a global sum of around 18 million livres made up of advances on the income of whole *généralités* or of individual

Elections. Advances might also be made on specific elements like the *Ponts et Chaussées* or *Tailles* of a particular administrative unit. These advances would usually be made by local officers like the *trésoriers-généraux de France* of a particular généralité, or by *Traitants* engaged in collecting the elements of taxation on which such advances were to be made. Advances were made regularly on the various farms, both general and otherwise, and on the *Dons gratuits* of the *Pays d'Etats* and the clergy. Similar in principle to these loans were loans on treaties made by the Crown. Advances were of course written into the treaties ab initio; these have already been discussed and are not the same as the loans at issue here. The Crown would solicit loans on treaties at a period after the treaty had been drawn up and agreed on. These secondary loans were distinct from the original advance. In the *Etat sommaire* of treaties of the years 1655–9, they appear as marginal notes alongside a brief statement of a particular treaty, but separate from it.[13]

Loans as advances on revenue formed a very large part of royal income during the years of Fouquet's tenure of the surintendance. It is much to be regretted that the researchers of the Chambre de Justice of 1661 should not have produced a coherent sequence of figures for loans of this type for the whole period 1635–61 with which they were concerned. Nevertheless they did draw up totals for the period 1655–9 which may be summarised thus:

Year	Loans	Remises	Net Total
1655	43,263,801	not available	not available
1656	not available	not available	(35,849,910)
1657	42,160,033	7,001,395	35,158,638
1658	39,370,788	6,061,755	33,309,033
1659	45,484,516	6,329,375	39,155,141

Such figures show that the government consumed something approaching its whole normal disposable income in advance. Nor was this all. Fouquet claimed that by autumn 1654 the state had secured advances on all its income for 1655 and 1656, and that Mazarin even proposed to consume the revenue of 1657 as well.[14]

The chief way in which this was done was by obtaining loans

on the security of advances. The Crown arranged advances on income, but these advances, although they anticipated income, took some time to arrive at the Epargne, so that the state would arrange short-term loans anticipating the advances. Such a situation was desperate. At the same time, it could arise only because the state possessed some credit, however weak. This credit was the responsibility of the surintendant des finances. Credit in this sphere was a complex phenomenon. In one sense it meant simply confidence. When money was advanced, lenders had to feel sure that it would be repaid, and it was Fouquet's task to make sure that their confidence was not abused. This was at times a difficult assignment because Mazarin was never convinced that the repudiation of state loans was other than a useful bolthole once the total became too large. Financiers had the terrible precedent of 1648 ever at the back of their minds, and it is clear that without Fouquet's continuous pressure on Mazarin to prevent some repetition of the governmental manoeuvres of 1648, the financiers would not have advanced funds. On a smaller scale, use of the influence of the surintendant was an everyday occurrence. Even when a loan had been made on the security of the future receipts of the Tailles of a particular généralité, it was fairly common for those receipts to be used for things more urgent than repayment of mere loans. In these circumstances the surintendant would have to be able to persuade the Conseil des Finances and the cardinal that the loan should be reassigned on some other element of royal receipts. Only if he could ensure this sort of reassignment, at least for more influential creditors, would the surintendant have the credibility which is basically what credit in this sphere meant.

The inspiring of confidence, of an atmosphere of credibility, was the main personal function of the surintendant in this realm of credit finance. On the other hand, his importance in the mundane questions of day-to-day administration was severely limited. It was not he who carried out the practical details of securing advances. This was left to the clerks of the Surintendance. Their most important function was, indeed, just this: the negotiation of advances to the state. In such negotiation, they benefited both from the unlimited trust and backing of the surintendant, and from the considerable liberty of action which their relatively informal position conferred. Such liberty of action led to the erosion of the position of the surintendant until he was virtually the prisoner of his clerks. It was a graphic example of the way Extraordinary roles and the men who exercised them came to control the Ordinary Machine.

A successful *premier commis*, or chief clerk, had to be the link between the surintendant and the financial world. He had to possess knowledge of the individual financiers, influence among them, and—most important of all—the ability to take action on his own responsibility in the mobilisation of credit, a mobilisation which would from the nature of things lie outside the bounds of cramping rules and regulations of the formal accounting system. The surintendant would know about much of this. But his position vis-à-vis his colleagues in the Conseil des Finances, the publicity attending the deliberations of that council, and the need for the inner caucus of the administration to preserve some shreds of financial respectability in view of the lingering hostility of the cours souveraines and the public at large necessitated discretion. It would have been politically disastrous to the surintendant personally, to Mazarin, and to the monarchy itself, for it to have been known widely that the surintendant took a leading role in the deceptions which were essential to the utilisation of credit by the state. The man who would be successful as chief clerk had to have stamina, courage, resource, perception of who mattered and who did not, and strength to negotiate with and if necessary browbeat the big financiers, whose money the state had to have but dared not steal.

Three men successively served Fouquet as premier commis. The first, Charles Bernard, proved rather unsatisfactory. He was certainly prepared to disregard the letter of the law when the occasion demanded. But he was unable to dominate the world of the financiers, partly because his health broke down, and partly because he simply did not possess a powerful enough personality. His tenure as commis ended effectively little more than a year after Fouquet ascended to the Surintendance.[15]

The case of his successor, Jacques Amproux seigneur de l'Orme, was rather different. During the early years of the joint surintendance, Delorme was nominally Servien's clerk, but at some time during 1654 he began to work secretly for Fouquet.

Delorme and Fouquet (at Delorme's suggestion) managed to trick Servien into putting forward the candidacy of the company preferred by Fouquet for the farm of the *Grandes Gabelles* which was to begin in 1656.[16] The fact that such operations arranged by Delorme were seen to work gave him influence among his fellows. This in a sense was what was meant by his credit. Later on, as Fouquet's chief clerk (he served from 1654 until 1657), he was able to persuade financiers to lend money against future receipts of the financial system at large under a personal guarantee that he would be able, should it prove necessary, to ensure repayment. Most important of all for the primary mobilisation of funds, he could arrange excessive interest rates for the financiers without the formal complicity of the surintendant.[17] This was possible because it was Delorme who actually wrote out many of the documents (in particular the ordonnances de comptant) by which fraudulent payments were made.[18]

It is clear, then, that Delorme was unofficially performing many of the functions of the surintendant during the years in question. How this situation arose is difficult to say. Perhaps it was partly because Fouquet was not yet at home in the financial world. While he was good at inspiring confidence and stimulating the generosity of capital holders in a general way, it is unlikely that he had mastered the complications made necessary by accounting procedures. Such a situation brought its dangers. The cunning and ruthlessness which were the prerequisites for a successful chief clerk were allied in Delorme with grandiose ambition. He had risen far above the provincial obscurity of his origins by the time he came to power under Fouquet. It might have been thought that he would feel himself adequately rewarded by being appointed intendant des finances in 1657. Similarly, the amount of money he made from manipulating the financial system should have been enough to satisfy even the most rapacious. But his appetites grew by what they fed on, and in November 1657 he joined in a plot to encompass Fouquet's fall. The mechanism of the plot (which was arranged by Fouquet's own brother Basile) was simple and involved Delorme merely in withholding his services. When Mazarin demanded large sums from the surintendant at very short notice to pay, or so he claimed, for the upkeep of the royal armies while they were

in winter quarters for 1657-8, Fouquet turned to his chief clerk
to ask for everything to be arranged. Delorme refused to do anything, and Fouquet, taken by surprise, faced ruin. If other financiers had followed Delorme's lead, the surintendant would have
lost his credit and Mazarin would have had him replaced. This
calamity was averted by Fouquet's turning to alternative sources
of supply: Barthélemy Hervart, contrôleur-général des finances,
and Nicolas Jeannin de Castille, trésorier de l'Epargne. Fouquet
could count himself lucky, for he had given far too much freedom to his chief clerk, and it was only the surprising fidelity of
Jeannin de Castille and Hervart which saved him. As for Delorme, he had no future in Fouquet's service, and so he de-
camped, taking with him documents which he hoped would, at a
more propitious time, enable him to destroy his master.[19]

Despite the shock of Delorme's treachery, Fouquet was either
unwilling or unable to alter the administrative pattern that his
delinquent chief clerk had established. The surintendant merely
appointed a new man, Louis Bruant, to take over duties formerly
exercised by Delorme. Of the chronology of Bruant's personal
life, little record has remained. Indeed it is difficult to say
exactly when he took up the post of premier commis. Certainly he
was active in the financial world before the end of 1657. In the
records that remain of transactions undertaken in that year for
the payment of interest on fictitious loans, Bruant was associated
with Delorme, and it is probable that he took over as chief clerk
immediately after Delorme deemed it prudent to leave the service
of the surintendant. Bruant was involved on the government side
of things as early as September 1657, in which month he was
largely responsible for arranging the treaty alienating half the
Octrois. [20] But this was less important than other roles that he was
to play later on. One of the most useful of these was avoiding the
paying out of money. Bruant turned out to be adept at fobbing
off creditors. Hugues de Lyonne described what this felt like in
a letter which he wrote to Fouquet in October 1660. He relates
that he had borrowed money for loan to the state, and that those
from whom he had borrowed were now pressing him to repay.
He reproached the surintendant thus:

I assure you that I have no idea where I can find 70,000 livres
which various people are asking me for. I went to see M Bruant

again four days ago, but that sort of thing has been going on for four months. I see only too clearly that if you do not do something personally, I shall be left cooling my heels interminably . . .

Clearly, Bruant was able to hold off even an important man like Lyonne, whose only hope of redress after a matter of months was a personal appeal over Bruant's head to his master.[21]

Bruant's functions were not entirely negative. In a letter of the same month, October 1661, from Fouquet to Bruant, the reply to which Bruant wrote in the margin, there are signs that the chief clerk of the surintendant was still being allowed an extremely wide scope for the exercise of independent initiative. Fouquet asked a number of questions, in particular, what plans had Bruant made for raising a loan of 300,000 livres on the security of the receipts of the Parties Casuelles, and what was Bruant going to do about the *Taillon*, since the money raised from the généralité of Caen had been spent? Clearly then, Fouquet delegated much of the taking of decisions on mobilising resources to his chief clerk. But this was not all. Fouquet ends his letter:

Send me the statement of all the Billets [of the Epargne] for which people are demanding payment [in cash]; in fact, send me everything you have, because tomorrow I have to draw up a composite statement, and it is going to prove difficult.

Fouquet refers to the fact that he had to present credible accounts to Mazarin. He reveals that he was entirely dependent on his chief clerk for the information on which those accounts were to be based. His only guarantees against being tricked were the word and reputation of that clerk.[22]

The implication of all this is clear. The role of the surintendant des finances in mobilising credit was important, but on his own the surintendant was capable of only relatively limited action. His official position was such that for the less legitimate operations, indeed even for the merely politically damaging ones which involved disturbing the peace of mind of officers, financiers and other lenders, he felt obliged, or was obliged, to utilise as an intermediary his chief clerk. That chief clerk came to have a large sphere of operation, and even took on many of the administrative functions of the surintendant, as Delorme arranged treaties and Bruant arranged loans. The surintendant had no safeguards against fraud. Indeed he must have known about much of the fraud which went on, even where he did not benefit personally from bribes such as those regularly given him by companies successful in the adjudication of new farms. Contemporaries were therefore incorrect when they referred to the sole disposition by the surintendant of the finances of the kingdom. The executive authority in finance clearly lay in the surintendant and his clerks. The seat of that authority may be said to have lain in the Surintendance as an institution.

But this is too placid a note on which to leave the Surintendance. The situation as it has been described here ran directly counter to the letter of the law. All the people involved in the Surintendance were aware of this, and this awareness coloured the way in which they behaved. In particular, the surintendant had to go along with his clerks in their more illegal acts. To bring them to book would have involved revealing how far the surintendant habitually deferred to them. He would have been treated as more guilty than they. (This is what happened after 1661. The prosecution in the Chambre de Justice tried very hard for three years to have Fouquet hanged. It harboured considerably less murderous feelings towards his clerks.) Fouquet was responsible in law for what was done in his name. This had an effect opposite to what the framers of such laws intended. The surintendant simply covered for his clerks, whatever they did. The clerks, on the other hand, conscious of their power, engaged in corruption to an extent far beyond what was needed to arrange for a reasonable rate of interest for loans. What had happened was not merely that Extraordinary needs had overshadowed Ordinary ones, but that Extraordinary Affairs had destroyed any kind of self-regulatory mechanism that the central direction of the finances might once have had. This becomes abundantly clear in the remainder of this chapter.

The price demanded by financiers for all kinds of credit was far above the fixed rate that the government's servants might legally offer. Observance of the law might be stayed when the state's needs became too great to avoid high interest rates and the like. In Germany in 1525 the Emperor Charles V had altered the laws against usury to allow a relatively free hand to financiers like the Fuggers on whom he depended.[23] But in France there

could be no question of this. It would have been foolish for
Mazarin even to have attempted such a course, given the rigidity
of the accounting machine, which is discussed below, and more
generally, the tense political situation which obtained in the
years following the Fronde. It was necessary to find ways round
the vigilance of the Chambre des Comptes. Such ways were to be
found in the perversion of the operations of the Epargne. This
was possible only with the co-operation, either active or passive,
of those in charge of that institution.

The operation of the Epargne was basically quite simple. The
three trésoriers de l'Epargne were responsible for ensuring that
no money was spent wrongfully. They were

> to watch with care and vigilant exactness to prevent any abuse or
> dissipation of funds. They might not relax this rule for any con-
> sideration of financial interest or fear or respect of persons with-
> out violating the trust they owed to their sovereign . . .[24]

The main requirement of this supervisory capacity was fulfilled
by the keeping of two registers of the Epargne, one for receipts,
another for expenditure. In these registers were to be written
details of every transaction undertaken by the trésoriers involving
royal funds. The purpose of this was to allow the king and his
council to know at any given moment how the finances stood. A
secondary requirement was that the trésorier in exercise of office
in a given year should make a true and faithful report once a
week before the royal council of the sums which he had received
and paid out in the week past. The weekly records of these
transactions were entered on rolls which were then transcribed
into the final registers of the Epargne. All the documents produced in monthly, quarterly and annual periods had to be scruti-
nised and crosschecked by the Chambre des Comptes before they
could be declared authentic (*arrêtés*). This administrative accounting procedure is discussed below in Chapter 4. Suffice it to
say here that the trésoriers de l'Epargne did not keep to it as
closely as they should have done. Their two main deviations
were to burn the primary rolls after they had been seen by the
royal council so that the final registers could not be checked
against them, and to compile their registers in such a way that it
was impossible to sort transactions out. The object in each case

was to confuse the state's accountants, and thus create a situation in which fraud might take place.[25]

There are several reasons why this situation came into existence. First came that fear and respect of persons to which the trésoriers were supposed, as the essence of their employment, not to succumb. What happened was that the *premier ministre* and the surintendant des finances forced the trésoriers de l'Epargne to disobey the law. Mazarin in fact assumed many of the functions of the Epargne himself. He took over the income of a number of généralités for sums which he needed for state and personal expenditure. This was done, according to Forbonnais, by simple *Lettres de cachet* which ran against all the laws and ordinances of the kingdom. Altogether, Mazarin is said to have taken from the Epargne an average of 23 million livres a year during the years 1655–8. The agents who received this money for him were Jean-Baptiste Colbert, Hervart, Colbert's reckless cousin Colbert de Villacerf, Louis Berryer, and perhaps Jean Hérault de Gourville and Paul Pellisson. Some of the money was spent on the prosecution of the war against Spain, but much went into Mazarin's private fortune. Such behaviour made nonsense of the legal responsibilities of the trésoriers de l'Epargne. Where the cardinal led, the surintendant willingly followed. Much of the money that he took must have been spent on his own pursuits. But at the same time, it is not to be doubted that without Fouquet's loose attitude to the conduct and control of the Epargne the state would not have been able to obtain the credit which in the 1650s was its main resource.[26]

A second reason for the corruption of the Epargne was that none of the three men who were its treasurers during the later 1640s and 1650s possessed a backbone strong enough to resist even the gentlest pressure. One of the three was merely venal. The other two were in varying degrees incompetent.

The venal treasurer was Nicolas Jeannin de Castille, who was born about 1617 and died in 1691. It is clear that he was as much a speculative financier as a state official. He freely admitted in his interrogation by the Chambre de Justice that he had been associated with Fouquet in making loans to the state in 1658. He calculated that Fouquet still owed him 1,303,000 livres in 1662. Such operations were considered to be relatively legitimate. It was not so with other activities from which Jeannin profited, like a treaty from which he drew an illegal 687,655 livres. Jeannin was less than forthcoming about this and other transactions of a similar nature. He was heavily compromised by Fouquet's fall, and was imprisoned in the Bastille in May 1662. This was not the sum of his troubles, for he owed a great deal of money to private creditors, whose vociferous claims for payment add up to getting on for 7 million livres. He was never able to repay more than a fraction of what he owed. But it is unnecessary to spend much sympathy on him, for he was clearly a clever and unscrupulous man, heavily involved in making money both from the general confusion of public finance and from the particular opportunities which his post gave him. This was not true of his colleagues Guénégaud and La Bazinière.[27]

Claude de Guénégaud (c 1619–86) succeeded his brother Henri as trésorier de l'Epargne in 1643, on the latter's appointment as secretary of state. There are certain indications that Claude may have been involved in illegitimate transactions during the 1650s, particularly in association with François Jacquier. But on close examination these indications do not add up to much.[28] Guénégaud, as will be revealed shortly, was moderately incompetent—he had a good deal of trouble remembering exactly who had worked for him during the 1650s. But he was not quite a disgrace.

The third treasurer undoubtedly *was*. Macé Bertrand de la Bazinière succeeded to the office on the death of his father in 1642, although, as he was still a minor, he had to employ a proxy until he came of age in 1653. Little record seems to have been left of his administrative conduct down to 1661. Saint-Simon was later to write of him brutally but apparently accurately:

> it appeared [to the Chambre de Justice] that he was in no sense a scoundrel, but had got into trouble because of his disinclination to work and his inability to stop spending money.

His performance before the Chambre confirms this judgement. Under interrogation, he gave a series of answers which showed that he had no understanding even of the nominal responsibilities of his office, and certainly none of the way in which his replies let him down. If he was so ignorant about the nature of his office, little hope can be held out that he was anything but grossly incompetent in its day-to-day administrative detail. This incompetence was something which Fouquet mentioned in his comments on La Bazinière's value as a witness. La Bazinière, he claimed, could not even understand his own registers relating to his years of exercise of office. The procureur-général of the Chambre de Justice, who was quick to contradict the fallen surintendant on the most trifling points of fact, in this case simply held his peace.[29]

Even if the trésoriers de l'Epargne had been seriously concerned with upholding probity in their administration, they would have found it difficult, for it would have been impossible to maintain personal supervision over every item which left record in their registers. The bulk of their administration was carried out, as was that of the surintendant, by a chief clerk, who enjoyed considerable independence. Claude de Guénégaud's chief clerk, Nicolas Rollot, was responsible for hiring subordinate clerks whose duty it was to write out the rolls of the Epargne submitted to the Conseil des Finances. The trésorier de l'Epargne was specifically responsible for the accuracy of these rolls, yet at his interrogation by the Chambre de Justice Guénégaud revealed that he did not know who had been hired by Rollot to write the rolls. The inevitable had happened. Records of fictitious transactions had been interpolated into the rolls after certification by the Conseil. The first that Guénégaud knew of such transactions was when he was confronted with them at his trial. The general impression of Guénégaud's administration, of a rather pathetic lack of ability instead of genuinely criminal tendencies, leads to the conclusion that, in his case at least, the trésorier de l'Epargne was the prisoner of his own underlings. On the other hand, it was to his advantage to allow his clerks to do in secret things for which he could not openly avow responsibility. In this the situation of the trésorier de l'Epargne parallels that of the surintendant des finances.[30]

The frauds committed in the Epargne were not in essence complicated, but discussion of them is possible only after the normal and accepted operation of the institution has been described. The Epargne had two basic functions: receipt and expenditure. These have been discussed in relation to the financial system as a whole in Chapter 1. What is of importance here is the precise way in which the Epargne handled transactions, and in particular the documentary instruments that were used. For it was in this field that the great bulk of the frauds that are the subject of the last section of this chapter took place.

The receipt of money at the Epargne was recorded initially in a *Quittance*, which declared that the particular trésorier de l'Epargne had received a particular sum of money from a particular financial officer, that the payment was correct, and that he held the said financial officer formally quit of the payment. Expenditure of money might be made by direct payment to a creditor in cash, but this was relatively rare, for very little cash made its way into the Epargne. Expenditure had to be made in a number of other ways, of which the most obvious was assignment by *Mandement*, a warrant given to a particular royal official in charge of, for example, making wage payments to a specific military formation. The warrant ordered a second official, in charge of a specific element of royal income, to give a specified sum of money to the first official. In return for this, the second official would be discounted for the payment which he had made against the total that in theory he ought to have paid to the Epargne as part of his yearly receipts.[31]

The trésorier de l'Epargne did not act on his own initiative in deciding how to apportion or assign the funds at his disposal. Given the shortage of money, it was impossible that all royal creditors should be satisfied immediately, if at all. It was a matter of high policy to decide who had to be repaid if he were not to make trouble, and who might be ignored for the moment. This thorny task belonged to the Surintendance. Creditors who were politically strong would be given good assignments, which might be collected easily and quickly. But these were few and far between. It was quite another matter to receive an assignment on the receipts of a frontier province devastated by war, or of a province held to ransom by dissident nobles. Worse still were assignments on the receipts of dubious things like treaties.

This was not all. When the revenue of the current year had been consumed by assignment and direct expenditure from the Epargne, it was necessary to assign current debts on the receipts of future years. For men dominated by memories of the Fronde, such Mandements were of problematical value, and the farthest ahead that the surintendant could assign payment tended to be two or three years. If further assignments had to be made, it was necessary to resort to trickery. Payments would be assigned on elements of royal income which the financial directorate knew had already been exhausted. Those who tried to secure payment on such Mandements would be disappointed. Since they were unimportant people whom the government did not fear, it could afford to take their tribulations with a light heart.

Similar to the Mandement was another royal document called the *Billet de l'Epargne*, which recognised that a certain person was creditor for a certain amount, and that repayment might be made on a particular element of royal income. The only important difference of the Billet from the Mandement was that the Billet did not order anyone to pay. It therefore was even less highly regarded by royal creditors than the worst of Mandements. The weak royal creditor tended in despair to sell both types of assignment for sums well below face value, and thus there grew up a trade in such things. This trade was liable to a large amount of fraud. Some of the varieties of fraud were used by royal officials as ways of allowing a satisfactory interest to those who would not otherwise have felt disposed to lend money to the state.

There were several things that could be done by financiers who had purchased depreciated assignments for later fraudulent use. But successful fraud depended on collusion by state officials. For example, when financiers bought Rentes sur l'Hôtel de Ville, they very often presented in payment obviously valueless Mandements and Billets de l'Epargne in lieu of cash. The Chambre de Justice of 1661 was more concerned with another and more flagrant practice—that of buying up cheap Billets de l'Epargne and persuading royal officials to reassign them on new and unexhausted sources of royal income. What made things worse was the fact that many of the financiers who profited were also royal officials who had formal responsibility for preventing the kinds of fraud from which they themselves in their private capacity drew huge sums. It is clear that the whole central financial administration was involved on a permanent basis in conspiracy to commit fraud. The key roles were undoubtedly played by the clerks of the Surintendance and the Epargne, with the tacit and slightly bewildered approval of their respective nominal masters. But the circle of fraud extended widely. For example, persons profiting from fraudulently reassigned Billets de l'Epargne in 1658 included both surintendants des finances, a trésorier de l'Epargne, a *trésorier de l'Extraordinaire des Guerres*, and a secrétaire du Conseil, together with uncounted farmers-general, Traitants and *Munitionnaires*.[32]

The mechanics of fraud were closely related to another documentary instrument, the *Ordonnance de Comptant*, whose abuse was the most striking feature of the financial administration of the mid-seventeenth century. The original purpose of the *Comptant*, or cash account of the Epargne was to make expenditure on the *arcana imperii*, secret matters pertaining to the state which would be endangered by public knowledge. The account was the means by which the king could make payments on his sole authority, payments which did not have to be verified in detail by the Chambre des Comptes as did all other royal expenditure. Use of the Comptant account demanded the issue of three related documents. First came the Ordonnance de Comptant itself, an order by the Conseil des Finances to the trésorier de l'Epargne to pay in cash to a specified individual a specified sum of money for a specified reason. The payment was to be made immediately. The document ended with the signatures of the chancelier, surintendants and contrôleurs-généraux des finances. The specified individual would take his Ordonnance from the Conseil to the Epargne, and receive his payment. The Ordonnance would then go on file at the Epargne. At the end of each quarter, the amount of money disbursed by Ordonnances de Comptant would be added up. The trésorier de l'Epargne would then be issued with the second document, a *Certification de Comptant* by the Conseil des Finances. This document would later be used in the registers of the Epargne to justify expenditure from the Comptant account. Finally, the Chambre des Comptes was informed of the king's wish that the trésorier de l'Epargne should be allowed to claim such unspecified sums in his accounts by a third document, an *Acquit de Comptant*.[33]

Use of Ordonnances de Comptant increased substantially over time. In 1582 the total issued was 751,538 livres. The annual average for the years 1630–42 was just under 5 million livres. In

1643 the total rose to 18,200,000 livres. In 1644 it was 59,457,000 livres, in 1645 it was 57,700,000 livres, and in 1646 it was 58,800,000 livres. After that there is a break in the data, a result, no doubt, of the dislocation caused by the Fronde. La Bazinière claimed that the total in 1653 was 16,156,499 livres, a figure which probably reflects the Fronde. The annual totals rose towards their former level as the more obvious effects of civil war died away. La Bazinière stated during his trial that the figure for 1656 was 49,575,365 livres, a total presumably added up for the incompetent treasurer by one of his clerks, and therefore possibly accurate. It seems likely that the levels for the later years of the surintendance of Fouquet were even higher. The Chambre de Justice is said to have found Ordonnances de Comptant amounting to 384 million livres for the years 1655–61. This would give an annual average of 64 million livres. If one may trust La Bazinière's figure for 1656 and assume a process of growth in the succeeding annual totals, it appears probable that the total for 1660 was of the order of 80 million livres—a figure roughly as large as the whole of the royal income as it existed in the theoretical cloud-cuckoo-land of the *Etat au vrai*.[34]

Part of the explanation of the growth implied in these figures may be found in the increasing number of categories of payment made under the device. Gifts to great personages at court or at foreign courts, expenses for journeys undertaken on royal business, supplementary payments to ambassadors over and above their appropriation written into the *Etat par estimation*, such were the original uses. Later came less legitimate use on the construction of royal buildings. Least legitimate of all was use for repaying loans, for paying Remises and interest on the various categories of royal income mentioned above, and for paying, at face value, old but reassigned Billets de l'Epargne.[35] The least legitimate use consumed far more money than the legitimate did. In fact, by 1661 the Ordonnance de Comptant had become simply a means of padding out the various periodic statements of royal accounts submitted to the Chambre des Comptes. The Ordonnance was used to justify a number of tricks in relation to royal credit. These could not otherwise be used because the Chambre des Comptes would have invoked laws which, though made by the monarchy, would, if strictly interpreted, have made the conduct of financial affairs virtually impossible in time of financial dearth.

It was stated above that Remises were legitimately made to financiers in lieu of interest on credit which they supplied to the Crown. The rate permitted was one-sixth (16·66 per cent) of the total credit given. Such reductions were more or less properly made by Ordonnance de Comptant. The improper use of such Ordonnances arose when the credit situation of the Crown became so bad that even this barely legal semi-official rate was no longer applicable in the world of affairs, when the lowest rate at which credit might be obtained might rise to 50 per cent, or, as Forbonnais put it, when *Affaires Extraordinaires* had to be negotiated at the second denier.[36] Adjustments had to be made if the state were to receive any credit at all. Some of these adjustments were made openly, as in the *Ordonnances de différence de fonds* which the state issued on Rentes sur l'Hôtel de Ville. On paper, financiers taking up new Rentes would pay the full legal price. But they would be reimbursed for anything up to 85 per cent of that legal price. The reimbursement would be made by Ordonnance de Comptant signed by chancelier and surintendants, contrôleurs-généraux and intendants des finances.[37] Both the terms of such a document and the names at its foot show how firmly the financial administration was committed to evading laws and regulations promulgated for its defence. The state's collusion in the process of cheating itself is here both clear and formal.

Such open complicity was not countenanced with regard to other forms of loan and advance, partly because such credit was considered less legitimate than Rentes, protected as the latter were by the safeguards of legal fiction mentioned in the section devoted to them above. High interest rates on loans and advances were paid by Ordonnances de Comptant. Since the form of the Ordonnance demanded a brief statement of the reason for its payment, and since interest rates in excess of the legal rate of 5·55 per cent could not be justified to the satisfaction of the Chambre des Comptes, it was necessary to resort to deception. A supplementary interest payment could be justified only by stating in the Ordonnance de Comptant that the payment was for interest on some other loan or advance on a treaty. These loans and treaties were fictitious, serving merely as pretexts for paying out money which would satisfy the Chambre des Comptes providing it did not look too closely.[38]

The Chambre des Comptes was encouraged not to look too closely by a number of manoeuvres designed to make such inspection complicated. The Ordonnances for fictitious loans, for example, were not paid in cash, as in theory they should have been. They were made out as Ordonnances de Comptant purely because of the secrecy accorded to the Comptant account. They were immediately reassigned not for cash payment but for Billets de l'Epargne. These Billets, which guaranteed the payment of the sums mentioned in the Ordonnances, were not honoured immediately, but deliberately held over for a time and split into various parts, and the parts joined with parts of other sums of other Billets de l'Epargne. Afterwards, these second Billets were themselves split up into parts and joined to others, all with the aim of confusing the state accounting machine so that it could not find out what had happened. Eventually those running accounting machinery would give up in despair, and the illegal Billets, now well matured, could be honoured (if that is the right world) in safety.

It was only when a special tribunal like a Chambre de Justice was set up that there was any real attempt to analyse what had gone on. And even the Chambre de Justice of 1661, goaded on as it was by the formidable cajoling of Colbert, could sort out only a few particularly corrupt transactions, leaving the bulk of such things on one side. One sympathises with the tired magistrates as one reads the voluminous and complex *procès-verbaux* tracing the tergiversations which had been undertaken by the financiers, the long series of forgeries of some documents, the elaborately casual defacing of others by blots covering payees' names and the sums they were to receive, the deliberate reference to obscure registers which would be difficult to find, let alone consult, and so on. The point that emerges time after time from such procès-verbaux is that most of the central administrators were once again involved in mass conspiracy. Clerks of the Surintendance happily forged hundreds of documents supposed to have been written in the Epargne. The contrôleur-général, who was supposed to prevent any alteration of documents after they had been ratified by the

Conseil des Finances, indulged himself in an orgy of totally illegal cross-hatching. Those who profited from such things, to the tune of millions of livres each, included all the important commis, trésoriers, Traitants and Munitionnaires. Nor was this all, for there is proof that three of the four secretaries of state in office during the ministry of Mazarin profited too, as did great nobles like the Princesse Palatine and the Duc de Guise.[39]

All this related merely to fictitious loans. There was another field of operation of comparable size and importance relating to fraudulent treaties. In such treaties a number of disparate schemes were spatchcocked together in so confused a way that it was impossible for the government's accounting system to decide which had been honestly carried out, which carried out dishonestly, and which not carried out at all. In one such treaty dated 29 August 1657 and arranged by François Jacquier for a Forfait of 9 million livres, eight major schemes and a host of minor ones were to be operated by the great Traitant. In the event, only 3,500,000 livres ever came into the Epargne from the treaty, and its arrival was followed closely by Jacquier himself on a successful mission to appropriate the sum in payment of his Remise and supposed expenses on the treaty. Payment was of course by Ordonnance de Comptant, and without the investigation undertaken by the Chambre de Justice Jacquier's speedy departure with his Ordonnance would have been the last heard of the treaty.[40]

Fraud in purchase of Rentes, in reassignment of old Billets de l'Epargne, in loans and in treaties, all of which was made possible by the abuse of Ordonnances de Comptant, gave the financiers an inducement to co-operate with the state in its search for credit. Financiers might engage in transactions for which they would not in the first instance receive a satisfactory return in interest. They might indeed not even be repaid the sums which they advanced in the different ways which have been indicated. But the profits which they might make in other sectors made up for these losses. They knew that without their willingness to sustain losses, they would not eventually be given the chance to make huge profits. A man who would not lend without the hope of quick formal repayment could not expect to be allowed to engage in treaties in which it was understood he might make a considerable killing. It may be argued that the profits made by financiers in these frauds were so large as to make nonsense of the idea that they were merely an indirect form of interest. Taking the period 1653–61 on its own, this would indeed be so. Yet as the careers of many of the more important financiers of the period pass under review, it is clear that the effect of the Fronde upon them is an essential part of the picture. Profits made in the fat years of the last phase of the public careers of Mazarin and Fouquet represented not only interest on current loans but reparations for the disaster of 1648, which was in a sense the application of the last and most disastrous expedient of all, the declaration of state bankruptcy.

This chapter and the last have attempted to set down just how the expedients adopted by the monarchy to keep itself afloat worked in the seventeenth century down to the end of the ministry of Mazarin. But it is necessary to add to the static analysis of the Extraordinary Machine adopted above some reference to the confusion that marked the conduct of the royal finances in this exceedingly murky period of their history. Discussion of Rentes, treaties and loans concentrates attention on three nodal points about which expedients focused. It should not be presumed, however, that contemporaries would have agreed with the division of the Extraordinary Machine into three parts, and the attempt it represents to understand what was going on. Contemporaries were simply incapable of visualising the Extraordinary Machine as anything more than a variety of Chaos. Men in the seventeenth century loved clear and distinct pictures of orderly and rational systems, of things, for example, like the Ordinary Machine. This, as it was described by contemporary analysts, was no more than a convenient and comfortable projection of orderly intentions on to a screen composed of disorderly and rumbustious elements, comprehension of whose dynamics was far beyond the primitive structural and social analysis of the time. But the Extraordinary Machine did not possess even the dubious advantage of a blueprint comparable to that designed by anxious theorists for the Ordinary Machine. Men gave up in horror at the sight of an interminable extent of expedients and devious schemes.

Affaires extraordinaires represented in a concentrated way

much that seventeenth-century men hated. It was not just a question of the obvious flaws that twentieth-century man would notice—the inefficiency, the corruption, the short-sighted alienation of precious capital assets. Nor was it just a question of the savagery which attended the extraction of many of the expedients of which the Extraordinary Machine was composed. Nor was it even the fact that the financiers who operated such expedients made large sums out of the misery and destitution of the populace and the incompetence and corruption of royal administrators. Behind all these things lay the feeling that the finances were simply out of control, and that the whole kingdom was being destroyed in consequence.

Wherever one cared to look, this seemed to be the case. The entire royal administrative system was in the grip of the venality of offices. The Crown borrowed with an all-consuming and deliberate recklessness, the only limit on its borrowing being the availability of funds for loan. And despite all the desperate efforts on the financial front, there was still barely enough money to keep the Crown's military apparatus in being, let alone in a condition to undertake strenuous and sustained offensive action. Over all this, the surintendant des finances was supposed to preside. Not surprisingly his power was as real as that of the Lord of Misrule at a medieval festival. What had happened to the Surintendance was in fact a microcosm of what had happened to the financial system as a whole. The powers of the surintendant, which were so clearly and distinctly described in official pronouncements and semi-official gazetteers, were as nothing compared to the powers of the commis of the Surintendance. This situation, in a society and a century obsessed with precedence and order, was incomprehensible and more than a little frightening.

Given the confusion of the situation, it would be futile to try to draw up totals for the Crown's income from Extraordinary Affairs in a particular year. Nevertheless, there is a way of coming to an evaluation of the importance of such affairs to the monarchy. Imponderably inefficient though the Extraordinary Machine was, it enabled the Crown to remain on its feet as it came to the victorious end of its century-long struggle against Spain. In fact the Extraordinary Machine served France better than the gold and silver of the New World served Spain. To that extent, the machine had done its job. But the cost to France was incalculable, and was still being paid, particularly in terms of reduced or destroyed administrative efficiency, as the monarchy dissolved into revolution over a century later.

Notes to this chapter are on pages 248–50

Chapter 4 ACCOUNTING

MALADMINISTRATION OF and corruption in the royal finances were basic problems of the monarchy of the *ancien régime*. To circumvent these maladies, ingenious attempts were made to lay down precise instructions for the correct conduct of business. The implementation of these instructions had to be supervised. This supervision was performed by two different accounting methods: first, the administrative control of day-to-day transactions, and second, judicial proceedings against those suspected of financial improprieties. Each method had two subdivisions. Administrative control was performed in the first instance by the *surintendant* and *Conseil des Finances*, and in the second by the *Contrôle-général des Finances*. Judicial control was performed as a matter of normal practice by the *Chambre des Comptes*. In extreme circumstances the government might set up a special tribunal, or *Chambre de Justice*, in the hope of re-establishing correct modes of operation. None of these bodies was effective in the control of financial administration during the first six decades of the seventeenth century except over limited periods when strong individuals chanced to be in a position to make the provisions of the law respected. It is a matter of some interest to see why this should have been so.

It has been shown how the various elements of royal income were brought in, and in particular how the expedients for extracting money worked. Many of the modes of operation involved were illegal and were known to be so by those who used them. Why were such things permitted by the state accounting systems? The answer is composite: the structure of institutions and the procedure for their accounting were inadequate; and more specially, the needs of the state were such, during the war against

Spain, that it was in a sense necessary for the administrative accounting systems in particular to be taken over by men who had little interest in keeping to the law.

Theoretically the surintendant des finances was under the administrative control of the king. The surintendant arranged the flow of funds (the process of *ordonnancement*), as and when the king directed. In the special circumstances of the period 1643–61, when the king was too young to give such direction, it was supplied by the *Conseil Secret*, of which Mazarin was the effective head. Such direction as Mazarin gave was in a negative sense, as for example in 1659, when he expressed his unwillingness to allow the surintendant to anticipate the income from the *Taille* for 1661. On the whole the cardinal was satisfied with the conduct of financial administration so long as his demands for money were met. Since many of these demands could not be considered even remotely legitimate, he could hardly have favoured too strict an observance of form. The surintendant was, then, by and large unchecked, particularly during the years 1653–60. This should not have been so, even though these years passed with something like a vacuum at the centre of authority where there should have been the powerful exercise of the monarch's will. The surintendant may not have observed the law, but he had no excuse for not knowing what the law was.

The administrative accounting control of the state's finances was the responsibility of the surintendant and the Conseil des Finances. A *règlement* of 7 October 1645 laid down with precision how this control was to be performed: each week on Friday morning, the surintendant and the Conseil des Finances were to assemble to examine the means by which the expenditure of the state might be made, and to see how those expenses newly commanded by the Crown might be met. The various means were afterwards to be analysed and considered, first by the *Petite Direction*, and then by the meeting of the Conseil des Finances on Wednesday afternoon. At the meeting on Friday, a statement was to be drawn up containing all the expenditure which was to be made. Alongside this statement there was to be a list of the specific elements of royal income from which the items of expenditure were to be paid, or to which they were to be assigned. The whole document was to be agreed to by those present, and ratified (*arrêté*) and signed by surintendant and contrôleurs-généraux des finances. No alteration was to be made without the formal approval of the Conseil des Finances.[1] The expedients described above, particularly in relation to interest rates on loans, should have been impossible, given the precise terms of this document. Yet such a document could not guarantee the exclusion of illegal payments. Technically illegal instruments like *Ordonnances de différence de fonds* would be signed by anything up to eight members of the Conseil des Finances without any questions being raised as to the justification of the proceedings. What happened was that when they were confronted with a règlement as difficult as that of 1645, the surintendant and the Conseil des Finances simply ignored it.

The surintendant and the Conseil des Finances had certain more general supervisory responsibilities over all the people who handled public money, the *comptables*. All comptables had, in theory, to justify the probity of their administration before the Conseil des Finances. This in fact was very easy, for the confusion which comptables, from the *trésorier de l'Epargne* down to the various local trésoriers, introduced into their accounts left the Conseil des Finances with very little idea of what had gone on, and virtually no possibility of deciding whether sums of money had gone astray. Had there been time, it might have been possible to sort things out; but the number of accounts which had to be examined and their diversity made quite impossible the analysis of specific items of expenditure, without which certainty could not be attained.[2]

The surintendant des finances should have been able to count on the work of the Contrôle-général des Finances, a composite royal commission consisting of one or two contrôleurs-généraux, a staff of clerks headed by the *commis à l'enregistrement des fonds*, and a number of *intendants des finances*.[3] Some indication of what in theory were the functions of the *contrôleur-général* may be derived from another règlement of 7 October 1645. All *Arrêts* produced by the Conseil des Finances had to be signed by him as well as by other highly placed officials. When the surintendant had drawn up his various *Etats par estimation*, these had to be signed by the contrôleur-général before they could be despatched to those officers and financiers responsible for collecting royal income and for whose guidance the Etats par estimation were prepared. Similarly the individual *Etats au vrai* sent in by officers and financiers, and the global Etat au vrai prepared by the surintendant relating to the sums of money which had actually been received, had to be signed by the contrôleur-général. In appending his signature to all these documents he implied that he had examined and approved them and that, having been through this process of *contrôle*, they could be considered authentic and accurate.[4]

On paper all this looked very well. The contrôleur-général had his staff to help him in checking up on practical things like the receipt of money at the Epargne. As the size of this staff grew by stages down to 1661, the effectiveness of the Contrôle-général ought to have increased. Division of labour must have lightened the burden of analysing the immense numbers of separate accounts. The law was clear. The men for the job were at hand. The maladministration of Mazarin and Fouquet should not have been possible. Why, then, did the situation revealed by the Chambre de Justice of 1661 come about? The answers are to be found partly in the basic nature of the institution of the Contrôle-général, and partly in the nature and primary value to the state of the men who worked for that institution.

One of the most important aspects of the institutions of the *ancien régime* is that there was no necessary concordance between regulations for the conduct of an institution and the way in which that institution actually worked. The point is an obvious one, but in the case of the Contrôle-général it is important, because the day-to-day operation of the institution in the period 1643–61 was quite distinct from the ideal laid down in the règlement of 1645 referred to above. Further, the way in which the contrôleur-général conducted himself underwent significant change during the period.

Particelli d'Emery was appointed contrôleur-général in May 1643. His tenure of the post lasted until his appointment as surintendant des finances in July 1647. During those four years, the Comte d'Avaux and the Président de Bailleul had the name of surintendants, but they possessed neither the time, nor the strength of character, nor the knowledge, nor the ability, to administer the royal finances. Particelli did the job for them. His eventual appointment to the surintendance did no more than recognise in form a situation which everyone knew had existed in fact ever since Anne of Austria took over the regency. All this made nonsense of the règlement of 1645. The contrôleur-général, far from being the watchdog implied in that document, was engaged in producing a series of desperate expedients ranging through the list of illegal devices described above. The basis for this exercise of power rested not on legally defined office but on the fact that, like Mazarin, Particelli was one of Richelieu's creatures singled out by him before his death as worthy to carry on the administration of the state. The reason why Particelli was not made surintendant before 1647 was that Mazarin was afraid that such an appointment would allow Particelli to seize control of the whole direction of the state, a control vested in Mazarin's hands only by the constitutionally dubious authority of the post of *premier ministre*.

It should not be assumed, however, that Particelli abandoned all the formal duties of his contrôle-général. As he was to do during his tenure of the surintendance, he resisted Mazarin's unrelenting pressure for money. As Mazarin gradually assumed control of the expenditure of the royal household and of the arrangements for supplying the royal armies with food and equipment, he found that the contrôleur-général began to resist his demands for cash. But there was far more to the correct exercise of the post of contrôleur-général than the courage to withstand the greed of a premier ministre. Particelli's day-to-day conduct in fact made it impossible for rigorous accounting methods to be followed. The circumstances of the period were such that the man who should have been upholding those methods worked in a way that subverted them almost completely.[5]

Those who succeeded Particelli as contrôleurs-généraux des finances failed for different reasons to make the process of contrôle a reality. Where he had had too much power, they possessed too little. Antoine Le Camus, who was sworn in as contrôleur-général on 21 April 1648, and François Ménardeau-Champré, who became his colleague at the end of the Fronde, were essentially lawyer-administrators who were appointed by Mazarin because they had proved themselves loyal to him, and at the same time gave off an aura of parlementaire respectability that would mislead diehard Frondeurs into thinking that the royal finances were now being run according to the law. The two men neither hindered corruption nor acted as sources of credit which the Crown might tap. In the negative role of acquiescing in corruption they had a certain utility, for they could have made things awkward had they so wished. But in 1657, there arose a need to have a man in the Contrôle-général who would actively further the search for credit, and Fouquet decided that the two contrôleurs-généraux must go.[6] After a certain amount of clumsy shuffling, they were replaced by two new men: Louis Le Tonnelier de Breteuil and Barthélemy Hervart. Le Tonnelier was, like his two predecessors, merely a lawyer-administrator intended to serve as a convenient front of respectability.[7] It was Hervart who did the work of contrôleur-général for the next four years. His promotion brought him no problems of adjusting to a new job, for he had been doing the work of the contrôleurs-généraux for the previous four years, although officially he was only commis à l'enregistrement des fonds.

Hervart was by origin a financier, who was able to combine vigorous religious belief with great financial dishonesty. He was a zealous German Protestant, born at Lyons in 1607 to the descendant of a patrician family of Augsburg. His father was a banker who died some time before 1632, leaving his sons Barthélemy and Jean-Henri (b 1609) a considerable fortune. This was used initially in war-contracting operations for Bernard of Saxe-Weimar, Protestant champion in Germany after the death of Gustavus-Adolphus. Eventually the Hervart brothers entered the service of France, and by 1649 Barthélemy had become one of Mazarin's chief sources of credit. In 1650 he was rewarded with the post of intendant des finances. His appointment as commis à l'enregistrement followed in 1653.[8]

The formal duties of such a post were the writing down of the financial instruments of the Conseil des Finances, in particular the various types of *Mandement* and *Ordonnance*.[9] This can hardly have taken up much of Hervart's energies, for as commis he had time to spare for playing an illegal role which he was to retain after he became contrôleur-général. This role was quite simply to prevent the Contrôle-général from operating. In this he was carrying out Mazarin's wishes. The methods used were economical of effort, but effective. For example, from 1654, no more registers of the money paid into the Epargne were kept by the Contrôle-général. This made it virtually impossible to keep any check on what the Epargne was doing.

Hervart also had spare time to play other roles, in particular that of lending money to the state. His posts in the Contrôle-général gave him a much larger range of sources of credit than he had had as a private citizen. This wide credit was used to save Fouquet at a critical juncture in 1657 when Delorme tried to destroy the surintendant. The knowledge that he had been so important led him to try to break Fouquet after Servien's death in 1659, by denouncing Fouquet to Mazarin. Hervart apparently hoped to gain Colbert's support in this attack, but he seriously misjudged his own reputation, for in a letter to Mazarin of 28 October 1659, Colbert described Hervart as a person for whom he had never had any respect.[10] One of the reasons for Colbert's hostility may have been his feeling that if anyone were to encompass Fouquet's fall it should be himself, Colbert, rather than Hervart. Another may have been that Hervart had been far too heavily involved in all manner of dishonest undertakings for Colbert to wish to be associated with him. Certainly the records of the Chambre de Justice contain references to Hervart's wrongdoing. He is known to have been responsible for altering the figures on *Ordonnances de Comptant* in collusion with Fouquet, and without the authorisation of the Conseil des Finances. He is known, too, to have profited from association with financiers like François Jacquier, Guillaume Languet and Nicolas Monnerot in fictitious loans and fraudulent treaties.[11]

If the contrôleur-général was a byword for corruption, his subordinates, the intendants des finances, were no better. The legal duties of these officials related to the humdrum processes of administrative control. For example, they had to check and verify the totals of sums of money arriving at the Epargne. They were occasionally called on to add their signatures to Ordonnances de Comptant, on the theory, no doubt, that a document signed by a large number of people might be assumed by the gullible to be legal even if it was in fact grossly fraudulent. They might also be sent out into the provinces to stimulate the local financial administration, or they might be employed in arranging *Affaires Extraordinaires*.[12]

The significant facts about them in the period from 1643 are that their numbers tended to increase, and that they were chosen not to assist the state to regulate its expenditure but to act as agents for the supply of money to the Crown. Moreover, far from assisting in the correct observance of procedure, they helped to render it impossible. From 1643 until 1649, there were four intendants des finances: Jacques Tubeuf, Séraphin de Mauroy, Claude Le Charon and Pierre Mallier de Moncharville. In 1649, four new posts were created and sold to Jacques Le Tillier, Jacques Bordier, Guillaume de Bordeaux and Etienne Foullé. In 1649 Le Charon died, and was replaced by Hervart. In 1650 Tubeuf and Mallier resigned, and were succeeded by Pierre Gargan and Denis Marin. Gargan died in 1657 and was succeeded by Delorme. In 1654 four new posts of intendants des finances were created. They were sold to Jacques Paget, Claude de Boislève, Guillaume de Brisacier and Claude Housset for 200,000 livres each. The increases of 1649 and 1654 were not permanent. In October 1658 the twelve posts were reduced to four, held by Mauroy, Le Tillier, Bordier and Bordeaux. In 1661 they were reduced still further to two, held by Jean-Baptiste Colbert and Marin.[13]

Most of these men were important financiers in their own right. Some, of course, have appeared before in this study as holders of high and corruptly used office: Delorme and Hervart in particular. Most of the others were *Traitants*, *Munitionnaires* and lenders to the state. Many were members of all three groups. Almost all are known to have profited, some enormously, from the range of illegal expedients described in earlier chapters. Probably the most corrupt of all was Boislève, who was more or less in charge (subject to the intervention of the chief clerk of the *Surintendance*) of arranging all the Extraordinary Affairs of the years 1655–8. The advantages of such a position to Boislève as Traitant, and to his friends Monnerot and Jacquier, can be imagined.[14] But Boislève was distinguished from his colleagues more by his success than by the nature of his activities. All the intendants des finances had links with the world of the financiers too strong for there to have been any hope that they would

exercise their nominal duties of preventing fraud in the royal
finances.

Administrative control of the financial machine and its operatives was clearly a total failure. And so the Crown tended, when
it became aware of the extent of its financial problems, to rely on
an older method of administration—the medieval one of judicial
process. In theory, the Crown could turn in this field to one of
the oldest institutions of the French monarchy, the Chambre des
Comptes. In fact, however, this body had become almost useless
as an accounting agency long before the seventeenth century.

The origins of the Chambre des Comptes are a matter of
speculation. It is known that the Chambre was originally part of
the royal court. As administration grew more technical during the
twelfth century, two subsections evolved out of that court, the one
devoted to the royal finances, the other to royal justice. The
officials of the first subsection were the first recognisable accounting agents of the Crown. They became known successively as the
maîtres de la cour de France and then as *maîtres des comptes du roi*.
They began to hold sessions at fixed times at the *Trésor-royal* in
the Temple in Paris. Gradually their task formalised itself as the
checking of the accounts of royal officials. The maîtres ceased to
follow the Crown on its journeys, and in the early years of the
fourteenth century they became known collectively as the
Chambre des Comptes. The high point of the power of the
Chambre came during the reign of Philippe de Valois in 1339–40,
when the king gave the Chambre considerable freedom to make
decisions on administrative questions during his absence on
military campaigns.[15]

The Chambre des Comptes never forgot these ancient glories.
It always insisted that it was the senior *cour souveraine*, and that
its authority was greater even than that of the Parlement.[16] Such
claims were generally ignored during the seventeenth century.
The government might succumb to pressure from the cours
souveraines in the matter of limiting the issue of Ordonnances de
Comptant, as in the royal Déclaration of 22 December 1648. But
once the Crown felt itself strong again, such submission was at an
end. The Chambre des Comptes was put firmly in its place on 17
December 1652 when the Crown issued *Lettres patentes* breaking
the Arrêts produced by the Chambre against the offending

Ordonnances.[17] Royal policy affected the Chambre des Comptes in other ways. It ceased to be a single body controlling the accounts of the whole kingdom. The successive creation of provincial chambres at Aix, Montpellier, Grenoble, Dijon, Blois, Rouen, Nantes and Bordeaux had limited the authority of the original Chambre des Comptes of Paris during the fifteenth, sixteenth and early seventeenth centuries.

And then, of course, there was the diluting effect of venality of offices, which made a joke of the probity that the original Chambre had considered so important. The composition of the Chambre des Comptes of Paris had changed markedly since 1388, when it had contained 2 *présidents*, 8 *maîtres* and 12 *auditeurs*. By the accession of Henri III in 1574 there were 8 présidents, 40 maîtres, 12 *correcteurs*, and 47 auditeurs, together with a number of less essential categories like those of *avocat-général*, *procureur-général*, *greffier* and *garde des livres*. Henri III created 16 more maîtres, 6 more correcteurs and 12 more auditeurs. Richelieu carried the process on. In 1635–40, there were creations of 1 président, 16 maîtres, 14 correcteurs, 20 auditeurs and a host of lesser officers including a whole new chancellery. The Chambre could not evade this widening of its ranks, but it was able to withstand some influences. It insisted that a man who bought an office of the Chambre should not have any outstanding accounts for royal money which might become liable to *correction* after the new officer had been admitted to the Chambre. It was on this ground that Particelli d'Emery was prevented from becoming a member of the Chambre in 1624. The Chambre went further in 1629 when it tried to exclude from office in the Chambre anyone who had ever been a royal comptable. But this had only a limited success, since the Crown, if it wished, could force the Chambre to accept the membership of a financier. This was done for Claude Cornuel, who took over one of the posts of président of the Chambre in 1635.[18]

In the seventeenth century the Chambre des Comptes retained two uncontested fields of operation. One was the function of examining all potential royal officers. Despite the extension of the venal system, the new officer had to submit evidence of his suitability to the Chambre des Comptes before he might swear an oath of allegiance to the king and before the Chambre would register his *Lettres de provision*. When all these things had been done, the Chambre would formally instal him in his office.

The other field was jurisdiction in matters of accounts. Through the intermediary of the contrôleur-général des finances, the Chambre received notification of all laws concerning the conduct of comptables. It had to register the règlements in which those laws were expressed, and to supervise their observance. This was part of its general judicial responsibility for accounts. All comptables had in theory to submit their accounts to the Chambre at the end of each year of exercise of office. The procedure for dealing with those accounts was highly formalised, and primarily judicial. This was a reflection of the medieval concept of administration by judicial process.[19] Such a concept naturally depended on a body of substantive though uncodified law, and thus on a mass of rules.

These rules would have been a good thing had they been applied to the basic mechanisms of tax-collection and expedients like the sale of office or the alienation of Rentes. The Chambre des Comptes had a potentially useful role to play in preventing the local corruption from which the French financial administration suffered. But this role remained merely potential, for the Chambre was rarely able to enforce the presentation of accounts, let alone their judgement. Even under Richelieu's administration, comptables refused to bring their accounts in until years after they were due. The weakness of the government in the years 1643–53 ensured that this situation would deteriorate further. Even when accounts were brought in, it took an unconscionably long time for anything to be done about them if they were defective. For example, in 1657 the Chambre seems suddenly to have realised that the accounts of the trésoriers des Parties Casuelles were not all that they might be, and so they exhumed accounts of trésoriers long since dead. The heirs of these men were ordered to present themselves at the Chambre des Comptes early in 1658 to defend their relatives' conduct as trésoriers. It was hardly an efficient method of inquiry to wait until comptables had been dead for a decade or more before deciding that their accounts needed investigation.[20]

Despite failure to fulfil its primary role, the Chambre des Comptes insisted that its purpose was to supervise all the elements of financial administration. This led it to attack the Crown as and when it could for what the Chambre felt were breaches of the law. In particular, it refused to countenance an interest rate on loans above the legal one of 5·55 per cent. Any rate above this was usurious and contrary to the laws of God. Capital holders who demanded a higher rate, the Crown which granted it to them: all were conniving at mortal sin.[21]

It has been shown in the section on interest rates how the Crown tried to get round this obstructive position. But it is permissible to remark here that if the attitude of the Chambre had been more realistic, some of the corruption of the financial system would have been avoided. The need to make informal payments in lieu of interest involved the Surintendance, Conseil des Finances, Epargne and Contrôle-général des Finances in the complicated modes of concealment described above. These modes created a contempt for the whole idea of control of the financial system and, though their justification lay in the need of the Crown for credit, they contributed to the dislocation of the state's finances. Had the state been able to offer a realistic price for money, had it not been forced to flout the old regulations about interest, then its minor officials might have engaged in corruption with greater circumspection and with a less damaging effect on royal income. The Chambre des Comptes was trying to do its duty, but its conception of that duty was derived from the fourteenth century. The nature of the monarchy had changed, and its costs had increased geometrically, but the Chambre des Comptes refused to understand or accept what had happened. It is hardly surprising that the Chambre was, by and large, simply a clamorous nuisance in the seventeenth century.

It is clear, then, that neither administrative control by surintendant, Conseil des Finances, and Contrôle-général, nor judicial control by the Chambre des Comptes, worked. Consequently, the government, in default of any effective accounting system, would occasionally have recourse to the extraordinary device of the Chambre de Justice. The word 'extraordinary' is used for two reasons. First, such Chambres illustrate the bizarre attitude of the French government of the seventeenth century towards finance and financiers. The government needed the financiers and the services they provided. But it was never very far from punishing them severely for the way in which they provided those services, even when the officials who arranged the punishing had often colluded in fraud with those who were punished. Furthermore, punishment was accompanied by an inordinate amount of moralistic puffing and blowing carried on by men whose own unpunished guilt, one might have thought, would have led them to fleece their former friends in a decorous silence. The second reason is that the institution of Chambres de Justice, or even the mere threat of their institution, was used by the government as a *moyen extraordinaire* of procuring money either as fines or as blackmail from those involved in the royal finances.

The basic justification for the use of the Chambre de Justice receded until it was often little more than a pretext for frightening the financiers into paying sums that they would not otherwise have proffered. Sully's investigations into the conduct of the financiers ended in mid-air in 1607 when the financiers themselves arranged the taxes which they should pay to have the Chambre de Justice rescinded. They compounded with the king for 1 million livres, and thirty-three of the more considerable of them guaranteed that the money would be paid. The Chambre de Justice of 1624 followed a similar course. It began as an attempt to purify the finances, and ended with a treaty by which fines amounting to 10,800,000 livres were to be paid by the financiers.[22] The Lettres patentes of 16 July 1648 authorising the setting up of a Chambre de Justice give the conventional royal statement on the need for inquiries:

> We have resolved, so that we may make known to our subjects both the love which we have for them and our desire to remove the causes of their sufferings, to establish in a short while a Chambre de Justice, to proceed to the investigation and punishment of the acts of violence [and] extortion . . . which may have been committed in our lands by whoever it may be, and of whatever quality and condition, in the imposition and levy of our resources, as much for the Tailles as for other taxes.[23]

Despite these brave words, and the attempt of the *Parlement* of Paris to proceed against particularly corrupt financiers like Catelan and Tabouret, Mazarin refused to allow matters to go very far. The Chambre de Justice of 1648 was even less effective than that of 1624. It was abolished by an edict promulgated at the royal *Lit de Justice* of 31 December 1652. Its only positive value to the government was to be in 1654, when a new Chambre de Justice began to extract money from the financiers. The excuse given for the general compositions which it levied from financiers was that the individual was to pay up

> to permit himself to be discharged from all inquiries that might be undertaken against him in consequence of the Declaration of July 1648 ordering the setting up of the Chambre de Justice.[24]

The extent to which the government was enmeshed in the complicated mechanisms of financial corruption is typified by the way in which the concept of the Chambre de Justice had become assimilated as a moyen extraordinaire.

From what has been already said concerning the financial system as it operated during the later years of the ministry of Mazarin, it is abundantly clear that if ever the setting up of a Chambre de Justice was necessary, it was in 1661. The frame of reference of the institution was given in an edict of November 1661: the king stated his intention to resume the direction of his finances, and to analyse their administration down to the smallest detail. The maladministration of those finances had led to 'all the ills that our peoples have suffered' and had caused 'the extraordinary surcharges which we have been compelled to load on them to meet the pressing needs of the state'. Those responsible for this maladministration were to be punished:

> A small number of persons, profiting from this maladministration, have, by illegitimate ways and using methods prohibited by our ordinances, amassed prodigious fortunes with great rapidity; made immense acquisitions; and given to the public a scandalous example by their gross pride and opulence and by a vulgar display capable of corrupting behaviour [*moeurs*] and all the maxims of public probity.

These men were to be interrogated and punished by a Chambre de Justice.[25]

The words are similar to those used at other critical junctures before 1661, and it has been conventional, at least among the biographers of Fouquet, to sneer at this new Chambre de Justice and to make great play of the involvement of Colbert, its moving spirit, in the illicit operations which the Chambre was supposed to punish.[26] All this is legitimate enough. But it is only fair to point out that the Chambre de Justice of 1661–5 was certainly not intended, at the outset at least, to repeat the shabby manoeuvres of its predecessors. It was, on the contrary, to clear up the royal finances once and for all. To this end, its ambit was not merely the investigation of central financiers in Paris. Colbert's concern for all levels of administration is revealed in the instructions for local agents (*subdélégués*) of the Chambre who were sent out all over France. These agents were to investigate and report back on all examples of maladministration which had harmed the interests of the king or those of his subjects. Not only were frauds diverting money from the Crown to be examined, but also instances of violence against private individuals and cases where comptables had exacted bribes before paying out sums ordered by royal assignments. Similarly the government published documents which were read in parish churches throughout the land enjoining those who knew of any examples of maladministration to come forward without fear of reprisals from interested parties. The powers of the subdélégués were large, and included the right to act both as prosecutor and judge in local cases. These powers were used to good effect. Some of the subdélégués were responsible for clearing up examples of persistent maladministration of finances which had been going on unchecked for years, despite the attempts of judicial institutions up to the level of provincial parlements and *cours des Aides* to reduce those guilty of such misconduct to obedience.[27]

There were nevertheless certain obvious limitations on the operation of even this best of Chambres de Justice. The political ramifications of the fall of Fouquet did indeed prevent the Chambre from following an unrestricted line of inquiry into financial administration. References to Mazarin, Colbert, Marin, Hervart and other important administrators and nobles to be found in the primary *procès-verbaux* preserved by Olivier Lefebvre d'Ormesson were excised from the official record written by Foucault and approved by Colbert. The Chambre de Justice had to investigate financial problems, but it had also to condemn Fouquet. The way in which Colbert carried out this latter aim is not pleasant. It began with Colbert's personally

editing Fouquet's private papers with a view to depriving the
fallen surintendant of the means of defending himself. It continued with the partisan chairmanship of the Chambre exercised
by the apparently senile chancelier, Séguier, and ended with the
odious Denis Talon's travesty of a closing speech full of wild and
incoherent accusations. It was only the calm insistence of Ormesson that prevented the proceedings from becoming merely a
political trial. His summing up, as Foucault records it, is a model
of patient analysis and judicious generalisation. The decision of
the Chambre de Justice was that Fouquet should be banished and
his property confiscated. But the political needs of the state
supervened; by a royal *coup de main*, Fouquet was condemned to
perpetual imprisonment in the fortress of Pignerol. This was
seen to be a miscarriage of justice even in the seventeenth century. Its only justification lay in the need for the king to establish
his own independent authority.[28]

There were other limitations, too, and these more relevant to
a discussion of the royal finances. Even with the best will in the
world, it was extremely difficult to prove that specific financiers
had committed specific crimes. It is one thing for the historian to
infer the involvement of individuals in the less reputable of
financial operations. It was quite another for the lawyers of the
Chambre de Justice to unravel all the frauds committed by
financiers in the years 1635–61 so that watertight cases might be
sustained against specific individuals. In the end the only important people against whom it was felt that a criminal case lay
were Fouquet himself, Bruant, Gourville, the two Monnerot
brothers, Gruin Marchand and Claude de Guénégaud, all of
whom were excluded from the general amnesty accorded by the
Crown in December 1665 to 'comptables, traitants, prêteurs et
gens d'affaires'. The other financiers were fined a total of
156,360,000 livres. Although the full list of these fines and the
reasons for their imposition fills over a thousand pages of the
registers of the Chambre de Justice, it is not clear that the list
was much more than an approximate attempt to dress up the
conventional taxing role of Chambres de Justice in paralegal
phraseology suitable to the precise administrative intentions of
Colbert.[29] Furthermore, the long duration of the Chambre de
Justice was bad for royal credit. A quest for greater precision in

the fines of all the financiers would have made the Chambre even more protracted. Therefore it was felt necessary to call a halt in 1665. Even quite early on in December 1662, the danger of spreading the terms of reference of the inquiry too widely had been felt. The general hostility of the population to the financiers was such that the officers of the *Châtelet* in Paris had assumed the right in November of that year to prosecute all those who had been involved in banking or mercantile operations. The Chambre de Justice had to order the officers of the Châtelet not to enter the houses of those who had 'trafficked in *Billets, Ordonnances* and *Quittances* of the Epargne' in search of criminal activities, since this would be a 'notable prejudice to the freedom of commerce'. Like Mazarin before him, Colbert did not mind fleecing the financial world, but even he objected to the general popular feeling which wished to destroy it.[30]

It is obvious that the accounting systems of the state were by and large incapable of preventing maladministration and fraud. What was more, government officials knew this, since they were habitually involved in both forms of dereliction. Why, then, did they continue to frame règlements like those cited earlier in this chapter, which were designed to prevent breaches of the law? The officials had no intention of obeying the terms of such documents, so that the purpose of such things has to be sought in fields other than that of administrative conduct. In fact, it was mainly a question of keeping up appearances. Those directing the state's affairs would, as was mentioned in this chapter, appoint respectable people to apparently important posts in the financial administration, in the hope that such appointments would convince hostile observers—a category that included the bulk of the population—that all was well and being done according to the law. The règlements of the Conseil des Finances and the Contrôle-général des Finances were intended to play a similar role. Thus is to be explained the divergence between the world of legal theory and that of practice.

The world of theory had its own structure and rationale, and the various règlements fitted into this very well, amplifying and reinforcing, elaborating and defining more precisely, until theory had consistency and order down to the smallest of details. In theory, the Chambre des Comptes, surintendant and Epargne, and the financiers too, could work together in rectitude and harmony. In practice, both these desirable qualities were conspicuously absent. The real world of the financiers operated in ways that were incompatible with the conceptions of order and probity that underlay accounting systems. These systems were in consequence reduced to a mockery. Not merely were they rendered incapable of performing their legal function; they were also used by financiers as means of making more money, as in the case of the Contrôle-général, and of acquiring social prestige, as in the case of the Chambre des Comptes, several of whose members had once been energetic financiers with small concern for any law.

The world of the financiers operated under its own rules. These, it is true, were determined partly by legal theory, in that the imposition of the rigours of basically irrelevant law presented the danger of sporadic and often catastrophic intervention in the fraudulent activities of the individual financier. But most of the determinants lay outside the bounds of governmental institutions and law. Financiers formed a group in French society, and lived and functioned according to patterns to be found in economic affairs, social structure and group psychology. These patterns are the subject of the rest of this book.

Notes to this chapter are on pages 250–1

PART 2

THE WORLD OF THE FINANCIERS

Chapter 5 ORIGINS

THE HISTORY of the *ancien régime* is full of unexpected difficulties, which are partly the result of obvious problems like the disappearance of documents and the failure of men three hundred years ago to record information that would provide answers to the kinds of questions that modern historians are wont to ask. Such difficulties and problems are compounded by differences, often hard to perceive, between the individual and collective mentalities of men long ago and today, and between the social structures and pressures of then and now. This means that it is necessary to tread with care in any undertaking in social history, making a continuous effort to ensure that one does not try to make the evidence bear an interpretative load greater than is warranted, and, even more important, that one does not impose preformed analytical categories too heavily on one's material.

This last point is obviously critical in any field of inquiry. But it is doubly so at the present stage of the study of the society of France under the *ancien régime*. In that study, the old verities have largely gone by the board, and at the moment it is impossible to come up with a theory of the society of the period that would be generally accepted by most scholars. Much of the new research that has been done in the last twenty-five years is still difficult to evaluate, a fact reflected widely in controversies in journals and reviews. Historians are still in the process of investigating the nature of *ancien régime* society piece by piece, group by social group, institution by institution. Each separate sector has its own problems of documentation and methodology. The results of investigations often seem to be reconcilable neither with previous knowledge of the subject, nor with investigations carried on in parallel but distinct fields. This is only to be expected. In the present case, investigation of the subject of this chapter turned up a series of conclusions that are not what might have been expected from a generally accepted interpretation of the economic history of Europe in the early modern period.

Financiers, as will be shown below, did not come from an easily recognised class in society. What is more, they did not necessarily have much to do with what is generally accepted as the rise of capitalism. Some financiers, it is true, had what might be called characteristically 'bourgeois' and 'capitalist' origins, if these terms are rather more loosely defined than some systematic Marxists would allow, that is to say, if one may concede the existence in the rise of capitalism of a phase called Merchant Capitalism. But financiers who were by origin Merchant Capitalists were in a minority. It is apparent that if there was a focus about which the question of financiers' origins concentrated, however loosely, it did not lie, in France at least, in the first stirrings of new forms of economic life. This becomes more clear from the chapter itself, which examines the origins of financiers from three points of view: the geographical places from which financiers and their families started; the earliest known points in society occupied by financiers and their families; and the length of time it took for people to become financiers.

The first factor to be discussed in the origins of the financiers is that of geographical place. It is obvious, even before putting the data through quantitative analysis, that the financiers, though they usually lived in Paris, were not necessarily by origin Parisians. A further point is that even of those who were born in Paris, a significant number came from families which had come to Paris in the recent past. These points can be made the bases of two analytical procedures for the number of cases known. These measure, first, where each person's family originally came from, going back to a limit of a century before the particular person under examination was born; and second, where each person was himself or herself born. Taking all those who had any involvement whatsoever in the financial affairs of the state (that is to say, all those who either held some financial post or exercised some recognisable role in the Extraordinary financial

affairs of the state), it was found that there was information
on eighty-nine cases. These are represented in the following
figure:

FIGURE 1: **Places of Origin of Financiers' Families**

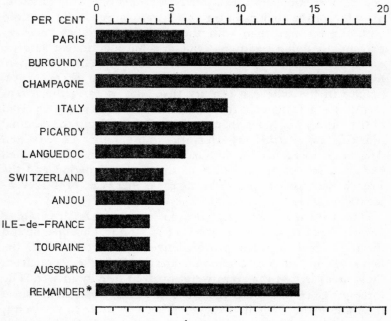

* COMPRISES: AUVERGNE, BÉARN, BERRY, BOURBONNAIS, BRITTANY,
DAUPHINÉ, NORMANDY, POITOU, GERMANY, AND THE ISLAND OF SICILY.

Interpretation of the figure on a basic level is simple enough. It
is evident that the overwhelming majority of families which produced financiers and whose origins are known came from outside
Paris. Further, roughly one-sixth (some 17 per cent) of the
families were of foreign origin. The largest group of such foreign
families was composed of Italians, most of whom appear to have
come from their native land as adjuncts of Mazarin. Two, however, the Cenami brothers, were members of a family which had
been active in France at least as early as the regency of Catherine
de Medici; while another, Particelli d'Emery, was involved in

French affairs from about 1616, some twenty-five years before
Mazarin formally entered the service of the French Crown.[1] Here
the mere counting of heads might lead to the attribution of too
great an importance to Italians in the world of French finance. In
fact, Mazarin's Italian bankers played a minor role in that world,
and their relationship was a purely personal one with Mazarin.
Very few of the Italians in the deck* were more closely involved
with the finances than with the cardinal, and such men represented a dying tradition. Though solid quantitative data are
difficult to come by, it would seem that Italians were more
numerous, and much more heavily involved in French royal
finance in the sixteenth century than they were in the seventeenth. In fact, the only really important foreigner in the period
of the ministry of Mazarin, apart from Particelli and the cardinal
himself, was Barthélemy Hervart, whose father hailed from
Augsburg. In France the dominance of foreign financiers, which
had been so notable a feature of the medieval period and the
French Renaissance, ended during the earlier years of the seventeenth century.

One point is immediately apparent about the families whose
origins were French: the large role of Burgundy, Champagne and
Picardy, which together provided over 47 per cent of all the
families. The one clear common factor that links the people from
these areas is that the areas were involved heavily in war. The
three provinces had been the scene of military operations since
the time of the Catholic League. What was more to the point,
they had been involved heavily and continuously in the multi-
form *apparat* of military procurement since the middle of the
sixteenth century. When the French Crown engaged in war, all
France suffered. Yet the incidence of suffering varied very
widely. The effects of war were worst where fighting actually
took place, and especially in areas where fighting continued over
a long period. The ordeal of north-eastern France in the early
modern period lasted in fact for at least two centuries, an agony

* The use of the word 'deck' demands some explanation. 'Deck' initially refers to the stack of IBM cards fed into the computer, and thence
comes to refer to the body of data punched in symbolic form on the cards.
I use the word here because no other word (like 'sample' or 'population')
fits my meaning.

made worse by the severely limited capacity that society had, at
the time, to repair itself.[2]

Even when individual communities were not directly visited by
military action, their life was distorted by the activities of those
who sought to maintain the various armies in a condition to keep
on flailing at each other in the mud and the trenches, saps and
mines of inconclusive siege warfare. Given the inefficiency of
early modern transportation systems, it is hardly surprising that
the hinterland of military operations should have been called on
more often than more distant regions to contribute food and
other supplies to combatant formations. Equally, it is hardly
surprising that such a hinterland should produce men capable
of organising the services necessary for continued military activity. Such were the Jacquier dynasty in Champagne and the
Berthelot of Montdidier and Amiens in Picardy, who were employed as *Munitionnaires* first in their native provinces, and later
on a national scale. Nor was it just a question of isolated families
who happened to become involved in *Munitions*. Members of
other functional groups analysed later in this chapter turned in
these provinces quite naturally to the most obvious, indeed the
dominant profitable activity, the supplying of military necessities
—of which the most profitable of all was money itself. Families
of importance here are, from Burgundy, the Bossuet, Bullion,
Cornuel, Girardin and Marin; and from Champagne, the Colbert, Doublet, Gargan and Le Camus.

The picture changes somewhat when one considers the places
where individual financiers were born. Data have been found on
the personal origins of 101 men. Their distribution is shown in
Figure 2 overleaf.

One factor is immediately visible: Paris was the most common
known birthplace of financiers. At the same time, it should not be
forgotten that as far as is known 71 per cent of the financiers were
born outside Paris. Some 12 per cent were born outside France,
and of these three-quarters were born in Italy. Such people have
already been sufficiently discussed. This leaves some 59 per cent
of the financiers who were born in the French provinces. This
group included some of the most important financiers of the age.
Nicolas Le Camus (1566–1648) was born in Reims, and went to
Paris towards the end of the sixteenth century. There he made a

great deal of money, though he delayed purchasing a post of *secrétaire du roi* until 1619. Claude and Guillaume Cornuel were born near Chaumont about 1580. Both went to Paris, made money, and eventually died holding high posts in the royal finances. This story was repeated in a large number of cases: Marin was born at Auxonne, and Gargan at Châlons-sur-Marne, François Catelan in Dauphiné, Pellisson at Béziers. And so one could go on.[3]

FIGURE 2: **Places of Birth of Financiers**

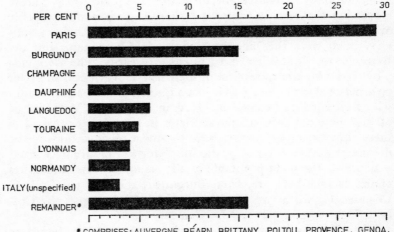

* COMPRISES: AUVERGNE, BÉARN, BRITTANY, POITOU, PROVENCE, GENOA, NAPLES, SWITZERLAND, THE SPANISH NETHERLANDS, AND THE ISLAND OF SICILY.

The financiers were men of largely provincial origin. But were there other common factors that linked them? On matters of religious or ethnic origin, the answer would seem to be moderately clear. The dual legends of Protestant and Jewish financiers seem to lack evidence. In the whole deck there are only nine known Protestants, of whom seven were financiers: Barthélemy Hervart, his father and his brother; François Catelan and his father-in-law Théophile Brachet; Jacques Amproux Delorme; and Paul Pellisson. There may have been more who kept quiet about their religion, or whose genealogically minded descendants suppressed their ancestors' religious deviance. As for the Jewish factor, stressed by some modern writers, it seems incorrect to assume the presence of hordes of Jews.[4] The only early modern reference to a supposedly Jewish financier comes from the pages of Saint-Simon, who refers to a financier whom he obviously detested as Morin-le-juif, a man whose daughter married the Maréchal d'Estrées.[5] I have been unable to find confirmation of this ethnic attribution. On the other hand, there were masses of obviously (and sometimes aggressively) Catholic financiers, like the Le Camus, Colbert, Fouquet, Boislève, Fleuriau, Forcoal, Languet, Maupeou, Pavillon, and many others. Some were even members of the hierarchy; not least Cardinal Mazarin, Prince of the Church and Munitionnaire.

The pursuit of common factors on other planes of analysis, such as social origins, is attended by what appear to be at first sight similarly negative results. One has in fact to carry out a small levelling operation. When seventeenth-century people dis-cussed the origins of financiers, they assumed that because such men tended to hail from the provinces, that is to say from areas relatively far from Paris, they must also come from levels of society which were equally remote. The theory was that the financiers were men from the dregs of society—though how this displeasing stratum was defined depended largely on the parti-cular writer's social status, psychological peculiarities and, one suspects in the case of Saint-Simon, state of digestion at the time of writing. There is little point in repeating such primitive social speculation, for enough facts are available for more objective answers to be produced about the social origins of the financiers.

Analysis of documentary references to origins reveals at first sight merely confusion. The early activities are known of 223 persons involved in the royal finances. These activities cover forty-five categories ranging from Actor to Valet de Chambre. But these can be concentrated into a number of broader cate-gories, which are expressed in Table 1. These broader categories merit some discussion.

The first group in the table is one called for convenience' sake 'Townspeople'. It forms some 25 per cent of the total of those about whose early career something is known. Within the group, only one man was an artisan. Trade occupied seven men. Some of these had specifically defined occupations. One Lefebvre, for

TABLE 1: **Broad Categories of Earliest Known Activity**

Broad Category		Total	Percentage formed by totals given here of basic group of 223 persons
A TOWNSPEOPLE		55	24·66
	Sub-totals		
Production	1		
Trade	7		
Banking and Exchange	23		
Town Dignitaries and Administrators	24		
B HOUSEHOLD SERVANTS		18	8·07
C COMMIS, ETC		57	25·56
D COURS SOUVERAINES MAGISTRATES		26	11·66
E MILITARY PERSONNEL		13	5·83
F CLERICS		12	5·38
G SUBORDINATE LAWYERS		22	9·87

example, who became an associate of Claude Cornuel, was said to have started off as an oil-seller in Melun.[6] But most of the seven were described simply as merchants. Artisans and merchants were far outnumbered by those who were involved in the buying and selling of money and credit. There are, of course, certain problems of definition and function in distinguishing, for example, a merchant from a money-changer, particularly because people often carried on both activities at the same time. Despite these occasional overlaps, eighteen men may safely be classified as bankers. These included the Italians to whom reference was made earlier. There were also a few native French: Correur, *Banquier Bourgeois de Paris*; Jean Vidaud, Banquier of Lyons, who was involved in the financial dealings of Mathieu Garnier, *trésorier des Parties Casuelles*; and last, lest the impression is given that only Paris and Lyons contained bankers who came to be involved in the royal finances, Hélie Gobert, Banquier of Poitiers.[7]

The last sub-group among the townspeople is composed of town dignitaries and administrators. Here again there is some problem of overlap. Jean Vidaud was both a banker and an *échevin*, or municipal magistrate, of Lyons. Correur's title, Banquier Bourgeois de Paris, makes one phrase out of his membership of two functional groups. Suffice it for present purposes that all those called Banquier have been put into the group just dealt with, and that the present group contains no one formally called Banquier. The group consists of twenty-four people. One, Jean Bazin, was an échevin of Paris. Three were *receveurs-payeurs des Rentes sur l'Hôtel de Ville de Paris*. One, Claude Neyret, was a *consul* of Lyons.[8] The remaining nineteen men were all possessors of the title *Bourgeois de Paris*. What this phrase meant is difficult to discern. In principle the title of Bourgeois was given to anyone who lived in Paris for more than a year and a day, who was not a domestic servant, and who paid municipal taxes. Often, however, people refused to assume the title, since they did not wish to assume with it the burdens of city taxes. One had, in fact, to be a person of some substance before it was worth becoming formally Bourgeois. Landowners who were Bourgeois enjoyed certain important privileges. They were exempt from paying *Taille* on their rural possessions. They were not subject to *Ban* and *Arrière-ban*, to the billeting of soldiers, or to any jurisdiction other than that of the law courts of Paris. Finally, they could sell wine of their growing and grain from their own lands without being subject to feudal impediments. The value of being Bourgeois derived rather paradoxically from being a landowner in the country.[9] The involvement of most of the Bourgeois in the deck was in formal lending to the state, as *prête-noms*, or men of straw, for loans made by more important men. But not all those first heard of as Bourgeois de Paris were so inconsiderable. Some, like Simon Le Noir, were the *adjudicataires-généraux* of big tax-farms. Others were of greater importance still, like Pierre Girardin, secrétaire du roi and *fermier-général des Aides* in the 1650s.[10]

The second group in Table 1, that of Household Servants, is composed first and foremost of lackeys (*lacquais*). Ten people are known to have begun their careers in this role. The best example is that of Denis Marin. Marin was the son of a master shoemaker of Auxonne, a little Burgundian town on the river Saône some 32 km east by a little south of Dijon. He went to Paris, where he became lackey, or liveried footman, to the Prince de

Conti. He soon moved on to the slightly higher role of valet to
Jacques Coquet, *Contrôleur de la Maison du Roi*—the King being
Louis XIII. Coquet taught Marin to write, and then passed him
on to Arnoul de Nouveau, Trésorier des Parties Casuelles, under
whose tutelage he came to take an interest in financial affairs. He
then branched out on his own. By 1632 he had enough money,
around 24,000 livres, to purchase a post of secrétaire du roi. In
1635 he became *adjudicataire-général des Gabelles de France*. His
career was now in full swing, and he became a valued colleague
of financiers like Guillaume Cornuel, Du Vouldy, Dalibert,
Boyer and Bonneau.[11]

Lackeys were not the only kind of household servant. One man
started as a valet. Two men were private secretaries. And so one
could go on. Clearly the category of Household Servants reflects
the structure and size of the households of the wealthy in seventeenth-century society. It is important to stress that service in a
household was not necessarily considered degrading in early
modern France. In a royal household, the highest nobles would
vie for positions that one would have thought menial. For
example, the Prince de Condé, Premier Prince du Sang, held—
when not in overt rebellion against the Crown—the post of
Grand Maître de France, which was equivalent to that of major-
domo. The prestige of such a post in the portentous domesticity
of the Very Christian King did not attach in anything like the
same degree to lesser households. But it is still true to say that
service was a relatively honourable calling, demanding high skill
and accomplishments. It was not a form of servitude from which
the fortunate might escape into the finances. It was a world in
itself. It even had its tragic heroes, like François Watel, Maître
d'Hotel of Nicolas Fouquet and, after Fouquet's fall, of the
Prince de Condé. In 1671, after an unforgivable gastronomic
disaster, Watel committed suicide by falling on to his bacon
slicer.[12]

The next two groups may be dealt with rapidly since they are
discussed in more detail elsewhere. The first of these is that
formed by *Commis*, the largest category of earliest known activity.
Something is said in the next chapter on the importance of such
men in the financial process. All that it is necessary to do here is
to stress that there was a link between the function of a commis

and the role of a domestic servant. Many commis lived in their masters' houses and were on call just like any other subordinate member of the household. Furthermore, although commis were involved in the financial world at the lowest levels, to become commis might be the first step that a man might take on the road to fortune. The more important of them, like the *premiers commis* of *surintendants des finances*, were often independent financiers in their own right. It was a category in which practising financiers might be found, and at the same time a ground from which potential financiers might be selected.

The second group is a composite made up of members of the magistracy of the *cours souveraines*, of the officer corps of the military, and of the hierarchy of the Church, who took up positions later on in life, after their basic careers had been established in these respectable institutions, in the finances of the state. Their part in the finances is discussed systematically in Chapter 8. But it is not out of place to mention here the fact that members of the three groups, if they entered the finances, tended to be catapulted into senior positions. Surintendants, *directeurs* and *contrôleurs-généraux des finances* were often men whose careers had begun in this apparently most unfinancial trio of professional groups.

The last group is made up of subordinate lawyers, most of whom were originally part of the lower echelons of the cours souveraines. This category included holders of the post of *avocat*. This was the first calling of fifteen financiers, amongst whom were notable men like Jacques Bordier sieur du Raincy, whose first known post was as *Avocat au Parlement* and who ended as *Secrétaire du Conseil d'Etat et des Finances* and *Intendant des Finances*.[13] A second important element of the group is made up of *procureurs*. The most important of these was Jean Hérault sieur de Gourville.[14] It is difficult to say why men who served early in their careers as subordinate lawyers should have gone on to play roles in the finances of the state. If a conjecture may be allowed, one might point out that the lower echelons of many legal systems are heavily involved in financial dealings which are often only partly legal. One has only to look at the continuing panic of the English Law Society at the prospect of light-fingered or merely forgetful solicitors to understand how easily

such men can become involved in quiet piracy. If a financier
wishes to do something particularly underhand, he has to know
how to avoid prosecution. This was as true of seventeenth-
century France as it is of twentieth-century England. Thus
Nicolas Monnerot is to be found employing Pierre Fournier,
Procureur au Parlement. Fournier evidently found that it was but
a short step from giving advice on how best to dress fraud up in
legal clothing to carrying out such frauds on his own behalf, for
he was later to be fined for such misdemeanours by the *Chambre
de Justice* of 1661.[15]

The enumeration of groups may be supplemented by attention
to the occupation of the fathers of financiers. Logically, it would
have been more fitting to discuss the fathers of financiers before
one talked about the earliest known activities of the financiers
themselves. In fact, however, genealogical data tend to be available only for rather famous and important people. To deal with
the occupations of fathers of financiers before discussing Table 1
would have suggested, first, that more is known about the origins
of the financiers than in fact is known and, second, that the
origins of the financiers were as a whole more elevated than was
the case. So it must be stressed that analysis of the occupations of
financiers' fathers essentially does no more than add two more
groups to those that have just been examined: those who were
derived from families involved in local administration in France,
and those who were the sons of financiers.

Fifteen financiers were the sons of local financial officials, and
sixteen more were the sons of local judicial officials. The less
distinguished group was that derived from financial administration. At the bottom of this group can be observed a dim succession of little men, sons following fathers in minor posts, as
Nicolas du Coudray followed his father as *receveur du Domaine en
la Vicomté de Conches et Breteuil* in Normandy.[16] Sometimes it is
possible to see a certain upward movement. The three sons of
Nicolas Cornuel, *grenetier* of the *Grenier à sel* of Villemor, became respectively président of the *trésoriers-généraux de France*
of Châlons-sur-Marne, intendant des finances, and *trésorier de
l'Extraordinaire des Guerres*.[17] But such movement was less important in the aggregate than the motion of men who were the
sons of rather more considerable fathers holding important local

posts like those of trésorier-général de France and receveur-
général des finances. Etienne Chabenas, Guillaume de Brisacier
and the three Rouillé brothers were all sons of such officials.[18] As
for judicial administration, fathers of financiers were to be found
at all levels of its local organs, in posts ranging from those of
avocats in *présidiaux* up to those of *commissaires* in the *Châtelet* of
Paris and procureurs of provincial Estates.

The second group worthy of mention is that formed by
financiers who were the sons of financiers. Since many members
of this group have been encountered in Part 1 of this book, it is
unnecessary to give their names, but it is of use to indicate what
posts the group held. There were:

Trésoriers de l'Epargne	3
Contrôleurs-généraux des finances	2
Intendants des finances	6
Trésorier-general du *Marc d'Or*	1
Trésorier de l'Extraordinaire	1
Trésoriers-généraux de France	2
Other local trésorier	1
Receveurs-généraux des finances	3
Receveur-particulier des Tailles	1
Fermiers-généraux	3
Officer of royal indirect tax system	1
Commis	2
Financial officers of Maisons Royales	10
Secrétaires du Conseil	2
Secrétaires du roi	12
Financial officers of military	7
Financial officer of cour souveraine	1
Receveur-payeur des Rentes	1
Financial officers of the Church	4

This comes to a total of sixty-three posts, most of which ranged
from important to very important. It indicates that, at a fairly
high level in the royal finances, the personnel to be encountered
were quite likely to be the sons of financiers, and that the
finances were to a significant extent a recruiting ground for
themselves.

To arrive at a quantitative conclusion about the succession of
disparate groups derived from the tables cited so far in this

chapter presents some difficulties of evaluation, particularly of
the relative importance in the royal finances of the persons of
whose origins record remains. The best way to carry out an
evaluation is to take a group whose basis is established in the next
chapter. The group, which I call the Primary Elite, is composed
of those people who held some post in the financial administration
and also exercised some recognisable role in Extraordinary
financial affairs. If one examines the occupations of the fathers of
this Primary Elite, in so far as they are known, and the earliest
known activities of the members of that elite; and if one conflates
the two, allowing primacy to the father's occupation, in cases
where both father's occupation and subject's earliest known
activity appear, a second table (Table 2) can be drawn up.

Examination of this table indicates that at the level of the
Primary Elite the world of the financiers tended to be self-
sustaining. Nearly one-half of the people in Table 2 were by
origin financiers. The only other major group was Townspeople.
Here production and trade played a slightly smaller role than
banking. Turning to the other groups in the table, it can be
seen that the law and administration both played roles roughly
equivalent in size to the roles played by production and trade,
and by banking. This picture prompts the drawing of subsidiary
conclusions. The French royal finances recruited their more
considerable personnel from a variety of different social and/or
functional groups. The focus of these groups was essentially the
state itself. Groups like the Law, Administration, Finances, and
even the Military, took their existence from the fact that the state
existed. Fifty-two members of the Primary Elite fit into one or
other of these groups. This total forms 72 per cent of those who
appear in Table 2.

Within this group of fifty-two, it is clear that the finances
themselves were of capital importance. It was not just a question
of financiers bringing sons into the world to follow in their
fathers' footsteps. Another factor comes into play. One of the
most important things about the French finances in the seventeenth century is that they were themselves the major source of
capital accumulation for those engaged in them. This can be seen
from the career of Jean Hérault de Gourville, which in form is
reasonably typical, though its course was unusually rapid. Gour-

TABLE 2: **Primary Elite—Origins through Father's Occupation or Own Earliest Known Activity**

Total Number of cases known: 72 (equals 100%)

Category	Sub-totals	Total	% of 72 cases
A TOWNSPEOPLE		19	26·39
Production: artisan	4 ⎫ 7		
Trade: small merchant	3 ⎭		
Banking: banker	8 ⎫ 9		
courtier de change	1 ⎭		
Town administration	2 ⎫ 3		
Payeur des Rentes	1 ⎭		
B THE LAW		8	11·12
Subordinate lawyer	3 ⎫ 4		
Law Student	1 ⎭		
Magistrate of cours souveraines	4 4		
C ADMINISTRATION		8	11·12
Local financial—Low	2 ⎫		
Local financial—High	1 ⎪ 5		
Local judicial—Low	1 ⎬		
Local judicial—High	1 ⎭		
Robe d'état	3 3		
D FINANCIERS		34	47·22
Financier	11 ⎫		
Munitionnaire	4 ⎪ 17		
Prête-nom	1 ⎬		
Other	1 ⎭		
Domestic service of a financial kind:			
Commis	14 ⎫		
Homme d'affaires	2 ⎬ 17		
Private secretary	1 ⎭		
E OTHERS		3	4·17
Military	2 ⎫ 3		
Surgeon	1 ⎭		

ville brought nothing to the finances but his brains and a loan from Mazarin. This initial stake was parlayed into something substantial through involvement in the Recettes-générales of the province of Guyenne.[19] As will be shown in the next chapter, money did enter the royal finances from elsewhere, particularly in the form of loans. But the really important wealth that existed within the world of the finances, and the most important denizens of that world, were created within its boundaries.

One last element needs to be built into this analysis of the origins of the financiers—that of time. In a sense the question of time has been dealt with at one end of the spectrum. Mention has been made of numerous persons who were the first members of their family to engage in the royal finances. Le Camus, Marin, and Gourville are examples of this phenomenon. But there was another kind of entry into the world of the finances, an entry which was relatively slow, and which was more that of a family than that of a single person. Because this pattern has never (to my knowledge) been discussed before, it seems worthwhile to give one example of it here. A further justification for such a course is this: it is necessary to take account in the study of the world of the financiers of long-term developments in French society, and, given the geographical distribution of the financiers' origins, in French provincial life.

It is clear that the phenomenon of the scion of some provincial family leaving his ancestral home and going to Paris was not the beginning of a process which saw financiers flocking to the capital to work their will on government and society. It was, on the contrary, a late stage of another process, the long progression of families through provincial society to a point where certain favourably endowed individuals could take off for Paris. Several generations might have passed since the financier's family emerged from the impenetrable obscurity of rural night. The earliest known member of such a financier's family might well be some kind of merchant operating in a small town. But his descendants turned as soon as they could to the purchase of administrative office, whether financial or judicial, which would eventually confer technical nobility. Marriages would be contracted with the daughters of local dignitaries. Attempts would be made to gain the patronage of some great noble. Eventually the

family would rise to the top of local administrative society, while
their children would achieve and maintain solid respectability in
the ranks of the local robe nobility. Other members of the
family would, for reasons which none of them seems to have
written down, seek to escape the stifling atmosphere of French
provincial life. They would go to Paris and find a relatively easy
road to advancement through the central mechanisms of the
royal finances. Although a certain amount of patronage from
ministers and officials would be necessary for them to ascend to
great heights, nevertheless their background, education and
social drive would be derived from their formative years in the
provinces.

There are many examples of this type of origin. One of the
best is provided by the Colbert family. Colbert's great-great-
great-grandfather may or may not have been a mason of the city
of Reims, who is said to have been active in the late fifteenth and
sixteenth centuries. But it is clear that the family soon moved
into minor administrative offices. Colbert's grandfather Jean-
Charles Colbert sieur de Terron was *contrôleur des Gabelles de
Bourgogne et Picardie*, and an agent of Cardinal Richelieu. Jean-
Charles' brothers included Gérard III Colbert, who was contrôleur des Gabelles de Picardie, and Simon Colbert sieur d'Acy
and Oudart II Colbert sieur de Villacerf, both of whom became
secrétaires du roi. The children of Gérard III were involved in
the royal finances before the great Jean-Baptiste was even born—
one of Gérard's daughters married the important financier
Nicolas Le Camus at the beginning of the seventeenth century.
Oudart II's children had passed through the financier stage by
the time the future contrôleur-général des finances had begun to
work for his first master, Michel Le Tellier. Three of Oudart II's
sons were members of cours souveraines: Jean-Baptiste Colbert
de Villacerf et de Saint-Pouange was a *correcteur* (1624–31) and
maître (from 1631) of the *Chambre des Comptes*, while his two
younger brothers, Simon II and Edouard I, both served as
respectable *conseillers* of the *Parlement* of Paris. But to return to
the basic point.

Jean-Baptiste Colbert de Seignelay (*the* Colbert) might be the
son of Nicolas Colbert seigneur de Vendières, Receveur-payeur
des Rentes sur l'Hôtel de Ville de Paris, a minor post despite its

E

inordinately long name; but his extended family connection possessed power in local administration, and a certain level of prestige in the local society of Champagne and in particular of the area around Reims. This family connection was undoubtedly powerfully reinforced by Colbert throughout his career. But it existed before that career began, and would have continued to exist had he never come to be Mazarin's personal intendant about the year 1650. Furthermore, the orientation of the whole extended family was towards the acquisition and exercise of various kinds of administrative post. Colbert would have been going against the trend of his family's history if he had *not* entered royal service or the service of some important minister. The only thing which seemed new about him was that he was making a strictly central or Parisian career close to the heart of the absolutist administration. It is here, no doubt, that his own clear-headed appreciation of the true road to power is to be seen —that he was prepared to accept an almost servile position with regard to both Mazarin and Louis XIV, knowing that honours and influence would flow more certainly to him as slave of the mighty than as possessor of some initially more prestigious and independent formally constituted office. In many ways, however, his career was merely the intelligent mutation of a method of advance adopted by his ancestors and their relations in Champagne since the middle of the sixteenth century.[20]

Study of the origins of the financiers prompts a number of conclusions. The financiers came from a series of different social and functional groups. Several of these groups had a certain prestige in French society. Many of the members of such groups, like the magistrates of the cours souveraines, had technical nobility before they became involved in the finances. Others, the military men in particular, and some of the clerics, were accepted as *nobles de race*. Nearly half the financiers of the Primary Elite were the sons of financiers, and a few of these were members of long established financial dynasties. Of those men who came from lower groups in society, many came from domestic service of various kinds. A certain number of people came from banking and exchange. A comparable number came from artisanal and mercantile occupations.

In none of the observed cases were the previous occupations of financiers or the occupations of their fathers in much sense new. There is in fact no representation of any modern economic activity—all the artisanal, mercantile and banking people followed crafts and pursued activities that had been known for centuries. The only remotely modern roles were those connected with the state itself. In so far as the origins of the financiers were not linked to state activity, whether administrative, military or financial, they related to sleepy little towns like Bar-sur-Aube or Auxonne, which themselves depended very largely on the basic activities of the countryside around them. France on this level was still dominated by the rhythms of agricultural life. Such change as existed was essentially, in agricultural terms, cyclical and, in social terms, of that kind that repeats itself in a succession of particular cases with only minor variation over centuries. People moved into the royal finances in the seventeenth century probably in larger numbers than was the case in the fifteenth century. But the basic process in individual careers was not necessarily very different in 1650 from what it had been in 1450.

Notes to this chapter are on page 252

Chapter 6 SUCCESS AND FAILURE

ONCE MEN had entered the finances, there were numerous ways in which their careers might develop. These ways may be expressed following the broad divisions of the finances as they were described in the first part of this book. That is to say, men might buy posts on the Ordinary financial machine, and they might engage in Extraordinary Affairs. Description of the paths taken by individual financiers is relatively simple. It is more complex to write a collective biography of the world of the financiers which is concerned with patterns of movement. To do this it is necessary to take into account a large number of people and the diffuse system of offices and commissions which they held, together with the different ways in which individual persons might act, the roles that they might elect or elect not to play, the sequences which they might follow in holding posts and playing roles, and the differing lengths of time which they might spend over each phase of their careers. The way in which these matters have been handled is by formalising the stages through which financiers passed, analysing the groups of financiers who passed through each stage, and thereby establishing profiles of each stage. The various stages are then arranged in a general succession of importance, as follows: *prête-nom*; *commis*; *Traitant*; *Munitionnaire*; acquisition of office; farmer-general; and lender to the state. Figure 3 is a simplified schematic drawing of the relationship of the stages to one another (see p 133). The analysis of stages having been accomplished, a review of the various groups of financiers is undertaken to determine elites of financiers distinguished by their success from their fellows. The collective biography is completed by an analysis of the numerous ways in which financiers, from the lowest to the highest, might fail.

FIGURE 3: **Relative Sizes of Groups and Common Directions of Movement in the Royal Finances**

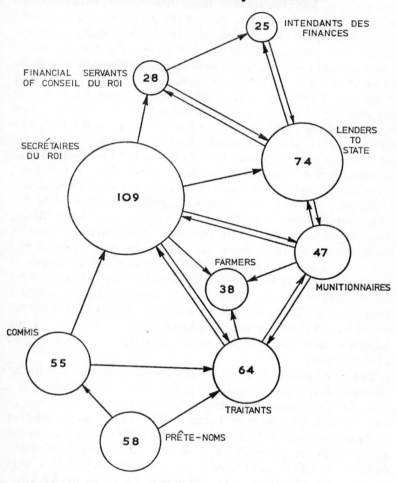

The lowliest central financial function was that of *prête-nom,* or man of straw, whose use, it will be recalled, was a safety device for the financier engaging in both treaties and loans to the state. Even at this low level there was a hierarchy. Most people who served as prête-noms were obscure figures. The majority were

lower household servants, with only the occasional lackey distinguished by a halting literacy. Slightly above this level but on
the whole no less obscure were those men of straw who possessed
the title *Bourgeois de Paris*. Most of the people encountered here
were covering for men making relatively large formal loans to the
state in the 1650s. Nothing more is known about such men of
straw beyond these single transactions. Somewhat higher still are
to be found men who made a profession of being prête-noms.
They served a variety of masters at different times, but always in
the capacity of man of straw. At the top of the hierarchy were
undoubtedly the men of straw of the various general farms, who
were known to the state as *adjudicataires-généraux*. They were
occasionally men who were later in life to hold positions of importance in the world of the financiers, and who, in their turn,
came to employ men of straw of their own. One such man was
Guillaume Cornuel, who became adjudicataire-général of the
Cinq Grosses Fermes in 1620, while another was Denis Marin,
who played a similar role in the farm of the *Grandes Gabelles*
which began in 1635. Such men were the aristocrats of the
hierarchy of prête-noms.[1] It is clear that the centre of gravity of
that hierarchy was to be found among the minor figures about
whom little is known. To be a prête-nom was on the whole a
despised role. If a man was in search of upward mobility he
would have to look for other paths of advance. The three most
notable of these involved serving as commis, as Traitant, and as
Munitionnaire.

The word *commis* is an unusually confused term, even in the
agitatedly serpentine context of the French financial world. Yet a
basic definition can be given: a commis was a person working in
financial affairs for another financier. There was a wide variation
in the importance of the functions performed by commis. On the
one hand the responsibilities of such a person might be essentially those of a prête-nom with administrative duties only
slightly beyond that supine willingness to sit in drafty ante-
chambers and represent one's employer in legal proceedings and
if necessary in jail, which was in fact what being a prête-nom
involved. Take, for example, a pair of minor commis called
Boisel and Legueux who signed their names in 1659 to a treaty
belonging to Nicolas Monnerot. Since the treaty was simply a

paper exercise laying a groundwork for fraud, their duties as commis were hardly exacting.[2] On the other hand, there were very powerful commis, the chief clerks of *Surintendance*, *Epargne* and *Contrôle-général*, who were of greater importance in some respects than their nominal masters.

These extremes are less interesting from a quantitative and functional point of view than the wide range of mediocrity lying in between. The fact is that almost everybody had his commis. At the lower end of the scale there were the obscure commis of inconsiderable bankers. Others, like Nicolas Tabouret de la Bussière, were commis of Traitants—in this case of the financier Gourville, whose interests in Guyenne in the 1650s it was Tabouret's task to superintend.[3] There were commis of local financial officials. There were even commis of commis. Daniel Chartier was commis of Charles Bernard, who was himself commis of Nicolas Fouquet, while one Taffus was employed as commis by Bernard's successor Bruant. In such cases the commis had a role to play analogous to that played by the chief clerk vis-à-vis the *surintendant des finances*. Both levels of commis were used largely to carry out operations so illegal that their respective masters could not countenance possible discovery by accounting agencies like the *Chambre des Comptes*. Something has already been said to indicate what the chief clerks of the surintendant got up to. It may be believed that operations that they found too dangerous to handle were piratical indeed.[4]

The pattern of mobility of commis in the royal finances exhibits some strange qualities. The first of these is that the highest level of commis did not possess upward professional mobility within the finances. The only course open, for example, to a commis of the Surintendance seeking to move on involved a lurch into relative respectability. Take the case of Antoine Guérapin (1605–70), onetime commis of Particelli d'Emery. He became a *trésorier-général de France* of Grenoble as early as 1643, though he was not *reçu* until 1669. Some time after 1643 he bought a post of *maître* in the Chambre des Comptes of Paris. Finally he acquired a *brevet* of *conseiller d'état* and the *collier* of the Ordre de Saint-Michel. None of these posts, not even that of trésorier-général, was important from the financier's point of view as an integral part of a financial empire. All were indeed respectable.[5] In fact, there was nowhere for an aspiring former chief clerk to go but out of the finances, into posts like those of maître des comptes. For reasons that are not clear, high-level commis seem to have been doomed to gentility.

At lower levels, however, there are many examples of the ways in which commis went on to play additional roles. Some became Traitants. One such was Nicolas Monnerot, who began his financial career as commis of the Munitionnaire Paléologue.[6] Several other men who later achieved various degrees of distinction were commis of intendants des finances. The most successful of these was Séraphin de Mauroy, who served first as *huissier* of the *Parlement* of Paris. He then became commis of Claude Cornuel and, after the latter's death in 1638, commis of another intendant des finances, François Sublet sieur des Noyers. When Sublet was promoted to secretary of state in 1641, Mauroy simply took over his post as intendant des finances.[7]

Such examples indicate that the role of commis at the lower levels was one from which men might ascend to more considerable posts or functions in the world of the finances. Such a role played a significant part in the upward mobility of financiers. It was a road in a sense in which the modern western world would understand the term, that is to say a continuous paved strip along which a man may advance with relative ease. The roads of advance represented by the roles of Traitant and Munitionnaire were far more in the seventeenth-century meaning of the term. In many respects one might then have given the name of road to a series of linked natural obstacles, as it might be potholes and rocks, over which men elected to scramble as best they could, given that progress by other routes was utterly impossible. What was more, given the difficulty of the going, men might be satisfied with an end to travelling far short of their original aim, or might be obliterated by some catastrophe while on their journey. The point is that large discontinuities are to be observed in the roles of both Traitant and Munitionnaire.

The discontinuities in the role of *Traitant* are the more obvious. There was, it is true, a hierarchy of Traitants. At the upper levels of this system were to be found the big central Traitants of whom most people thought when they thought about financiers. At the lower levels there were large numbers of

more or less obscure people who served as *Sous-Traitants* or
local Traitants for a big central Traitant in Paris. These underlings must have outnumbered the central men many times over,
but there is relatively little information to be found about them.
Nevertheless, it is clear that there were two groups of Sous-
Traitants. The first was composed of local financial officials,
ranging from *receveurs des Tailles* in *Elections* up to trésoriers-
généraux de France in *généralités*. There had to be someone to
take on sub-treaties, and these local men were available for the
job. No fortunes were made by such men. None became significant on a national level. The second group of Sous-Traitants
was composed of men more closely connected with the central
finances. Many were mere hangers-on, men who were given
something to do because of family pressure. One example of this
comes from the circle of the financier Jean Hérault de Gourville,
one of whose nieces inveigled him into employing her husband or
father-in-law (it is not clear which) in such a capacity.[8] None of
the people in this second group was of great importance. In fact,
Sous-Traitants and local Traitants were not professionally
mobile. Out of twenty-four people who appear in such roles in
the deck, only one went on to play other roles in the royal
finances.

There was, then, a division between central Traitants and
their local underlings. That is about the only straightforward
thing that can be said about the central Traitants. Several of
them started their careers as private commis of some financier.
Such was Claude Housset (c 1615–85), who began his working
life as commis of the financier Rabatus.[9] Another central
Traitant had been a prête-nom, though his exercise of that role
was hardly typical. His name was Nicolas de Frémont, and he had
acted as cover for François Catelan in treaties made, surprisingly,
during the Fronde. Such a beginning gives some idea of what
Frémont was like—he was nothing if not a gambler to be involved in such enterprises at such a time, when a prête-nom
might well attract the attention of a *cour souveraine* and find himself hanged.[10] But on the whole there is not much information
about the earlier activities of Traitants. The only inference that
can be drawn from the few pieces of data is that for a financial
beginner anxious to play the role of Traitant, the road to success

probably lay through serving initially as subordinate to some already successful financier. On the other hand, it should not be thought that successful Traitants were drawn exclusively from such recruiting grounds. Many men were successful financiers before they turned to the exploitation of treaties. Some of the most important Traitants began their careers as Munitionnaires, as did Claude de Boislève and François Jacquier.[11]

As for the way Traitants conducted themselves as Traitants, enough has been said on that subject in Chapter 2. All that needs to be pointed out here is that the central Traitants were the most successful of all the functional groups in the royal finances in terms of important offices held. Of the sixty-four central Traitants in the deck, ten became *fermiers-généraux*; five became *trésoriers des Parties Casuelles*; five became *intendants des finances*; one (Particelli d'Emery) went on to become *contrôleur-général* and *surintendant des finances*. But many Traitants did not bother to purchase such high posts. They were far too busy making money. One such was Hugues Betauld, an exceedingly wealthy man who reached his high point in the years 1639–45 with a series of grossly fraudulent treaties. He was content to own the unprestigious but lucrative post of *receveur des Consignations de la ville de Paris*.[12]

The element of discontinuity observed in the hierarchy of Traitants recurs in the third road to success in the royal finances —serving as a *Munitionnaire*. There are clearly two groups within this category. One comprises subordinate Munitionnaires who merely acted on the orders of a controlling agent. There are thirty-three of these subordinates. The second comprises men who operated as principal agents in their own right, and who might well have a network of subordinate Munitionnaires doing their will. There are forty-seven of these. Only two people functioned in both categories. These were Pierre Gargan and one Nacquart, who operated partly as subordinates of Mazarin, and partly as independent agents.[13]

On the whole, the subordinate Munitionnaires were, in functional terms, just as much an immobile group as the Sous-Traitants. Closer examination reveals a further point: the subordinate Munitionnaires included a significantly higher proportion of non-professionals that did the principal Munitionnaires. Of the subordinate group of thirty-three, fifteen (45 per cent) held office in the financial administration of the state. Only two of these fifteen held posts of any importance: Pierre Gargan, who became intendant des finances, and Nicolas Monnerot, who became trésorier des Parties Casuelles.[14] Turning to roles played in the Extraordinary financial machine, only one subordinate Munitionnaire became a central Traitant, and only one became a fermier-général. On the other hand, fifteen of the subordinate Munitionnaires held offices outside the royal finances.

The principal Munitionnaires show rather different tendencies. Admittedly, of the forty-seven people in this category, only twenty-six (55 per cent) held posts in the financial administration. This overall figure is not significantly different from the 45 per cent scored by the subordinate Munitionnaires in this sphere. But an examination of the posts held reveals an important difference. The principal Munitionnaires included two surintendants des finances, one contrôleur-général, four intendants des finances, and one trésorier des Parties Casuelles. Evidently the principal Munitionnaires held posts of far greater importance than the subordinate Munitionnaires. This relative importance was maintained in the area of roles in Extraordinary Affairs. Eleven principals were also central Traitants. Eight became fermiers-généraux. But only eight of the forty-seven principals held posts outside the royal finances. It is clear, then, that the principal Munitionnaires were a more professional group of people than their subordinates, that they had far greater chance of success in the royal finances, and that they played a far larger role in Extraordinary Affairs.

Given the lack of personal mobility between the categories of subordinate and principal Munitionnaire, the question arises of where principal Munitionnaires came from, if not from the ranks of the subordinate. The answer to this is composite. Some principals, like François Jacquier and François Berthelot, were the sons of principal Munitionnaires. Another group of principals was made up of men who began their careers as hangers-on of the great. Such was Gourville, who got his start in the finances by attracting Mazarin's attention. Others got their start by ascent through local office. Such was Simon I Berthelot, founder of the family's fortunes, who began his working life as a surgeon, bought

a post of receveur des Tailles of Montdidier, and then moved
into the military supply business. Others were originally bankers,
like Barthélemy Hervart.[15] The common characteristic of the
members of this disparate aggregation was that their first involvement in the royal finances at other than a puny administrative
level tended to lie in the *Munitions*.

The mode of ascent as a principal Munitionnaire parallels the
ascent of central Traitants. One began as a principal, often, as in
Gourville's case, in a very small way, and proceeded by making
progressively larger contracts with the Crown. The high point of
success was reached when one began to make contracts with the
Crown worth millions of livres—like the contract for 10 million
livres arranged by Jacquier and Boislève in 1654 to keep the royal
armies supplied while in winter quarters.[16] The speed at which
one progressed upwards in the hierarchy of munitions supply
varied according to a number of factors, of which three were
particularly important. One, obviously, is the question of whether
one's father was a Munitionnaire or not. François Jacquier could
hardly have been promoted to his key position of *commissaire-
général des Vivres* in 1650, when he was only 31 years old, had his
father not previously held an important place in the administration of munitions. A second factor is whether or not one was
willing and able to make partnerships with men more powerful
than oneself. This is where Boislève, for example, really began to
make big contracts, that is to say, through his alliance with the
predatory Jacquier. A third factor is whether or not one had the
sympathetic attention of some important minister. One reason
for the success of several Munitionnaires in the 1650s was their
readiness to solicit the attention of the greatest Munitionnaire of
all, Cardinal Mazarin.

Even before the achievement of success, expressed in the
munitions business as in the underworld of Traitants by hydropic
contracts and progressively larger opportunities for fraud, a new
phase in the life of the financier might begin. He might begin to
seek means of protection against the dangers facing denizens of
the world of the financiers, dangers which are described as they
affected the weak, unlucky or merely stupid in the last section of
this chapter. One form of protection was provided by the possession of one or more of a number of institutional posts. Some

of these posts were part of the financial administration and have
been discussed in the first part of this book. Other posts which
have not been discussed so far fall into two categories: first, posts
directly concerned with the royal finances which have not yet
been dealt with; second, posts not directly concerned with the
finances. If I may indulge in a metaphor, the first are rather like
the carapace of a lobster, in that the protection afforded is intimately connected to some financial function, or, as it were, necessary aspect of the beast's economy; while the second are like the
successive shells of the growing hermit crab, in that they are
assumed artificially as a means of protection, but have no organic
link with the functions carried on under the shelter that they
afford. Examples of the lobster analogy are provided by the
highest ranks of Munitionnaires. Like the higher ranking commis, most principal Munitionnaires had some kind of office
which acted simultaneously as a focus and a front for their financial life. François Jacquier's post of commissaire-général was of
such a kind. Other Munitionnaires held posts more closely connected with the central administration of the army. Such was
Louis Longuet, *trésorier de l'Extraordinaire des Guerres*.[17]

Other men might buy posts as trésoriers-généraux de France
or *receveurs-généraux des finances*. These officials formed a relatively large company in the financial administration of France. In
the deck, too, there are quite large totals for both groups—forty-
nine trésoriers, and thirty-three receveurs. But these groups are
by no means uniform. Men who differed widely in social origin
and aspiration, in financial status and power, and in motive for
purchase bought such posts. Often a local man might buy a post
of trésorier-général de France merely for the social prestige that
it would give him. He would not necessarily find himself involved
in any particularly heavy way in the state's finances either as an
ordinary administrator or as a lender to the Crown. An example
of this is provided by Nicolas II Cornuel, *président* of the
trésoriers-généraux de France of Châlons-sur-Marne. There is
no sign that he had anything to do with the financial empires of
his brothers Claude and Guillaume II.[18] Other local men who
served as trésoriers-généraux or receveurs-généraux might have
a greater involvement in the royal finances. They would fulfil
their functions as administrators, but were prepared also to

operate the treaties which the king and his council might create for the extraction of taxes and Extraordinary expedients from their particular généralité. This they would do not because they were particularly interested in making money but because they feared what would happen if a Parisian financier were appointed to carry out such treaties. This type of office holder was distinct from a third group, composed of men who bought such posts purely to make money, who appear to have shouldered much of the financial responsibility of the généralité, and to have had important links with local bankers and with financiers in Paris. A fourth category was composed of Parisian career financiers who bought office in the provinces as a means of extending their unofficial influence more widely. A man in this category probably had little to do with the administration of the généralité, largely because he lived in Paris. His office would be really no more than a variety of social ornament.

It is a matter of considerable difficulty to decide where the balance lies in this question of use of office. But in the present context it is possible to come to a conclusion at least about the relative importance to financiers of posts of trésorier-général and receveur-général by counting heads and looking at names. Of the forty-nine trésoriers-généraux de France who appear in the deck for one reason or another, only one person who was a major practising financier operated simultaneously as a practising trésorier. This was Jacques Tubeuf.[19] Thirty-three receveurs-généraux des finances appear in the deck. Of these, ten were involved in Extraordinary Affairs, and five could be called major financiers. All five were involved in a serious way in carrying out the duties of a receveur-général, though how they defined those duties would not have been acknowledged by the state. Nicolas Monnerot, for example, is known to have been involved for decades in profitable credit swindles on the *Recettes-générales* of Lyons, of which unfortunate city he was receveur-général.[20] It would appear, therefore, that professional financiers preferred the post of receveur to that of trésorier. It is not hard to see why. The receveur had to handle large sums of money, whereas the trésorier tended only to have a say in how money should be levied and spent. Handling money was agreeable in the seventeenth century largely because people found that it tended to stick to their hands, and society seems to have had no effective cure for this condition.

Above the level of *bureaux des finances* and Recettes-générales were to be found a host of formal offices which the aspiring financier would find gave him attractive profits and which at the same time provided better and better protection. Many such posts have been discussed in the first part of this book: for example, those of trésoriers des Parties Casuelles and de l'Epargne. Nor was this all, for the ultimate in profit and self-protection was provided by the posts whose holders were supposed to steer the unwieldly tub of French finance on a course of fiscal rectitude. The most important of these posts were the commissions of contrôleur-général and intendant des finances and *commis à l'enregistrement des fonds*. But this sort of job was not available to everybody. The cost of such posts was substantial. The majority of financiers preferred not to commit themselves to the expenditure involved. Moreover, many financiers were simply too poor to countenance it. In any case not everybody wanted to be tied to any particular area of jurisdiction or field of financial enterprise. Most Traitants preferred a less limiting type of office. Many Munitionnaires did too. They therefore turned to the other kind of office—the category containing those offices which had no organic link with the royal finances, but which were nevertheless purchased by financiers.

The most obvious example of the use by financiers of non-financial posts is provided by the five colleges of *secrétaires du roi*. The importance of these posts cannot be exaggerated. Of the forty-seven principal Munitionnaires in the deck, ten (21 per cent) were secrétaires du roi. Of the sixty-four central Traitants, twenty-five (39 per cent) were secrétaires du roi. Of the thirty-eight fermiers-généraux, twenty-nine (76 per cent) were secrétaires du roi. Turning to the higher echelons of the financial administration, it is to be observed that of thirty-six commis of important institutions ranging from the Surintendance des Finances to the *Surintendance des Bâtiments du Roi*, thirteen (36 per cent) held posts of secrétaire du roi. Eight out of twenty-five, some 32 per cent, of the intendants des finances held such posts, as did four trésoriers des Parties Casuelles, two trésoriers de

l'Epargne, and one person (Particelli d'Emery) who was successively contrôleur-général and surintendant des finances.

The origins of the post of secrétaire du roi, like the origins of
many other interesting institutions of the *ancien régime*, are lost
in the night of time, as the French put it. This fact is distressing,
but does not affect the present inquiry too closely. The oldest
function of the secrétaire du roi was to assist the *chancelier* of
France in writing down the multitude of legal acts (*Arrêts*), edicts,
declarations, and so on, produced by the whole gamut of royal
institutions. At a very early date, the offices tended to be created
by the Crown for sale, and despite periodic attempts to reduce
the number, it tended to increase. This increase was at the cost of
administrative efficiency, and the Crown attempted in the later
medieval period to separate a working group of *secrétaires signant
en finances* from the body of secrétaires du roi. This attempt,
protracted though it was, failed by 1547, when the Crown was
forced to set up posts of *secrétaire d'état* to carry out functions
which the men signant en finances had shown themselves unable
to perform. It took the Crown another seventy years to shunt the
disgruntled secrétaires signant en finances off into the administrative limbo where their colleagues the basic secrétaires du roi
had been languishing for a century or two. In limbo they might
be, but the posts still attracted purchasers. It is difficult to see
why. The full title of some such secretaries—*secrétaire du roi
maison et couronne de France et de ses finances*—though satisfyingly
convolute, hardly seems worth the 25,000 livres or so that it cost
in the seventeenth century. Yet the Crown was able to create
and sell such offices at great speed during the reign of Louis
XIII.

The reason behind the popularity of the office was that secrétaires du roi had certain important privileges. For a start, they
had personal nobility, which had been conferred on them by the
king in 1484. Furthermore, providing a secrétaire du roi served
for more than twenty years in his office, his children were considered noble too. Obvious advantages flowed from such status,
such as personal exemption from the *Taille* and from municipal
taxation for things like watch and ward. Nor was this all, for in
the case of the Taille, exemption extended to the peasants working
on the estates of secrétaires du roi. There were also legal privi-

leges which did not devolve from noble status. The most important of these was the right of *Committimus*. This allowed secrétaires du roi to use the *chambres des requêtes* of the parlements within whose jurisdiction they lived or held land as courts of first instance with regard to civil cases. This saved them from having to struggle through the tangled web—though web is a word implying too much organisation—of local courts of *prévôtés, bailliages, sénéchaussées* and *présidiaux*. Proceeding through such courts could waste years of a man's life and empty his purse into the pockets of greedy provincials.

But it was not merely a question of privileges that the individual secrétaire might possess by right of office. There was also the strength of the organised colleges of secretaries to one of which each secrétaire du roi belonged. The colleges were quick to denounce any infraction of the privileges that had been accorded to them, and an attack on an individual member was treated as though it were an attack on his college as a whole. And for all this privilege and protection the price to be paid was small. The office of secrétaire du roi at 25,000 livres was cheap compared to the posts of *trésorier de l'Epargne* (1 million livres) and *secrétaire du Conseil* (from 850,000 to 900,000 livres). It was in fact a bargain.[21]

The post of secrétaire du roi was relatively commonplace, and there was a hierarchical superstructure of higher writing offices, permeated by financiers of progressively greater eminence. The most important part of this superstructure was connected with the Conseil du Roi. There were two major elements: the *secrétaires du Conseil* and the *greffiers du Conseil*. In the deck there are twenty secrétaires du Conseil and five greffiers du Conseil. Of these twenty-five men, at least thirteen (52 per cent) were involved in the Extraordinary financial affairs of the state. Nine (36 per cent) were central Traitants and five (20 per cent) were fermiers-généraux. As for official positions, four of the twenty-five intendants des finances in the deck served earlier in their careers as secrétaires du Conseil, while the secrétaire du Conseil who was most successful was Particelli d'Emery. The major reason why such posts attracted financiers is indicated in a document of the *Chambre de Justice* of 1661. François Catelan, Secrétaire du Conseil, was accused of having used his office for grossly corrupt purposes. Since he had to be present at sessions of the Conseil du Roi to write down decisions that were taken, he came into possession of valuable information on the nature of royal policy long before other financiers. This information enabled him to prepare bids for treaties and other expedients, and to warn his collaborators of forthcoming extraordinary demands for funds and so on, ahead of his competitors. In time of war, when the Crown was concerned far less with the price of credit than with the speed of its mobilisation, the advantages to the financier of Catelan's position can hardly be overestimated.[22]

Secretaries of all kinds played their part in the royal finances. Some of them were not necessarily primarily financiers, rather strange adventurers who were involved in all kinds of complicated intrigues, some of which happened to be connected with the royal finances. On the other hand, most of the thirty-five people in the deck who held secretarial posts in the various households were seriously involved in the royal finances. Some important financiers held posts of *secrétaire de la Chambre du Roi*. Others were *secrétaires des Commandements* of lesser households like those of Anne of Austria and Philippe d'Anjou.

Posts of secrétaire du Conseil and de la Chambre du Roi represented the keystone of some financiers' success. But relatively few of those who purchased posts of secrétaire du roi went on to hold these more elevated secretaryships. It was partly a question of the large expenditure involved, and partly the fact that there were only a few of such offices available. The average person who bought a post of secrétaire du roi would in fact tend to continue as a Traitant or Munitionnaire. For secrétaires du roi who were more affluent than most, yet who did not purchase higher secretaryships or other offices, the most common direction taken was towards involvement in the tax-farms of the state. Of the thirty-eight fermiers-généraux in the deck, over 76 per cent held posts of secrétaires du roi. It is difficult to say with certainty why they should have chosen such a field for investment. But it was probably because the tax-farms had a certain formal quality that did not attach to treaties and the other expedients of the Extraordinary Machine. To become a fermier-général was to enter the Ordinary financial machine. Such a role represented the height of many men's ambitions. Indeed, a large proportion of the men who were Fermiers-généraux in the 1650s settled down to administer their farms in a way that was, by seventeenth-century standards and compared to the hectic world of treaties, quite responsible.

Analysis of the group formed by those who served as fermiers-généraux reveals discontinuities in functional mobility similar to those observed in the hierarchies of Traitants and Munitionnaires. Fermiers-généraux did not work their way up from the lower levels of *adjudicataire-général* and *sous-fermier*. The men who made successful careers in tax-farming and ended up as fermiers-généraux were almost always men who had been principals operating in their own right from the beginning. They started in small farms which, despite their lack of size, reported directly to the Epargne, and worked upwards until they were involved in the big *fermes-générales*. On the other hand, this progression of principals through a succession of larger and larger farms was not the only way in which fermiers-généraux were recruited. It was possible for financiers who had made fortunes in other fields of financial endeavour to involve themselves in tax-farms at the highest levels without passing through apprenticeship in lesser farms.

This indeed was what happened during the 1650s. The fermes-générales became the object of a siege laid by the more piratical financiers of the age. The men who held the farms before this siege and who were either displaced by, or submerged in the new influx had been fermiers-généraux for some considerable time. They were vociferously appalled at the *démarches* carried out by a man like Claude Girardin in the readjudication of the farm of the Grandes Gabelles in 1655.[23] The new generation of farmers reflects the significant deterioration that was going on throughout the royal finances. The older generation of the 1640s and 1650s had been corrupt and grasping—the records of the Chambre de Justice are testimony enough of the extortion by *Gabelleurs* and others that went on for decades, despite continued protests by local law courts. But at least the professional concern of the older generation was the farms in themselves. The new generation treated the farms simply as elements of financial empires. The farms, in fact, became adjuncts of the loan business, in much the same way as treaties and

Rentes had lost their original purposes and become elements in the granting of excessive interest.

Lending to the state was the function about which everything turned in the royal finances. Short-term credit was both the thing that kept the state going from day to day and the most profitable field for the development of a financier's resources. It is not surprising that big financiers played a highly important role in this field.

In the deck there are seventy-four people known to have lent directly to the state, and sixty-six who lent to financiers on the understanding that the sums lent would be passed to the Crown. The basic qualification for a direct lender to the state was, it need hardly be said, to possess capital in a relatively mobile or easily mobilisable form, or to be able to borrow. The point, though obvious, needs to be made, because it was not just financiers who lent to the Crown. Indeed, of the seventy-four direct lenders, thirty-eight (51 per cent) had no financial post at all. Admittedly, twelve people appear not to have had a post of any kind. But even so, this leaves twenty-six people who lent money to the Crown and are known to have possessed posts outside the royal finances. Nevertheless, care must be taken in evaluating the importance of this. Mere counting of heads will not do. One must consider, over and above the fact of lending, the amount people lent and how often they lent. The point is that much of the lending by non-professionals was an ad hoc response to the particular crisis of credit which occurred during the Fronde. The relatively normal times that returned after 1653 saw the re-establishment of normal credit lines between the state and the professional financier. Few people outside the ranks of the financiers would be prepared, as a matter of habit, to take the risks involved in lending to the Crown.

It is of some utility to correlate the group of thirty-six professional financiers lending directly to the state with the other professional categories that have been referred to earlier in this chapter. Three (8 per cent) of the lenders were highly placed *commis*. Fourteen (39 per cent) were or had been central Traitants. Twelve (33 per cent) were or had been principal Munitionnaires. Three (8 per cent) served as subordinate Munitionnaires. Seven (19 per cent) were financial officers of *maisons royales*. Thirteen (36 per cent) were secrétaires du roi. Four (11 per cent) served in secretarial offices of the Conseil du Roi. Five (14 per cent) were fermiers-généraux. Three (8 per cent) were trésoriers des Parties Casuelles. Seven (19 per cent) were intendants des finances. Two (Hervart and Colbert) were contrôleurs-généraux des finances. Three were trésorier de l'Epargne (Jeannin de Castille), directeur des finances (Etienne III d'Aligre), and surintendant des finances (Fouquet). Clearly loans to the Crown were forthcoming from most of the people important in the financial world, and certainly from all the categories which have been seen to be important earlier in this chapter. As for the sixty-six people who lent to other financiers, they included within their ranks thirty-two (49 per cent) who had no financial position. Of this thirty-two, three were members of the modern administrative machine, ten were officers of various cours souveraines, four were officers in the military, one was a bishop, another a member of the administration of a town, and yet another held a post in the old local administration. Fourteen had no known post. Of these, four were women who were either widows or daughters of financiers, or else were related in some other way to men who were or had been in the finances. As for the thirty-four people who had some official position in the financial administration, four of them (12 per cent) were highly placed commis; eight (24 per cent) were central Traitants; five (15 per cent) were principal Munitionnaires, while five more served as subordinate Munitionnaires. Four (12 per cent) were financial officers of maisons royales. Twelve (35 per cent) were secrétaires du roi, and three (9 per cent) were secretarial officers of the Conseil du Roi. Three were fermiers-généraux. Five held posts in various bureaux des finances. Two served as trésoriers des Parties Casuelles, three as intendants des finances, and two as contrôleurs-généraux. One, finally, was a trésorier de l'Epargne.

This enumeration indicates two things: first, that there is a difference between the performance of the non-professional group lending directly to the state and that lending to financiers for eventual loan to the state. Members of the modern administrative machine, cours souveraines, military and Church seem to have preferred to lend to financiers rather than to the state. The second thing is that the group of thirty-four financiers lending to other financiers was significantly less distinguished than the professional group of thirty-six financiers who lent directly to the Crown, on the basis of relative percentages in each lending group of central Traitants, principal Munitionnaires and fermiers-généraux. Clearly, while professional financiers did lend to each other, the really important ones preferred to lend to the state. It is reasonable to suppose that it was easier to defraud the state than it was to cheat one's colleagues.

Lending might be the central function of the financial system by the middle of the seventeenth century, but not all those who lent money to the Crown directly were financiers of importance —many, indeed, were not really financiers at all. Equally, it is probable that some really important financiers either did not lend, or are not known to have lent money directly to the Crown. Yet there has to be some way of finding out, amid the plethora of groups discussed in this chapter, who the really important financiers were. The problem is difficult because there are no obvious quantitative data that can be subjected to basic analysis to reveal a group of particularly important people.

The computer is no help here, because it is bereft of the powers of original thinking and framing of concepts. The only thing to do is to survey the careers of a few men whose names appear so often, and in the context of such large operations, that it is evident they must be considered particularly important people. Examination of the careers of men like Jacquier and Nicolas Monnerot reveals two obvious things: that they were involved in a very wide range of activities; and that they held a number of posts in succession or in parallel. It would seem possible to argue that a criterion for establishing a group of particularly important financiers could be the number of roles that each played and the number of posts that each held.

The first and most obvious test to make of this hypothesis runs as follows. By cross-tabulating those who held some kind of financial post against those who exercised some kind of recognisable role in Extraordinary Affairs, a group of 176 people is created, which can be called tentatively the Primary Financial Elite. The intention behind this proceeding is to produce a group which is distinct from the men who held doggedly to some financial post and apparently did nothing in the financial world beyond that, and from the members of the non-financial world, the courtier, soldier, central administrator, magistrate, or ecclesiastic, who punted on the fringes of the financial world but did not buy an office within it. The resultant group can be checked by cross-tabulating it against the persons known to have been fined by the Chambre de Justice of 1661–5. According to a list in the Fonds Clairambault, some 494 people were fined a total of 156,360,000 livres. Of this 494, 87 can be clearly identified as members of the Primary Financial Elite. The fines of these 87 people totalled 107,918,000 livres. To put it another way: 18 per cent of the people fined paid 69 per cent of the fines, while 82 per cent (made up of people who do not appear in the Primary Financial Elite) paid 31 per cent of the fines. Clearly then, members of the elite were far more heavily fined than those who were outside it. The point is made more clearly by looking at the average fines paid by the two groups. Members of the Primary Elite known to have been fined paid an average of just over 1,240,000 livres. People fined who were outside the Primary Elite paid an average of 119,000 livres—which is just under a tenth of what was paid by the members of the Primary Elite.[24] The Primary Elite can therefore be presumed to exist, at least as a methodological tool.

In simple numerical terms, the 176 members of the Primary Elite were dominated by 56 secrétaires du roi and 43 central Traitants. There were also relatively large numbers of lenders both to the state and to other financiers. But if one considers the proportion of members of a given category who appear in the Primary Elite, compared to the overall number of people in that category in the deck as a whole, the following picture emerges: the highest percentages were central Traitants (66 per cent) and principal Munitionnaires (58 per cent). These categories were followed fairly closely by a set of groups: straight lenders direct to the state, lenders to other financiers, manipulators of *Rentes publiques*, and subordinate Munitionnaires. On the official side of things, the list is headed by the intendants des finances (52 per cent), the surintendants des finances (50 per cent), the trésoriers des Parties Casuelles (47 per cent), and the financiers holding writing offices of the Conseil du Roi (46 per cent).

These figures from the Primary Elite are of significance, and will be discussed in a moment. But first, it is helpful to perform two other processes of selection. The Primary Elite is a relatively large group. It is evident from examining the names and careers of its members that there is a wide range of importance within the group. It is therefore useful to distinguish between levels of importance. Such distinction depends on selection of a properly discriminant function, which is this: the key factor that emerged from analysis of the data in this chapter from prête-noms to lenders was that the financiers who were most successful were those who played a number of roles and held a number of posts, usually in parallel. So it would seem reasonable to examine the groups formed by those who held two or more posts in the financial machine and/or played two or more roles in Extraordinary Affairs. The resultant group of 96 men can be tentatively called the Secondary Financial Elite. The process can be repeated substituting three for two, and the third group, thus formed, some 36 strong, can be tentatively called the Tertiary Financial Elite.

Certain differences are readily apparent between Primary and Secondary Elites. In almost every category of officers, the percentage of the overall elite formed by that category is higher in the Secondary Elite than it is in the Primary. Given the different criteria for the establishment of the two groups, this is only to be expected. But certain categories show far greater increases than others. Intendants des finances, trésoriers des Parties Casuelles, holders of writing offices of the Conseil du Roi, and secrétaires du roi all exhibit more or less substantial increases. In the functional or role categories there is a similar situation. Central Traitants, principal Munitionnaires, lenders to other financiers, and lenders direct to the state all increase substantially. The conclusion to be drawn is clear: the higher level of differentiation of the Secondary Elite compared to the Primary tends to concentrate attention on certain categories of posts and functions. The posts were not necessarily the most obviously important. But significant financial power attached to posts like those of intendant des finances as the first part of this study showed, and, as has been seen in this chapter, to posts like those of secrétaire du Conseil. As for the functions that are more highly stressed in the Secondary than in the Primary Elite, these revolved about the mobilisation of credit at the highest level.

The Tertiary Elite, composed of people known to have owned three or more financial posts and/or exercised three or more roles in Extraordinary Affairs, contains 36 members. Of the ten surintendants des finances in the deck as a whole, only one, Particelli d'Emery, qualifies as a member of this central group. No *directeur des finances* survives, nor is there a trésorier de l'Epargne to be found. Some categories of officials more or less maintained their position, or even did marginally better in the Tertiary Elite than they had done in the Secondary. Such were the trésoriers des Parties Casuelles, commis, financial officers of maisons royales, senior officers of bureaux des finances, and writing officers of the Conseil du Roi. Others did substantially better. The secrétaires du roi increased their proportional representation by about one-half, from 40 per cent in the Secondary to 65 per cent in the Tertiary Elite, while the contrôleurs-généraux des finances more than doubled theirs from 4 per cent to 10 per cent. The most successful of all were the intendants des finances, who nearly tripled their proportion from 13 per cent to 32 per cent. As for the roles in Extraordinary Affairs, there was attrition or relative stagnation in minor roles. Local Traitants simply disappeared, while sous-fermiers nearly suffered the same fate. But other roles showed more or less substantial increase. Principal Munitionnaires went up from 25 per cent in the Secondary Elite to 41 per cent in the Tertiary. Central Traitants went up from 37 per cent to 65 per cent. Lenders direct to the state increased from 34 per cent to 49 per cent.

The Tertiary Elite emerges from this analysis and comparison as a body of people not very interested in scaling the highest pinnacles of financial administration, but only in securing those posts, like those of intendant des finances, which were of direct use in their financial enterprises. The Tertiary Elite was dominated, to an extent far greater than that observed in the two previous elites, by roles exercised rather than by posts held. Three out of every five members of the Tertiary Elite were central Traitants. One out of two lent directly to the state. Two out of five were principal Munitionnaires.

Certain general conclusions follow from this discussion of the modes of ascent in the royal finances. Ultimately, administrative posts, which are so clear and obvious at first sight, possessed of satisfyingly orotund titles and backed by royal documents filled with detailed recitals of powers and duties, were less important than roles exercised in Extraordinary financial affairs. But this basic point is by no means the whole story. The motion of financiers from the beginning of their careers to the end was not a simple ascent through progressively more and more important roles. Mobility did exist in this financial world. But it was distorted by the rigidity and fixity that were so much a part of French society at large. There were certain roles—and, indeed, certain offices or posts—whose exercisers or holders did not move on to more important things. Examples of activities that seem not to have been generative of further upward mobility are the roles of prête-nom, Sous-Traitant and subordinate Munitionnaire. Official or semi-official positions that shared this immobile characteristic include those of fermier-général and receveur-payeur des Rentes sur l'Hôtel de Ville de Paris.

To isolate these discontinuities in the financial world is relatively easy. To suggest a full explanation of them is more difficult. One point that should be made is that the reason for the phenomenon varied according to the position of the individual in the financial hierarchy. Obviously a minor prête-nom, picked out almost at random from the servants' hall, was not likely to be able to persuade anybody that a man of straw should ever be endowed with an independent existence in the finances. As for the other categories of the relatively immobile, it is important to distinguish between groups. Many Sous-Traitants were local officials press-ganged or frightened into an involvement in treaties which was strictly limited in scope and duration. Many subordinate Munitionnaires were non-professionals bribed or cajoled by the cardinal minister of state to co-operate in his designs, but only for a limited duration. Such persons do not need further explanation. The real problem comes down to why more members of the upper levels of the finances—specifically the members of the Tertiary Elite—were not drawn from the lower echelons.

The solution to this problem turns on three factors. First comes the question of how people committed themselves to specific activities. The really big men kept themselves and their capital free from long-term commitment and available for rapid deployment and redeployment in ephemeral and profitable activities like loans, treaties and munitions contracts. To buy an office or engage in an activity which tied one down to a particular role and gave one too obvious a place in the administrative hierarchy was to shut oneself off from the more profitable, though infinitely more dangerous, rising trajectory followed by big Traitants and Munitionnaires. The second factor lies in the origins of financiers. Evidently a man born into a relatively elevated situation within or without the royal finances had a much better chance of succeeding than a man who had not been so born. It will be recalled from the previous chapter that study of the origins of the members of the Primary Elite revealed substantial groups of men whose fathers were financiers or members of other institutional groups. Persons with such origins pose no problems on the score of mobility. The people who pose problems are those who started from low levels of society. Why was it that a few rose, while the vast majority found themselves bogged down in lowly occupations? The answer involves a third factor— the exercise of independent initiative. The only way for a person of humble origins to rise was to turn to self-employment, as Gourville did; that is to say, to start in a small way as an independent operator and to plough profits back into successively bigger operations. Such a course was possible only for the exceptionally lucky and brilliant man, like Gourville himself.

Finally, to speak more generally, the process of moving upward in the royal finances depended on the financier's clearly perceiving what was important and what was not. To reduce things to a formula: office was nothing like as important as role. The secret of the successful financier was to concentrate on basic capital accumulation through the mutually reinforcing exercise of a multiplicity of roles chosen solely for their profitability and not for their social or administrative status, whatever these might be. The only purchases of official posts that such a man would tend to make would be of those which, like that of secrétaire du roi, offered a certain degree of protection, or which, like the posts of receveur-général des finances, trésorier des Parties Casuelles, and intendant des finances, provided a front for corrupt operations. These, were they not practised behind such cover, would draw down immediate, condign and exemplary punishment.

Success was expressed not merely in upward movement in the finances. Successful financiers did not confine their enterprises to purely professional matters. Such men built fine houses. Their children rose to high positions in all branches of the governance of France, and their descendants were to be found in families of the highest nobility. But before discussion of these and related matters is undertaken, it is important to stress one thing: the world of the financiers was exceedingly insecure. The rate of failure was very high. Even before quantitative analysis was undertaken it became abundantly clear that many men involved in the finances of the French monarchy came to a bad end. In the deck compiled for this study, therefore, an attempt was made to code the careers of men after they left the finances. The fragmentary nature of the data made a large number of answers impossible to find. Nevertheless, there is information on eighty-six people. Forty left the finances under relatively fortunate conditions. Of these, three took up full-time activities in various cours souveraines, while four entered central administration. Seven simply retired. Twenty-seven died from what were considered in the seventeenth century natural causes while they were still involved in the finances. This leaves forty-six who suffered grave misfortune. Thirty-seven found their careers terminated by ruin, imprisonment, exile, or a combination of these things, brought on by the activity of the state. Of this unhappy band, several died in prison, while at least four were ceremoniously hanged.

It is difficult to know how representative the forty-six cases are. Inevitably they relate to the more rather than to the less important financiers. This may mean that too little stress is placed on the element of slow, simple failure. History does not relate how many small financiers were cheated and ruined by Nicolas Monnerot or François Catelan in the pursuit of fortune, before these great cachalots were caught and rendered down by the state, nor how many men were dragged down by the bankruptcy of a leviathan like Jacques Le Tillier. Nevertheless, it is possible to isolate the various kinds of failure that occurred.

The most common failure was that of the small man attempting to swim in waters far beyond his capabilities. The career of Pierre Dehement, holder of the minor post of *trésorier et payeur des Cent Suisses de la garde de Sa Majesté*, is typical. The early stages of his involvement in the royal finances were as a minor Munitionnaire and lender to the Crown in the 1630s. The readiness with which the government accepted the loans he offered misled him into believing that he could make a success of the office of trésorier that he bought c 1643. The government could now dispense with smiles. Dehement was in their power, and was forced to pay a devastating series of exactions for raising and lowering his wages. He had already strained his credit by borrowing for the state in the 1630s—the loans had, of course, never been repaid by the state—and now he fell into destitution. He was imprisoned for debt, and each time he secured his release he was immediately reincarcerated for failing to pay some new exaction imposed while he had been out of circulation.[25]

His was not the only kind of failure. Whereas Dehement apparently had little imagination or drive, other failures were full of new ideas that, they hoped, would revolutionise the royal finances and make fortunes for everybody, including themselves. One of the strangest of these people was Balthazar Gerbier, a man who had been successively painter, architect and English diplomat, before he attempted to set up complicated state pawnshops in France in the 1640s. Having failed in this as in everything else, he returned to England to open a school (which failed) in Bethnal Green.[26] Another projector was Lorenzo Tonti, a Neapolitan soldier of fortune who invented those disagreeable lotteries called *Tontines*. Having collected a lot of money from gullible investors in the first Tontine in Paris, he ran away to Poland.[27]

But failure was not confined to the lower depths. Among the eighty-six men about whose careers after the end of their involvement in the finances something is known, there were thirty-four members of the Primary Elite. Of these seventeen, exactly half of the group, came to a bad end. Another twelve (35 per cent) died more or less peacefully while actively involved in the finances. Of the remaining five, one entered a full-time career in a cour souveraine, while another took up a career in nonfinancial state administration. One more was allowed to retire voluntarily, and the remaining two went bankrupt. Clearly the odds were fairly high that a financier of the Primary Elite would not be permitted to enjoy in tranquillity the money that he made in the finances. Failure was a menace to even the most successful financier. It could come in various forms: first, mere bankruptcy; second, loss of patronage; the third, the consequences of such loss.

Mere bankruptcy could come about for two major reasons. The first derived from the unvarnished business failure of the individual financier, the second from the role exercised by the state vis-à-vis the individual financier. The first kind of bankruptcy was rare. The collapses that are heard about are usually those of men who ran up against the financial bad faith of the state. Antoine Feydeau, for example, tried to run a series of tax-farms together as one unit during the reign of Louis XIII. But the legal complexities of all the different farms, the foolish indifference of the government to his problems, and the irresponsible hostility of Court factions to him, led eventually to failure to meet his obligations, to bankruptcy, and to flight.[28] Such individual tribulations, however, were as nothing to the general crises precipitated when the state decided that it did not want to meet its obligations, as, for example, at the beginning of the Fronde. Many of the men ruined at that time were close associates of Mazarin himself, who allowed them to survive like birds with broken wings, blundering about for the next decade trying to repair the damage for which he was responsible but for which they had to pay. Such was the case of the brothers Cenami, Italian bankers who had acted as subordinate Munitionnaires for Mazarin at Lyons in the 1640s. In 1648 they went bankrupt and, despite the amelioration of conditions after 1653, were never able to return to financial health.[29]

Such a story was no doubt repeated in a large number of cases, but the records do not dwell on the phenomenon. It is never comfortable to remember the misfortunes of others, particularly when one fears that a similar thing will happen to oneself. On the other hand, a good deal is known about the effects of the combined state bankruptcy and penal investigation carried out under the auspices of the Chambre de Justice of 1661. Much of what happened in the Chambre de Justice is obvious enough, and has in any case been discussed above. What is of interest here is the pattern of failure of financiers as a result of the events which began with Mazarin's death in March 1661 and which more or less ended with Fouquet's going to Pignerol in December 1664. The point is that patronage was of great importance in the world of the financiers, particularly if one lost one's patron, or if one had the wrong patron.

There are examples of what might happen in isolated cases during the 1650s. For example, Marandé, whose patron was Abel Servien, failed to attain the post of commis à l'enregistrement des fonds because Servien was a man of no power in financial affairs. Hervart, who was eventually appointed to the post, gained it largely because of the patronage of Mazarin.[30] But the importance of patronage to the success of a financier and the disastrous consequences of the disappearance or withholding of patronage are to be seen best in what happened to the twenty-two men patronised by Fouquet about whose careers after the end of their involvement in the royal finances something is known. One of them died in 1662 before the Chambre de Justice caught up with him, although his descendants were forced to pay fines for his misdemeanours. Two survived the Chambre de Justice, although one, Jacquier, paid one of the two highest fines imposed by the Chambre.[31] The remaining eighteen suffered ruin, imprisonment or exile, or a combination of the three. Clearly it was unhealthy to be the client of a person careless enough to fall. This conclusion is reinforced by analysis of events following the death of Jean-Baptiste Colbert in 1683. A number of people had escaped the wrath of the Chambre de Justice of 1661 because they had effective patrons. Not least among these were two of Colbert's clients, Bellinzani and Berryer. Both were disgraced and ruined by Colbert's enemies after the contrôleur-general died.[32]

The price of failure in the royal finances in the seventeenth century was high. Much of the price was paid quite literally in money, although the amounts that people were forced to pay were often twisted by political factors, and need some interpretation. For example, the magistrates of the Chambre de Justice of 1661 in imposing fines seized on men who were easily recognised, usually by the possession of some important financial office. Then they weeded out those who were in favour with Colbert or the king. These men received either very light fines, like the 50,000 livres paid by Denis Marin, or else no fine at all, as in the cases of Colbert himself, Berryer, Béchameil and Jeannot de Bertillac. After this, certain notorious heads were broken with especial violence, including those of Fouquet, Bruant and Gourville (both of whom prudently ran away and were never caught, though their goods were confiscated), and people like Jacquier, Monnerot and Catelan, together with the trésoriers de l'Epargne. These tasks completed, the rest of the financial world could be fined mechanically, with only a perfunctory examination of corrupt *démarches* by particular financiers.[33] This last category of fine, by far the largest, was also probably the most fairly assessed.

The imposition of crippling fines was only the beginning of a man's suffering. If a man was fined heavily enough, it was more or less guaranteed that he would exist for the rest of his life in a kind of living death. Nor was it just a question of deliberately bankrupting a man. The authorities could go further by insisting that a given person be exiled to some particularly insalubrious spot. Such was the fate of two of the trésoriers de l'Epargne, Jeannin de Castille and Claude de Guénégaud, who were sent to Limoges. Though it may have been more tolerable to be free and destitute in such a town in the seventeenth century than to be in the Bastille, the distinction would have been difficult to perceive for much of the time, particularly on a rainy Limousin evening.[34]

Even so, the exiles were in the final analysis better off than the next group—those who stayed in close confinement until they died. The rigours of French prisons in the seventeenth century are beyond the scope of the present inquiry. All one can say for the moment is that it should not be presumed that life for imprisoned financiers was as pleasant as Voltaire was to find his first sojourn in the Bastille. Fouquet's travail at Pignerol, whither he was taken in December 1664, was intended by Colbert to be as unpleasant, and therefore as short, as it could be. Fifteen years of imprisonment broke Fouquet's heart, and it was very clear that while Colbert lived there could be no thought of release.[35] Two other figures died in captivity. The first was François Catelan, who was sent to the Bastille on 12 October 1662. He was transferred to the Petit-Châtelet in January 1666, where he died that summer.[36] The second figure was Nicolas Monnerot, one of the few men who can compare with Fouquet for stubbornness and courage under harrassment by the hostile Colbertian faction among the magistrates of the Chambre de Justice. Voracious as the European pike in his appetite for the wealth of lesser fry, he shared the pike's daemonic energy in his fight to regain his freedom. Though the outcome was never in doubt, he covered his retreat every inch of the way, and he was silenced only by death.[37]

Death could also come as the direct result of legal proceedings. This possibility was the one that really alarmed financiers. The Chambre de Justice was responsible for the execution of at least four people. One was a Munitionnaire called Balthazar de Fargues, who was active in the area around Abbeville and Hesdin during the period 1645–9. After 1661, one of the local *subdélégués* of the Chambre de Justice had Fargues arrested in Paris and taken to Abbeville. There, to Fargues' great surprise as he tells us in a document which he wrote challenging the legality of his arrest, a large crowd gathered, united in its intention of pulling him to pieces. The crowd need not have bothered, for the legal authorities had enough material on Fargues' behaviour as Munitionnaire, of his supply of grossly defective food for troops and so on, for a hanging case to be made and sustained. The local court condemned him to death, and the Chambre de Justice confirmed the sentence.[38]

The financiers took this rather hard. Fargues and the other men who were hanged were provincial babes in the wood compared to the successful financiers of Paris. If such relatively minor figures could be so readily destroyed, what might the more guilty not expect? No doubt a moment's reflection would have satisfied financiers anxious about the length of their necks that the four men were insignificant yokels whose deaths were simply occasions for the cathartic venting of spite by judges and other local worthies, and incidentally gave a measure of light-hearted entertainment to the populace. But when it is recalled that throughout the course of the Chambre de Justice the case against Fouquet was built around the attempt to prove that the surintendant himself was guilty of peculation to a degree so great that only death could pay for the crime, then it is possible to understand the financiers' trepidation.[39] Might it not seem that Colbert and his

F

supporters were planning to establish the principle of universal hanging by killing men at the top and at the bottom of the financial pyramid? They would then be able to move into the middle ground to kill at their leisure. This, coupled with the erratic severity of the Chambre which was revealed in the variations in the fines it extracted, a severity which could, it would appear, strike at anyone, seemed to exemplify the danger of being a financier at all.

This chapter has shown that in some ways financiers were upwardly mobile figures. In particular, people who served as commis and/or Traitants rose to positions of considerable importance. At the same time, it should be remembered that many people involved in the royal finances were *not* mobile. They existed to perform necessary functions at low levels, as prête-noms, Sous-Traitants, and sous-fermiers, in particular. In terms of numbers of people involved in the finances, the immobility of the lower levels predominated over the mobility of the successful financiers. The success of the best-known financiers has to be offset by the failure of countless minor figures who perished leaving barely a ripple after them. The apparent ease with which men like Nicolas Monnerot, Jacquier, Catelan and Boislève made money takes on a certain fragility when seen in such a context. Success for the financier could be achieved and maintained only by constant vigilance and a consistent ruthlessness which stopped at nothing in the pursuit of self-interest.

Such ruthlessness in itself reinforced the probability of failure for lesser men. Monnerot, with his plans for running a Chambre de Justice to mulct his fellow financiers, is a graphic example of such reinforcing. At the same time, knowledge of the normal, depressing lack of success of lesser men, together with the frightening possibility of prosecution of more considerable financiers by Chambres de Justice, gave a hectic quality to the life style of even the most successful financier. The future being so dark and problematical, the successful financier tended to live very much in the agreeable present, spending money as he made it because if he did not spend it soon it was possible that the state or another financier even greedier than he would take it away from him. Ironically, it was partly because successful financiers spent in this somewhat frenetic manner that they attracted the resentment of the public and the Crown. The financiers' reaction to their dangerous environment in fact made that environment more dangerous still. At the same time, financiers' modes of spending were a highly important part of the structure of their social personae. It is therefore with the ways in which the money made by financiers was spent that the following chapter is concerned.

Notes to this chapter are on pages 252–3

Chapter 7 THE USES OF MONEY

THE LITTLE information that can be found on the size of the fortunes made by financiers is exceedingly unreliable. This unreliability stems from a conflict of sources: on the one hand, statements about financiers' fortunes derived from pamphlets, doggerel verses and ribald songs; and on the other, statements made by financiers themselves, particularly in court and, as they went to their reward, in wills and other testamentary dispositions. On the public opinion side, it was said that financiers were not only plebeian and depraved but also scandalously rich. But this is not what might be concluded from a study of financiers' wills. These reveal how decent and modest their authors had been in life, and how much of such money as they had legitimately made was to go to support soup kitchens for deserving paupers and other worthy causes. Such documents were designed to create an atmosphere of restrained but intense piety which, it was hoped, the authorities would not be so crude as to disturb with postmortuary proceedings on charges of peculation.

To steer a course between these violently opposed sources is impossible. It is therefore necessary to attack the question of the fortunes of financiers in a different way, by examining the ways in which financiers spent their money. Six categories of spending emerge from the data. They divide into two groups. First come those categories which represent private investment in public affairs—that is to say in those matters related closely to the state and the various branches and strata of its administration. The categories here are offices, and directly alienated royal taxation. In the second group are those categories which represent investment in affairs not related to the state: renting and purchase of accommodation in Paris; purchase of estates and titles in the country; provision of marriage portions for relatives; and building, the most obvious kind of conspicuous consumption.

Of the public matters, the more important category is the purchase of office. Financiers bought such things for a variety of reasons. Posts of *secrétaire du roi* were acquired partly as means of self-protection. The cost was fairly modest—about 25,000 livres in the middle of the seventeenth century. Investment in posts near the centre of financial administration which were of more direct use in making money was very much more expensive. To become *intendant des finances* in the 1650s cost some 200,000 livres. This was the sum paid by Jacques Paget, Claude de Boislève, Guillaume de Brisacier and Claude Housset in 1654.[1] To become *contrôleur-général des finances* cost Louis Le Tonnelier de Breteuil and Barthélemy Hervart 450,000 livres each in December 1657.[2] It was more expensive still to become *trésorier de l'Epargne*, the senior *comptable* post in the kingdom. Such a post was valued at 1 million livres in the 1650s.[3] The sums mentioned mean more when they are compared with one another: it cost about forty times as much to become trésorier de l'Epargne as it did to become a mere secrétaire du roi. Even posts which might seem out of the mainstream of the finances cost a great deal of money. Gourville bought a post of *secrétaire du Conseil* for 900,000 livres in 1660.[4] The post of *surintendant des finances et secrétaire des Commandements* of Louis XIV's consort Marie-Thérèse was not an obviously important office. But it changed hands for 450,000 livres in 1659.[5] The reason for the high price of both these offices is that they gave their holders proximity to the centre, both politically and financially. Proximity was everything, so that high-sounding posts in the provinces sold for relatively trifling sums. The office of *trésorier-receveur-général des Etats de Bourgogne*, for example, was sold for a mere 65,729 livres 4 sous on 28 January 1652 by one Guillaume Burgat to Antoine Bossuet, elder brother by some three years of the future Bishop of Meaux.[6]

Expenditure on office was by no means confined to fulfilling purely professional aims. Financiers were also concerned with less obvious but none the less important questions of social status and prestige. Even posts of secrétaire du roi, useful though they might be to new financiers in their day to day business, had the additional advantage of ennobling those who purchased them. This, as the financier came towards the end of his career, may have come to be the most important virtue of an office originally acquired for different reasons. Moreover, for some considerable time before the middle of the century financiers had bought posts that meant little to their careers in the finances. Several very successful financiers bought prestigious posts in the *Chambre des Comptes* of Paris. Claude Cornuel, for example, came to own one of the offices of *président* in that body. The office was valued at 420,000 livres at its owner's death in 1638. Even the posts of *maître ordinaire* of the Chambre were worth over 200,000 livres to financiers in the later 1650s.[7] Purchases of offices like these, which were really outside the finances, were made only by the most successful financiers. The reason for their action seems to have been the desire for a kind of post less tainted than those in the main line of the financial administration.

Other, less successful financiers were not immune to the desire for respectability. But they found cheaper ways of indulging it. The most obvious of these ways was to buy socially acceptable but not too expensive offices for their sons and sons-in-law. For a son aspiring to a career in the Church, a financier might buy a post of *aumônier du roi*. One such changed hands for 60,000 livres in 1659. An office of *greffier* in the *Parlement* of Paris would set a parent back some 50,000 livres in the mid-1650s. Guillaume Languet paid 85,000 livres in 1654 for a post of *procureur-général* of the Parlement of Dijon for his son Denis. For those parents who were prepared to spend a more substantial sum, the post of *maître des requêtes* had considerable attraction. During the early 1630s a price of between 150,000 and 180,000 livres was usual. But by 1661 the price had risen to 320,000 livres.[8] Such expenditure, though large, was worth it, for possession of a post of maître des requêtes put a financier's son on the road to becoming a member of the central administration of the absolutist state.

The venality of offices was, it is clear, of great importance to the financier. Not merely did it make possible investment in financial office which would increase his wealth and financial power, but it also allowed him to spread his net into the non-financial world, in fact, to create a respectable aura about himself and his clan.

The second field of investment in public affairs was in the

fiscal system of the state. This investment was quite distinct from the grossly fraudulent and highly profitable kinds of involvement in fiscal matters entered into by financiers in their professional capacity, which were described in the first part of this book. The kind of investment under discussion here was made by financiers essentially as private individuals seeking a safe long-term income. Originally, financiers might have found such income in *Rentes sur l'Hôtel de Ville de Paris*. But by the middle of the seventeenth century financiers had ceased to show interest in them as long-term investments. They knew only too well, since they were partly responsible for the situation, that Rentes were virtually useless as a source of steady income. Only two important financiers, Claude Cornuel and Guillaume Languet, are known to have purchased Rentes as long-term investments, and their holdings were tiny compared to their other interests. Cornuel owned a block of Rentes worth 55,000 livres, which represented only 2·96 per cent of his declared fortune at death of 1,856,000 livres. Since his real fortune was almost certainly considerably more than this, the proportion of it held in Rentes was probably less than 1 per cent. At all events, it is legitimate to infer that financiers paid little attention to Rentes in the long term.[9]

There was in fact a much more attractive alternative to Rentes. This consisted of buying directly alienated royal taxes. The reason why direct alienations were bought by financiers while Rentes were despised is not immediately obvious. At first sight it would seem that both Rentes and direct alienation, and indeed the sale of offices, were merely different ways of selling off royal income in return for immediate cash payments. The net result for the investor might appear the same, that is to say, he received long-term income which had once been the Crown's. However, the state cheated holders of office and long-term investors in Rentes so badly that potential investors who understood what they were about preferred to know exactly where the income of their investments was to come from. They also wanted an uninfringeable right to receive their money, a right formally ceded by the Crown to the investor and which the Crown could not unilaterally resume for fear of legal action in which it would almost certainly be held to account by the magistrates of the cours souveraines. It was for this reason that people invested heavily in alienated taxes.

It is unfortunately impossible to find out how much money was invested in each case. Often enough a person bought both an estate and the royal taxes that were levied from the taxpayers on that estate, and then added both these elements together. The only clear statement of the value of someone's purchases of directly alienated royal taxes comes from Colbert's analysis of Mazarin's fortune in 1658. According to his intendant, the cardinal owned *Droits* worth 2,342,273 livres 6 sous 3 deniers, which brought in an income of 253,750 livres a year. This represents a yield of just under 11 per cent, which must reflect the activities of the tireless Colbert and the power of the cardinal himself.[10] Such a return could not be expected for more ordinary mortals, nor is it likely that any other person came close to Mazarin in the size of his or her investment in this field. Nevertheless, those who invested were important people, and it may be presumed that the resources which they brought to such investment were considerable. Some of the most important financiers of the age, such as Claude Cornuel, Pierre Monnerot and Louis I Béchameil, were involved.[11] But they were not alone. Even members of the cours souveraines, like Guillaume de Lamoignon, *premier président* of the Parlement of Paris from 1657, and Achille de Harlay, who took over Fouquet's post of procureur-général of the same Parlement in 1661, did not think it beneath their dignity to invest in such things.[12] Neither did nobles of the sword. In fact, analysis of the professions followed by all the investors of whom record has been found reveals that in this particular field —which relates to purchases made by persons not as mobilisers of funds for the state but as capital holders anxious to secure safe but profitable investments—the financiers formed only one of a number of functional groups.

Furthermore, as the financier grew wealthier and became better established, there was a tendency for him to move away from total reliance on investment in the apparatus of the state. Ultimately, even long-term investment was only as safe as the state itself. And in the age of the Fronde, when taxes went uncollected for years at a stretch, the state was unable to provide the annual payments which alone gave alienations of taxation a capital value. The re-establishment of order after the Fronde restored that capital value. Nevertheless, if he could, a wise man would turn to investment in things which, though they might depend on economic conditions in a general sense for their value, were not entirely dependent on fluctuations in the fortunes of the Bourbon régime. Such investment was largely connected with property in land and buildings, and with social prestige. It was not connected with making money, for that was made in the royal finances. The object in every case was to create a leisured and opulent style of life which would facilitate the passage of the financier into the ranks of the true nobility. Mere possession of technical nobility derived from owning a post of secrétaire du roi or the like was not enough.

There were four major fields in which the quest for nobility was carried on: acquisition of respectable property in Paris; purchase of landed estates; investment in marriage; and building, both in town and in the country.

The first field that the financier turned to was that of property in Paris, for the world of the financiers was essentially a Parisian one. If one wished to be a success, it was indispensable to base oneself on Paris. At first, the new or poor financier might merely take rooms in a house owned by someone else. But eventually the financier would be able, and social convention would practically force him, to buy a house of his own. The addresses of 106 persons connected with the royal finances have been found. They were spread over seventeen parishes, sixteen of which were in Paris, and one of which was technically not part of the city. This was Saint-Sulpice, which was outside the wall of Philippe-Auguste, still at the time the legal boundary of the city on the south-western side. Cross-tabulation of the professional and functional groups into which the 106 people fall against the parishes where they lived, citing all the abodes of the 106 even when they moved once or twice (a total of 129 addresses), produces the following results.

The most obvious thing is that financiers tended to prefer some parishes to others. There are three groups of parishes: first, Saint-Merri, Saint-Nicolas-des-Champs and Saint-Eustache; second, Saint-Paul, Saint-Gervais, Saint-Jean-en-Grève and Saint-Louis-en-l'Isle; and third, the remaining ten parishes—

Saint-André-des-Arts, Saint-Benoît, Saint-Etienne-du-Mont, Saint-Germain-l'Auxerrois, Saint-Jean-le-Rond, Saint-Martial-en-la-Cité, Saint-Nicolas-du-Chardonnet, Saint-Roch, Saint-Sévérin, and Saint-Sulpice. Further than this, the parishes in each group have certain differences from one another. For example, while relatively large numbers of financiers lived in Saint-Merri and Saint-Nicolas-des-Champs, they formed less distinguished communities than the financiers of Saint-Eustache. It is easy, turning to the topography of Paris in the seventeenth century, to find some indication of why this was so.[13]

The first question to be asked is, where were the respective parishes? Saint-Gervais, Saint-Jean-en-Grève, Saint-Merri, Saint-Nicolas-des-Champs and Saint-Paul were all in the Marais —the area bounded by the rue Saint-Martin on the west, the Seine on the south, and a line forming a rough quadrant from the Arsenal in the east along what are now the Boulevards round to what is now the place de la République in the north. The significant parishes outside the Marais were not far away. Saint-Louis-en-l'Isle, as its name suggests, is on what is now known as the Ile-Saint-Louis, though the island was known somewhat confusingly in the seventeenth century as the Isle-Notre-Dame. Saint-Eustache lay just west of the Halles.

As for the financiers to be found in these parishes, there were concentrations in both Saint-Nicolas-des-Champs and Saint-Merri. In the former, in an area bounded on the north by the rue des Gravilliers, on the east by the rue du Temple, on the south by the rue des Francs Bourgeois and on the west by the rue Saint-Martin, were to be found twelve financiers, of whom only one achieved high position in the royal finances—that was Charles Bernard, unsuccessful *premier commis* of the surintendant des finances in the 1650s.[14] In the western section of the Marais, the richer financiers were concentrated towards the south, in the streets directly adjoining the church of Saint-Merri itself. In the rue de la Verrerie were to be found men like Bonnaventure Quentin sieur de Richebourg, secrétaire du roi and *Fermier-général des Gabelles*, who lived there down to 1640. But the bulk of the important financiers of Saint-Merri lived, as did Pierre Girardin in the 1640s, in the rue Quincampoix, on the western edge of the parish.[15]

In the far south of the Marais, that is to say the parishes of
Saint-Jean-en-Grève, Saint-Gervais and Saint-Paul, are still to
be seen a number of important houses, most in bad condition, a
few, like the Hôtel de Sully, restored. This was an area where
parlementaires and members of the modern administrative
machine, like the Ormesson and Fouquet, used to live. The
Ormesson house still stands, sadly dilapidated, on the rue Saint-
Antoine, while the house owned by François IV Fouquet on the
rue de Jouy was pulled down in the seventeenth century. But it
was here that Nicolas Fouquet and his brothers grew up.[16] The
interesting thing is that while two surintendants des finances
(Sully and Fouquet) lived in the area, neither did so while he was
surintendant. Nevertheless, some important practising financiers
lived in the area. Nicolas Jeannin de Castille lived in the Place
Royale, now the Place des Vosges.[17] Pierre Dalbiert lived in the
rue des Lions.[18] Barthélemy Hervart lived in the rue du Paradis
(which is now that part of the rue des Francs Bourgeois
running from the rue Vieille du Temple to the rue des
Archives) from 1657.[19] The rue d'Orléans was especially
favoured. Claude Cornuel was living there in 1637, the year before his death.[20] Pierre Gargan owned a house there and lived in
it until his death in 1657.[21] Claude Girardin was living in the street
in 1659.[22] In the rue de Thorigny, somewhat to the west, lived
Pierre Aubert, Fermier-général des Gabelles.[23]

The area where the most important financiers chose to live
was the parish of Saint-Eustache. Some financiers lived there
before the building of the Palais Cardinal began in 1633. One
such was Jacques Dalibert, who came to live in the rue des
Vieux Augustins in 1629.[24] But it was not until Cardinal Richelieu established himself there that the *quartier* became really
popular. It was agreeable for persons politically close to the seat
of power, or wishing to become close or closer to it, to establish
themselves in physical proximity. The seat did not move far after
Richelieu's death. When Mazarin was in Paris (and not on one of
his hectic journeys round France, getting under the feet of his
commanders in the field), he lived just north of the Palais Cardinal (or, as it was soon called, Palais Royal) across the rue des
Petits-Champs in a jumble of buildings known for politeness'
sake as the Palais Mazarin.[25] All kinds of people moved into the

area. Barthélemy Hervart rented a house in the rue des Vieux
Augustins for three years until he bought his house in the rue du
Paradis.[26] He was only one of six members of the Tertiary Elite
who lived in the parish. The others were François Berthelot,
Nicolas de Frémont, Gourville, Particelli d'Emery and Jacques
Tubeuf.[27]

Obviously, all this trafficking in property cost money. Many of
the men who gave their addresses to notaries or prosecutors only
rented their accommodation. One suspects that many of those
living in the northern part of the parish of Saint-Nicolas-des-
Champs were in this situation. And even quite important people
might live in rented accommodation, as Hervart did for a time.
But most successful people bought houses as soon as they could.

It is worth discussing two of these purchases, because they
give some idea of what money could buy in the seventeenth century, and of the relative costs of different categories of things,
particularly offices. The first purchase was by Jacques Dalibert.
He had come to live in the rue des Vieux Augustins in 1629, but
it was not until 1633 that he bought a house there. The house
consisted of

> . . . two blocks, one at the front, the other at the back, a court-
> yard in the middle, a part of which was formerly a garden. The
> front block can be used as cellar, kitchen, reception room, bed-
> rooms, closets and an attic at the top, and the back block can be
> used as two cellars, a reception room, kitchen, master bedroom,
> closet with a little office [cabinet] beside it, an attic above. The
> buildings are . . . all roofed in tile, and extend from the house of
> the Golden Lion and others to the house of the Three Fish and
> others . . .

All this cost 24,000 livres, about the same price as Dalibert had
paid for his post of secrétaire du roi. Dalibert had reckoned his
fortune in 1629 on the eve of his marriage to stand at 180,000
livres. The price of the house was about 13 per cent of that figure,
although, given that Dalibert's fortune probably increased during the period 1629–33, it is likely that the house committed less
than 13 per cent of his fortune in 1633. In any case, the price was
not to be paid in cash. A sum of 8,000 livres, plus interest, was to
be paid in one year as down payment, while the remaining
16,000 livres was to be paid for by Dalibert's constituting to the

sellers of the house a private Rente of 1,000 livres, which works out as equivalent to paying interest at 6·25 per cent.[28]

The other purchase was by Henri du Plessis-Guénégaud. In 1648 he bought an estate in Paris, consisting of the Hôtel de Nevers (which, as can be seen from a 1618 plan of Paris, was large enough in itself) and the area surrounding the house bounded by the rue Dauphine, a *quai* on the Seine, and a section of the defending walls of the city stretching north-west from the point where the rue Dauphine met the wall (at the Porte de Buci) and ending at the old Tour de Nesle. The estate included title to houses on the western side of the rue Dauphine, the quai and a small *chantier* connected to it, the Tour, and not merely the section of city wall but the ditch and counterscarp as well. This would take the boundary of the property up to what is now the eastern side of the rue Mazarine. For all this, Guénégaud paid only 600,000 livres. He had acquired a bargain whose value was composed not merely of real property, but of something less tangible though nevertheless appealing. To be able to describe himself, as he did in a document drawn up in March 1662, as

Chevalier Marquis de Plaincy, Seigneur du Plessis et autres lieux, Conseiller du Roi et Secrétaire des Commandements de Sa Majesté, Commandeur de ses Ordres, demeurant à Paris en son hôtel paroisse Saint-André-des-Arts,

clearly gave Guénégaud as much pleasure as the wife of Bath got from being called Madam. His title indeed had a fine ring to it—but it needed that last phrase to round it off.[29]

Most of the houses owned by financiers and used by them as their usual Paris homes fell between the extremes that the two examples just described represent. But there was a significant concentration at the lower end of the scale. For example, Claude Cornuel's house in the rue d'Orléans was valued at 110,000 livres in 1638, while Claude de Boislève, who bought the Hôtel de Carnavalet in the rue des Francs Bourgeois in 1654, valued the house at 100,000 livres in the early 1660s.[30] These acquisitions by wealthy financiers were modest in price compared to the sums that such men would invest in office.

It is evident then that, despite its importance, property in Paris was merely a beginning. Even before the financier acquired the last and most opulent of a series of Parisian houses in which he would reside until his death or ruin, he would turn to acquisition of land outside Paris. Often, it seems, the wish to become owner of even the most trivial *seigneurie* was exceeded only by the lust for office.

Clearly motives in the purchase of land differed and were as numerous as the financiers themselves. But there were two major categories of motive: people wanted social status and/or investment with guaranteed returns. The status question is highly complicated, for it is very difficult to say whether or how the purchase of a particular piece of land related to the acquisition of noble title by its purchaser. This difficulty is part and parcel of the larger problem of who was noble and who was not, something which was extremely confused and was felt to be so by the authorities of the state and by society at large in the seventeenth century.[31] A few points can be made, however. Mere purchase of a seigneurie did not in any sense make a man noble. If *seigneurs* in the deck were noble, it was because they possessed some post such as secrétaire du roi or *conseiller au Parlement* which conferred personal nobility. Given the terms of the nobility of the secrétaires du roi, the factor of land was irrelevant. Loyseau says (and on this kind of purely legal point he is reliable):

> The secrétaires du roi . . . by edicts of the years 1484 and 1549 were expressly declared to be noble, and capable of *enjoying*, as these edicts say, *all qualities, prerogatives and precedence of nobility, as if they were nobles of four generations, even to being worthy of receiving the order of chivalry.*[32]

This being the case, the acquisition of land can be seen more as a way of helping to create the life style and image that a noble was expected to have. Eventually the two elements, that is to say, *noblesse de dignité* conferred by office, and the possession of land, would grow together until they became inextricably intertwined, forming a fair enough variety of noblesse. Evidently such nobility was not the same thing as immemorial *noblesse de race*. But it took its place legitimately in a hierarchy of nobilities.

A large number of financiers possessed technical nobility, purchased land, and assumed a title different from their original names. One of these was Jean Hérault. On 16 July 1659 he became secrétaire du roi. Soon after this acquisition of legal nobility, he purchased the Seigneurie of Gourville in Anjou.[33] The measure of the estate's use to him is quite simply that instead of being plain M Jean Hérault, he was known for the next forty years as M de Gourville. Like Gourville, most financiers stayed at the low level of seigneur. Nevertheless, a few were to be found in higher places. Some of these were qualified as *chevalier*. These included Charles Bernard, Louis I Berryer, Jacques Dalibert, and Michel I Particelli d'Emery. Others went on to become *barons*: Delorme, Gaspard I de Fieubet, Thomas I Morant, Jérôme de Nouveau, Sublet des Noyers, and Tubeuf. A few achieved the status of *marquis*. These included Adrien II Hanivel de Manevillette, Louis Picart de Dampierre, Nicolas Fouquet and Jean-Baptiste Colbert. Two became *comtes*—François Berthelot and Jean Rouillé. One, and he because he was able to ally his unique opportunities for making money to his equally unique role in affairs of state, became *duc et pair de France*. This was Mazarin himself.[34]

In many respects such a catalogue is not very impressive. If one compared this group of nearly twenty people with the French nobility as a whole, the group would be dwarfed into insignificance. Moreover, the group is a disparate one, composed of people with widely differing origins, some of whom owed their noble status to membership of groups other than financial ones. Fouquet, for example, was really a member of the *robe d'état*, while Mazarin's status derived from his being *premier ministre* and cardinal. The degree of insignificance of the financiers in the nobility can be evaluated in quantitative terms by an examination of the most highly specialised financial group, the Tertiary Elite. The styles of sixteen members of that Elite are known. Of this group, fifteen were seigneurs, of whom two also possessed the title of chevalier, while two others were also barons. Only one was a comte, and he was a man who never even saw the estate giving him his title, which was in fact something of a joke. A comparison of the performance of this group with that of another group in the deck makes the point more graphically. Whereas only 6 per cent of the Tertiary Elite held titles at the levels of comte, marquis or duc, such titles were held by over 60 per cent of the military men. These figures, it should be stressed, were derived from data whose bias is heavily towards the finances. But even so, they show clearly that the financiers could hardly be said to have subverted the bastions of noble power. The nexus of high nobility and the military is indicative of the continued existence of an age-old military caste.

Why, then, were people so angry with the financiers, and why was it felt that they were upsetting the established social order? It would appear to have been largely a question of newness and speed. The question arose at its most critical at the lower levels of the hierarchy of the landed. In the deck as a whole, there are data on the style of 496 people. Three hundred and thirty-seven (some 68 per cent) were seigneurs. The largest concentrations of seigneurs were to be found in the ranks of financiers and members of the *cours souveraines*. There is, however, a critical difference between financiers and magistrates. Compilation of a group of men known to have been the first in their families to call themselves seigneur, and analysis of the functional variables into which these men fit, reveal that of forty so-called new seigneurs, thirty-one (78 per cent) were involved in some way in the royal finances, while only five (13 per cent) were magistrates of cours souveraines.

There was, then, a correlation between new seigneurs and involvement in the royal finances. Given the hostility of society at large, and in particular of the various kinds of older nobility, to social movement, the fact that financiers were obviously newer than other groups would be enough to attract unfavourable attention. But it is known from the history of the Fronde that the most serious hostility towards financiers was felt by magistrates of the cours souveraines. Possessed of titles similar in the mass to those of the financiers, the magistrates were observing a group of men newer than they rising in one or two generations to status that the forebears of magistrates had attained with some difficulty and maintained for some considerable time without much further advance. What made the magistrates feel worse was that their observations telescoped what was a whole series of movements of usually quite small size by individual financiers into one large movement which it was assumed financiers had made, were making, or were about to make. To put it in a more specific way: if Gourville, a former household servant, bought a seigneurie, and if Mazarin, a foreigner who wrote French only with difficulty, could become duc et pair de France, then it could be represented that financiers were rising from the depths and in one monstrous leap ascending to the pinnacles of noblesse.[35] But it was mostly a question of appearance interpreted by hostile and even hysterical observers. The movement of men in the aggregate was not large, except in single stages of advance, and even then the concentration was at the lower end of the scale.

So far the discussion has been concerned with the purchase of land for reasons connected with social status. There was, however, another side to things. Some men bought land as investment, though not many of these men could be called hard-core financiers. The pattern revealed by analysis of purchases is in fact rather a strange one. Most financiers seem, like Gourville, to have bought a *terre* to get themselves on to the ladder of landed society, even if only on a low rung. But at this point acquisition seems to have stopped. There are, it is true, ample signs that investment in land did go on, and in a way suggesting that attention was paid to the revenues of an estate in cash, unrelated to any return in the form of status. For example, people, or their agents acting on instructions, spent a lot of time rounding out estates by acquiring outlying farms, a process which made no difference to their title. Similarly, people acquired estates bearing titles inferior in rank to the highest one in their collection, although they would usually be known only by the highest title. But these things were not done by the general run of financiers.

Even the big career financiers seem to have been content with one or two big estates, surrounded by a scattering of lesser seigneuries. This was certainly the case with Michel I Particelli d'Emery. His most prestigious purchase, made in March 1648, was of the *Vicomté* of Saint-Florentin in Burgundy. But this purchase, made for the relatively small sum of 60,000 livres, took place right at the end of the life of the surintendant and was merely to buttress an earlier investment, the Seigneurie of Tanlay, whose sixteenth-century château he made his country seat. For much of his life he seems to have owned relatively little land, even when, as secrétaire du Conseil and intendant des finances, he could have afforded a great deal of property.[36] The case of Claude Cornuel reinforces the argument. It seems that he

bought only two estates, La Marche for 70,000 livres, and Le
Mesnil for 150,000 livres. The latter, as far as it is possible to
tell, was bought at the end of his life.[37] These men were highly
important financiers, who spent much more on land than their
junior colleagues seem to have done. But even these two financiers were completely outclassed by rich members of the modern
administrative machine who became involved only at a developed
stage of their careers in the royal finances. Claude II de Bullion
was a lawyer-administrator who was surintendant des finances
from 1632 until his death in 1640. For thirty years before he
ascended to this post he had been buying land, and by the time
he died he owned estates worth well over 1 million livres.[38]
Nicolas Fouquet spent over 2,200,000 livres on land.[39] His colleague Servien spent over 1 million livres.[40] As for Mazarin, as a
result of the purchase of estates like the duchies of Mayenne and
Nivernais, and of the outright gift by Louis XIV of 200 parishes
in Alsace, the cardinal's holdings in land outside Paris were
worth some 7,500,000 livres by 1660.[41]

This difference in performance between the most successful
financiers and wealthy members of the modern administrative
machine seems to indicate that financiers, as relatively new men,
did not have resources for investment in land on a large scale.
There were too many other things that had to be attended to
first, like offices, houses in Paris, and the like. It was only when
financiers had these things, and moreover when they were sure
that they could provide properly for their families, that they
would turn to purifying their money by sinking it in wide acres.
The modern administrative people, on the other hand, tended to
belong to families which had been buying land long before the
administrators in question began to make their own acquisitions.
The only exception to this is Mazarin, a foreigner whose case
was, to say the least, exceptional.

A great deal of land was changing hands in the middle years of
the seventeenth century. Old noble estates were being broken up.
New agglomerations of land were being brought together. In
this dual process, the financiers played their own relatively restrained part. They had little need of original thoughts in this,
for it was a process that had been going on for centuries. The
factors involved varied in their incidence. No doubt in the six-

teenth century land changed hands at an enhanced rate, given the classic situation of an inflation of prices and the relative inability of some—though by no means all—of those who held land to adjust to the new price structure. In the seventeenth century, when the price revolution ended, land went on changing hands. It is not necessary to seek explanations for this very far from the purely demographic level, where any number of causes might operate. Families might die out. The owner of an estate might die leaving orphan children and a widow. A family might be saddled with a head who was a compulsive gambler. On the other hand, it must be pointed out that much of the land on the market of whose sale there is record came from what one might call the old noblesse de race. And it was bought by relatively new men—men who were financiers, or members of the modern administrative machine or of the cours souveraines. But this was nothing new. Financiers had been buying terres and seigneuries at least since the late fifteenth century, when, for example, Jean Bourrée bought the estate which is now called Le Plessis-Bourrée, just north of Angers. Such a man was absorbed happily into landed society. Contemplation of the process of absorption was to drive men like Saint-Simon into torrents of imaginatively obscene abuse, but nothing that they could say or do would stop it.

In addition to investment in office and the purchase of property in Paris and in the country, there were other ways of spending money in the pursuit of social status. The first of these was investment in marriage. Marriage was a business arrangement in early modern France, as it had been in settled if not civilised societies from time immemorial. The social aspect of the patterns of marriage traced in the society of seventeenth-century France by financiers and their siblings, sons, daughters and grandchildren is discussed below in Chapter 9. What is at issue here is the role that money played in arranging marriages, and the way financiers sought marriage partners for themselves and eventually their offspring.

The attitude of mind in which people approached such alliances is well shown by a rather sordid document setting down the price fathers would have to pay to get their daughters married off to various different levels of officials. It comes from the *Roman bourgeois* of 1666, and appears as Table 3.[42] The docu-

TABLE 3: **Data from Tariffe ou Evaluation des partis sortables pour faire facilement les mariages***

Amount of Girl's Dowry Necessary (in livres)	Husbands available in particular Price-range
2,000 to 6,000	Marchand du Palais
	Petit commis
	Sergent
	Solliciteur de procès
6,000 to 12,000	Marchand de soie
	Drapier
	Mouleur de bois
	Procureur du Châtelet
	Maître d'hôtel et secrétaire de grand seigneur
12,000 to 20,000	Procureur en Parlement
	Huissier
	Notaire
	Greffier
20,000 to 30,000	Avocat
	Conseiller du Trésor
	Conseiller des Eaux-et-Forêts
	Substitut du Parquet
	Général des Monnaies
30,000 to 45,000	Auditeur des Comptes
	Trésorier de France
	Payeur des Rentes
45,000 to 75,000	Conseiller de la Cour des Aides
	Conseiller du Grand Conseil
	Conseiller au Parlement
75,000 to 150,000	Maître des Comptes
150,000 to 300,000	Maître des requêtes
	Intendant des finances
	Greffier et secrétaire du Conseil
	Président aux Enquêtes
300,000 to 600,000	Président à Mortier
	Vrai marquis
	Surintendant
	Duc et Pair

* Source: A. Furetière, *Le roman bourgeois*, 33–4.

ment is undoubtedly at fault in a number of respects, particularly in that it pays no attention to the social position of the girls who were to be married off, a variable which was, in fact, of critical importance. Nor does it face up to the complexities of people's social *personae*, in that a man might hold a number of posts which cut across the purely monetary blocks into which the social and functional hierarchy was divided by the author. Nevertheless, it establishes the frame of mind for dealing with a marital climate which was on the whole too cold for much love.

In the world of the financiers, marriages were undertaken for two reasons over and above the reason given by St Paul: to further one's business, or to acquire some kind of social prestige. Both predicated some financial arrangement—that is to say, usually the woman had to have a dowry. If the partners to the marriage were fairly evenly matched, then the dowry could be calculated with the kind of predictability hinted at by the *Roman bourgeois*. But where there were large disparities in status, strange things might happen. Relatively large dowries might have to be offered to attract socially prestigious sons-in-law. Occasionally the reverse might happen—a socially prestigious wife might need no dowry to attract a socially unprestigious husband. The possibilities were endless, although there were certain common patterns that are discussed in Chapter 9.

Some financiers who married when they were in positions of little importance had inevitably to be satisfied with rather poor marriages. Such was the case of Simon II Berthelot, *Receveur des Tailles* of Montdidier, who married Anne Fournier, daughter of a former *avocat au Parlement*, in 1652. The dowry was small: two tiny pieces of farmland, together with private Rentes of an annual value of less than 100 livres. Further than this, Berthelot's new mother-in-law promised to pay him 1,600 livres in cash.[43] But for the financier with more money, life had considerably more to offer, as is shown by the marriage of Jacques Dalibert, *Intendant des Gabelles* of Languedoc, to Estiennette, daughter of Jean Charpentier, *Commissaire ordinaire des Guerres*, in 1629. The Charpentier parents offered a dowry of 60,000 livres, which they retained the option to supply in cash or in property in Paris and in the surrounding villages. Equally, the financier with more money could buy more for his children.

Dalibert and his wife had a daughter, Marie, who was of an age
to be married in 1647. Analysis of the marriage that was arranged
for her shows significant differences from the marriage of her
parents. What is to be observed is a classic pattern of change
made possible by the successful career of a financier. Dalibert
was able to raise 150,000 livres to serve as a dowry, with which
he was able, by a marriage contract of October 1647, to ensnare a
socially acceptable son-in-law, Jean Le Boulanger, *Maître des
Requêtes ordinaire de l'Hôtel*. What Dalibert had bought was, by
the standards of seventeenth-century French financiers, well
worth having: social prestige. That, of course, is a phrase easy to
write, but difficult to define. Some idea of its nature can be
gained simply from looking at the list of people who witnessed
the Le Boulanger-Dalibert marriage contract. On the bride's side
were eight people who with their minor posts were quite over-
whelmed by the glittering tribe assembled by the husband-to-be.
There were twenty-three of these, of whom eleven held posts of
importance in Parisian cours souveraines, while four more were
members of the modern administrative machine. Another was
prior of Moustier. Yet one more was a *grand audiencier de
France*.[44] Alliance with this circle, however much its members
might sneer at someone whom it would give them pleasure to
define as a gross financier, was evidently worth it, for a large
number of financiers contracted similar marriages for their
daughters.

The categories of spending so far discussed have a relatively
modest quality about them. Had they been the only ways in
which financiers expended their ill-gotten gains, society might
not have been as uniform as it was in its condemnation of financiers as a group. But there was a last category of spending which
attracted a great deal of unpopularity, an unpopularity so deep
that it coloured society's view of the whole question of financiers.
Financiers were hated because of the way they made their
money. But what sharpened this hatred to a fine cutting edge was
the flamboyant way in which some of that money was spent, that
is to say on conspicuous consumption. There are evidently many
fields in which such consumption took place—extravagance in
clothes, gambling, purchase of furniture, pictures and objets
d'art, patronage of painters and other graphic artists, play-

wrights and poets, religious foundations, and so on. But the data that have been turned up so far are fragmentary and diffuse, except in one field: building. It is, therefore, on this last field that the rest of this chapter will concentrate.

Even the most cursory acquaintance with the history of France during the sixteenth and seventeenth centuries makes one aware of the frenzy for construction that existed. It is clear, too, from the names, social status and official careers of those commissioning new buildings for themselves that financiers played a large role. But the data need to be presented in a variety of systematic forms before the precise role of financiers can be elucidated. For a start, it is logical to make a division between building in town and building in the country. Second, it is obviously necessary to break those who commissioned buildings up into the functional groups that have been used heretofore. And third, it is sensible, since the data found make it possible, to analyse construction by time period. This produces two tables: Building of Houses in Paris (Table 4); and Building of Châteaux (Table 5).

The first point that emerges from Table 4 is that about half of the houses built in Paris during the period from the later sixteenth century until the later seventeenth century, and which are mentioned by historians of architecture as being of particular artistic significance, were built by persons involved in some way in the royal finances.[45] Such people were almost three times as numerous as the nobles d'épée who built town houses, over three times as numerous as members of the various cours souveraines, and over six times as numerous as members of the modern administrative machine. A second point is that while the involvement of some groups stayed on the whole fairly constant over the period, other groups varied more or less widely. There was in the seventeenth century a great flurry of construction in Paris, which was at its most intense in the period 1630–50. In this activity the role of the old nobility was severely restrained. Their involvement in building in Paris did not change significantly over the seventeenth century, although they did achieve a relatively high level in the period 1610–30. Members of the modern administrative machine did surprisingly badly. Members of the cours souveraines increased their share during the peak period of 1630–50, and though the absolute value of their involvement declined in the period 1650–70, the decline was much less than that recorded for the overall level of activity. Consequently, their performance rose proportionately to equal that of the noblesse d'épée. But the fact remains that the level of activity during the peak period was largely the result of the willingness of persons involved in the royal finances to sink some of their profits into new building. Their share rose from a quarter before 1590 to over half in the years 1630–50.

TABLE 4: Building of Houses in Paris

	All construction: Before 1590—After 1670	Before 1590	1590–1610	1610–1630	1630–1650	1650–1670	After 1670
Number of people involved	138 (100·00)	12	8	22	65	14	10
Tertiary Elite	8 (5·80)	—	—	—	2	5	1
Secondary Elite	11 (7·97)	—	—	—	6	6	1
Primary Elite	17 (12·32)	—	—	—	11	7	1
Any financial involvement whatsoever	70 (50·72)	3	3	10	35	11	4
Modern administrative machine	11 (7·97)	1	—	—	7	2	1
Cours souveraines	21 (15·22)	1	1	3	12	4	1
Sword nobles	24 (17·39)	3	3	6	4	4	4
Diplomatic service	6 (4·35)	—	1	—	4	1	—
Unknown	15 (10·87)	4	1	2	6	1	1

These two decades were the high point for the financiers. Between 1630 and 1645, for example, Jacques Bordier built his house at 10 rue du Parc-royal, while Jean Galland built one at 11 rue des Haudriettes. Starting in 1635 Particelli d'Emery had an *hôtel* built at 4 rue de la Vrillière, a site later to be submerged beneath the Place des Victoires. In 1637 construction began on an hôtel at what is now 2–4 rue de Bretonvilliers on the Ile Saint-Louis for Claude Le Ragois de Bretonvilliers. The architect is believed to have been Jacques Androuet du Cerceau. The pace of construction quickened after 1640. Claude de Mesmes comte d'Avaux commissioned the architect Le Muet to build a large hôtel at 71 rue du Temple for some 800,000 livres. Denis Marin employed the same architect to remodel substantially an hôtel that the financier bought at 58 *bis* rue des Francs Bourgeois. The Guénégaud family distinguished itself by having three hôtels built. Henri de Guénégaud commissioned François Mansart in 1643 to build an hôtel at 31 rue des Francs Bourgeois (the house is now known as the Hôtel d'Albret). In 1648 Mansart began work on the site of the old Hôtel de Nevers. Henri's brother Claude stayed in the Marais. His hôtel, in what was then the rue Saint-Louis, was on the site of what is now 60 rue de Turenne. It was begun in 1646.[46]

As the general level of construction fell in the period 1650–70 to under one-quarter of what it had been in the preceding two decades, the financiers were less struck than other functional groups, so that their share went up to nearly four-fifths. From 1655 until 1661, François Mansart carried out extensive re-modelling for Claude de Boislève at 23 rue de Sévigné, which is in fact the Hôtel de Carnavalet. In 1656, Pierre Aubert de Fontenay's house at 5 rue de Thorigny was begun by the little known architect Bouillier de Bourges. Aubert, who was a *Gabelleur*, called his house the *Hôtel Salé*, a joke remarkable more for its grossness than its wit. In the same year, Louis Le Vau began a remarkable house (now known as the Hôtel de Lauzun) at 17 quai d'Anjou for Charles Gruin des Bordes.[47]

In the years after 1670, the level of construction of houses by financiers declined, although it was still double that achieved by the noblesse d'épée. The most notable construction for a financier at this time was undertaken at the orders of Jean-Baptiste Colbert. Beginning in 1674, Pierre Bréau remodelled for him a large hôtel situated at what is now 6 rue des Petits-Champs and 2–2 *bis* rue Vivienne.[48]

It was the financiers, then, who provided the major part of the impetus towards the construction of the new residential Paris of the seventeenth century. This is in itself of importance. Its relevance here is that it shows just how conspicuous this aspect of the consumption of goods and services by financiers was. In what was by far the largest concentration of people in France, a city whose population was seething with all manner of political and social discontent, and within the larger context of what may now be called with a fair degree of consensus the crisis of the seventeenth century, the financiers built extravagantly, overshadowing all other groups in society. The financiers profited and enjoyed their profits while the *bas peuple* starved, took sick and died.

Though the financiers might tend to mingle strangely well with other groups in society—for example, marrying off their daughters to their social betters and buying respectable careers for their sons—yet in this question of building in Paris they were out on their own and utterly conspicuous. What made their architectural pretensions even more significant to the baleful eye of popular vengeance was the simple fact that the pretensions were architectural. A large building cannot be easily overlooked. It is a very obvious sign of wealth, a wealth whose source was clear enough without the arrogant behaviour of an Aubert de Fontenay with his Hotel Salé.

On the other hand, one should not presume too much about the financiers' power from the great extent of their construction in Paris. Examination of the building of châteaux during the sixteenth and seventeenth centuries restores some balance to an assessment which, were it to be based exclusively on Parisian evidence, might lead to some too obvious statement of claims about the eclipse of the old nobility.

The table on the building of châteaux (Table 5) shows an immediate and striking contrast with building in Paris. The noblesse d'épée played a role which was, numerically at least, about twice as important as that played by those with any involvement whatsoever in the royal finances. Though the noblesse d'épée might from one point of view appear to be losing a battle for survival under a regime of vile bourgeois, from the relative number of châteaux built it would seem simply that the noblesse d'épée was deploying its wealth in the country and that from a non-urban point of view its dominance over French life was barely challenged. A second point is how much less well members of the various financial elites did in the construction of châteaux than they had done in the building of hôtels. The Primary and Tertiary Elites did more or less half as well in the former as in the latter.

Analysis of construction of châteaux by time shows the need to produce some modification of the picture revealed by the undifferentiated totals of the first column of the table. At one stage in the first third of the sixteenth century, financiers seem to have been as heavily involved in the construction of châteaux as the nobility was. It will be recalled that this was when Thomas

TABLE 5: Construction of Châteaux

	All construction: Before 1500—After 1700	Before 1500	1500-1530	1530-1570	1570-1600	1600-1630	1630-1670	1670-1700	After 1700
umber of people involved	119 (100·00)	2	15	20	8	27	20	21	4
ertiary Elite	3 (2·52)	—	—	—	—	—	3	—	—
condary Elite	7 (5·88)	—	—	—	—	—	7	—	—
imary Elite	8 (6·72)	—	—	—	—	—	8	—	—
y financial involvement whatsoever	26 (21·85)	1	4	1	—	3	13	3	1
odern administrative machine	17 (14·29)	2	2	1	—	2	5	4	—
urs souveraines	11 (9·24)	—	—	—	—	—	7	3	—
bles	51 (42·86)	—	4	13	4	13	4	11	1
plomatic service	3 (2·52)	—	—	—	—	—	3	—	—
known	14 (11·77)	—	—	3	1	7	3	—	—

Bohier was building Chenonceaux, Gilles Berthelot, Azay-le-Rideau, and Jean Cottereau, Maintenon. On the other hand, whereas the noblesse d'épée maintained its general level of construction (admittedly, like the flight of the woodpecker, with wild swoops) for the next 140 years, the financiers seem during the last seventy years of the sixteenth century not to have concerned themselves with building châteaux. They re-emerged in the field in the first third of the seventeenth century, reached a climax in the period 1630–70 when they equalled the two highest points of the noblesse d'épée (for 1530–70 and 1600–30), and declined as rapidly as they had risen.[49]

Such a picture in many respects confirms that presented by the table on construction in Paris. In the first place, the noblesse d'épée seems to have gone its way relatively unaffected by political and socio-economic crisis. The qualification 'relatively' is important, because it would seem possible that the low level of construction by the noblesse in the periods 1570–1600 and 1630–70 may have been connected with the civil and religious wars of the later sixteenth century and with the crises within the nobility which had their most obvious manifestation in the *Fronde princière*. But the nobility seems to have bounced back. The financiers, on the other hand, had one important period, after which

their architectural efforts in the country sink back to compara-
tively minor size. At the same time, it should be pointed out that
the phase of greatest effort made by financiers in the building of
châteaux coincided closely with the same phase of their efforts in
Parisian construction. Here again the question of conspicuousness arises. Given the relatively restrained rate of noble, that is to
say normal, construction in the years 1630–70, the high rate of
construction by financiers tended to stand out. It was for this
reason that so much was said at the time about the building of Le
Raincy (c 1640) for Jacques Bordier. It also helps to explain
the notoriety of Fouquet's magnificent château at Vaux-le-
Vicomte, although much of the brouhaha about *that* derives
from the dramatic circumstances of the fall of the surintendant.[50]

This is not to deny that financiers did build in the country.
Examples of such construction include Claude Cornuel's building
at Le Mesnil, Michel I Particelli d'Emery's at Tanlay, the
Guénégaud family's at Fresnes near Meaux, and Claude Girardin's at Vaudreuil in Normandy.[51] Much of this building was no
doubt expensive. Some of it was in magnificently good taste,
reflecting if not necessarily the artistic ability of the financier
patron then at least his understanding of how to gain some kind
of aesthetically pleasing return on money spent. A particularly
apt example here would be Tanlay with its elegant Italianate
towers, its gatehouse and its wide moat filled with water lilies and
fat carp. Yet the fact of the matter is that, despite the appearance
of the quantitative data which gives the important roles in building châteaux to nobility and then to finance, there is another
factor that has to be considered.

The really big individual constructions of the seventeenth century were, apart from those undertaken by the Crown itself,
largely the work of men who straddled a series of functional and
social categories, combining noble status with political power,
together with influence in, or over, the conduct of financial administration. Two men were *hors catégorie* here: the Duc de
Sully and the Cardinal-Duc de Richelieu. They were not content
with building several châteaux apiece (one of which, at Richelieu,
was to be compared for sheer size only to Versailles), but built
whole towns as well, Sully at Boisbelle-Henrichemont and
Richelieu at Richelieu.[52] Such efforts make Fouquet's building

at Vaux look restrained—and even Fouquet was not just a financier.

The conclusion emerges then that, in architectural terms at least, the presence of the financiers was by and large an urban one. It is clear that the new quartiers of Paris, the Marais and the parish of Saint-Eustache, and even the Ile Saint-Louis, would have been quite different had the financiers not possessed money to throw into urban construction. At the same time, the relatively few examples of construction or major rebuilding of rural châteaux by financiers are insignificant beside the construction by nobles d'épée and members of the modern administrative machine.

Certain more general conclusions may be drawn about the uses made by financiers of the money that they accumulated. These uses form a fairly complex nexus. If one can establish an order of uses which most would have followed, one could say that financiers tended first to buy ennobling office, then a house in Paris, then an estate in the country. After that, they might provide for their children. Wealthier ones would build houses in Paris, and the wealthiest would go on to remodel or construct châteaux in the country. These activities differed for the most part from those of the old nobility, who, it seems clear, were not involved as heavily as the financiers were in the purchase of either office or land, but were much more heavily involved in the construction of châteaux. If the financiers' activities may be reduced to a formula, this is that they were a process of becoming noble. There was no commonly concerted plan of campaign here, but rather a series of steps which were conditioned very largely by the structure of society and which significant numbers of financiers took. Certain attributes one had to have, and there were clear priorities, perceived automatically because they were obvious. At the same time, the priorities were perceived not merely by financiers but also by other groups that were in similar states of becoming—that is to say by members of the modern administrative machine and the cours souveraines. The difference between the three groups was partly a question of relative success. The most successful in terms of material performance were the modern administrative people, the least successful, the magistrates of the cours souveraines. This leaves the financiers somewhere between the two. The only real distinction of the financiers lay in their relative newness, and in the speed and exuberance with which they carried out what was in fact in general a quite small upward social leap.

Notes to this chapter are on pages 254–5

Chapter 8 RELATIONSHIPS BETWEEN THE FINANCIERS AND THE WORLD AT LARGE

THE ATTITUDE of French society in the seventeenth century towards financiers was curiously ambiguous. Although there was hostility among the vast bulk of the population, there was a certain degree of acceptance from particular groups close to the centre of political power. But this is not the full extent of the ambiguity. Even within institutions which formed the vanguard of hostility to financiers, that hostility was not an emotion which mastered everybody. The *Parlement* of Paris might co-ordinate the cours souveraines of France in attacks on financiers, as, for example, in 1648. But a significant number of individuals involved in the royal finances were also, at some time in their careers, possessors of office in that same Parlement. The military, that bastion of old noble intransigence, possessed a collective attitude summed up in the Maréchal de La Meilleraye's belief that financiers who were late in paying troops their wages should be summarily executed. But even here, there were ambiguities. The maréchal himself helped to mobilise funds donated by the Estates of Brittany in the 1640s. He also served, for a brief period in the early part of the Fronde, as *surintendant des finances*.[1] In a sense, he was himself a financier.

It is evident then that the ambiguity referred to above had a certain complexity, for financiers had friends, or at least there were people who were only intermittently hostile to them, in unexpected places. Moreover, the closer one examines the matter, the more widespread the acceptance of financiers appears to have been. It becomes, therefore, a matter of some importance to analyse the relationship of the financiers with other groups in French society. Given the nature of the data, this analysis can be most profitably pursued on two levels: first, the relationship between the financiers and other institutional groups, and in particular the complex network of patterns traced by financiers working out from the finances to other posts, together with the reciprocal patterns traced by members of other institutional groups working in to the finances; and second, the professional and marital patterns traced by financiers and their families in society at large. The first of these areas is dealt with in the present chapter, while the second is dealt with in the next.

An immediate problem in examining relationships between groups in seventeenth-century France is to determine how to treat institutional bodies. There is as yet no considered and sustained analysis and description of such things. It is possible, therefore, to come to only a provisional position. This creates an institutional context adequate for the present purposes and at the same time not so rigid that its possible inaccuracies would limit the utility of the discussion of the roles of financiers and others, once later work had supplied correction of the context. Certain procedural and descriptive decisions are even now unimpeachable. Professor Goubert, in a discussion of modes of analysis of the France of the *ancien régime*, has said that the traditional concepts used to analyse French society do not face up to the starkness of the situation. He suggests that France was essentially divided into two groups: those who had enough to eat, and those who didn't. This kind of division can be applied to an aspect of French society other than the dietary: the governing and the governed, or those who did things and those to whom things were done. This last formulation makes it possible to think of an active congeries of institutions which, in a very broad sense, ruled France. It is a question not merely of royal administration, but also of social and religious subordination and discipline. Examination of the data reveals nine distinct groups of such institutions: the modern administrative machine; the *Conseil du Roi*; the royal court; the cours souveraines; the old local administration; the military; the Church; the diplomatic service; and, last, the finances. In a work devoted to finance and financiers, it would be out of place to spend time on a description of the roles played by the first eight of these groups. There is space only to enumerate categories of membership.

The modern administrative machine is a composite created to sum up the central line of the administrative organisation set up by the later Valois and Bourbon kings of France during the long centralising revolution of the French monarchy which lasted from the later fifteenth century to the personal rule of Louis XIV. By the time of Mazarin, this machine was composed of a group of posts at the centre, not necessarily all of which were filled at a given time. These were: *premier ministre, chancelier, garde des sceaux,* royal favourite, governor of a minor king, *ministre d'état,* unofficial police chief, and *secrétaires d'état* and their *commis.* To these must be added the *intendants de justice, police et finances,* who at this time must be considered more central than local officials, rather in the way that an English Judge of Assize is central whereas a Justice of the Peace is local. The intendant de justice was assisted by *subdélégués,* and his work was supplemented by special *commissaires.* These last two types of official complete this rough enumeration.

The Conseil du Roi in the present context is composed partly of full members of the various royal councils that existed under Mazarin, that is to say, the *Conseils Secret, d'en Haut, des Finances, d'Etat et des Finances,* and *Privé,* together with those set up under Colbert's aegis—the *Conseil Royal des Finances* and the *Conseil de Commerce.* The full members of these councils were usually qualified by the style *conseiller d'état ordinaire.* To these must be added men who served as royal councillors of state for six months in every twelve, the so-called *semestres.* I have specifically excluded holders of *brevets* of *conseiller d'état.* These particular royal brevets were merely a source of extra income to the Crown and of illusory prestige to their purchasers, who gained the right to be called conseiller d'état but were sedulously restrained—except in time of dire governmental weakness or inanity—from taking part in the deliberations of the Conseil du Roi.

The term 'royal court' also needs some explanation. Strictly speaking there was not one royal court, but a hierarchy of several royal households or *maisons: Maisons du Roi; de la Reine-Mère; de la Reine; de Monsieur*—the king's brother (care must be taken to distinguish which Monsieur one means—Gaston d'Orléans, brother of Louis XIII, or Philippe d'Anjou, brother of Louis XIV); *de Mme la Duchesse d'Orléans*—wife of Gaston; *de Mademoiselle*—daughter of Gaston. Later on, of course, there would be maisons for the Dauphin, and his son and daughter-in-law, the Duc and Duchesse de Bourgogne, and even for quite minor twigs of the genealogical tree of the Great King. The term 'royal court' is used here as a kind of umbrella to include officials of all these organisations. It should further be pointed out that the term excludes financial officials of the various households, since these are properly to be considered members of the financial administration, and therefore financiers. The term includes holders of non-financial office: *gentilshommes, valets, chambellans, écuyers, maîtres d'hôtel, chevaliers d'honneur, dames d'honneur,* and so on.

The term cours souveraines is confined to magistrates of all the more important sovereign courts, and of some courts which were technically sovereign but of relatively restricted importance. In descending order there were: the magistrates of the parlements of France, together with the *Conseil provincial* of Arras, the *Conseil souverain* of Pignerol and the *Conseil supérieur* of Colmar. Then come the magistrates of the *chambres des Comptes, cours des Comptes, cours des Aides, Grand Conseil, cours des Monnaies, chambres de l'Edit,* and *Chambre aux Deniers*.

The heading 'old local administration' includes *gouverneurs* and their *lieutenants-généraux* of frontier provinces, towns, strongpoints, and areas, and of internal provinces, towns, strongpoints, areas and royal palaces. At a much lower level there were *baillis* and other officials of *bailliages*; *sénéchaux* and other officials of *sénéchaussées*; officers of *prévôtés*; and magistrates of *présidiaux*.

The heading 'military' excludes financial officials like *commissaires des guerres*. But it includes all army ranks from *maréchal de France* down to *enseigne*, together with units within which these ranks were held, and all naval ranks from *amiral* to *lieutenant de vaisseau*.

As for the Church, all the obvious levels of the secular and regular clergy are included.

Last comes the diplomatic service, which includes not merely ambassadors, plenipotentiaries and residents, but also numbers of the secret agents with whom seventeenth-century diplomacy abounded.

These functional variables outside the financial world can be cross-tabulated against variables inside the finances. This permits the following numerical analysis. Out of the 744 persons with some kind of financial involvement, 209 (28 per cent) also had some kind of post outside the finances. Of this group of 209, there is a preference for involvement in the royal finances not on an institutional basis, but in Extraordinary Affairs. Whereas 123 persons (22 per cent) out of 570 in financial administration held outside posts, such posts were held by 109 (31 per cent) of the 350 persons involved in Extraordinary Affairs. Furthermore, an examination of the three elites reveals that persons with outside posts were not negligible in the royal finances. While they might tend to be slightly swamped in the Primary Elite, having forty-three (24 per cent) out of 176 members, at the same time they formed over one-third (34 per cent) out of the ninety-six of the Secondary Elite, and exactly one-third of the thirty-six members of the Tertiary Elite.

These totals and percentages can be broken down into subgroups. Table 6 shows that ninety-two members of the cours souveraines had some involvement in the finances. They were followed, but at a distance, by the modern administrative machine with forty-six—only half the number provided by the previous group. The other variables provided respectively: royal court (twenty-eight); diplomatic service (twenty); old local administration and military (both nineteen); Church (seventeen); and Conseil du Roi (fourteen). This particular order of size needs some further analysis. It is important to be able to compare not merely the brute numbers of people in cross-tabulations of financial variables against the outside functional variables, but also the percentage rates relating brute numbers to numbers of people having some financial involvement. The enumeration of brute numbers reveals that in almost every case the cours souveraines played the biggest role. The only place where their performance was even equalled lay in the Tertiary Elite, where cours souveraines and modern administrative machine both had five members.

It is also necessary to evaluate the quality of each outside

TABLE 6: Roles of Members of Outside Groups in Financial Affairs

	Total in variable in deck as whole	Any kind of fin. inv. whatsoever	Member of financial administration	Mainline financial administration	Involvement in Extra-ordinary Affairs	ELITE STATUS		
						Primary	Secondary	Tertiary
All members of outside groups	637	209 *100·00*	123 *58·85*	69 *33·01*	109 *52·15*	43 *20·57*	33 *15·79*	12 *5·74*
Modern administrative machine	100	46 *100·00*	35 *76·09*	18 *39·13*	21 *45·65*	14 *30·43*	11 *23·91*	5 *10·87*
Royal court	58	28 *100·00*	20 *71·43*	13 *46·43*	6 *21·43*	4 *14·29*	1 *3·57*	0 *0·00*
Conseil du Roi	31	14 *100·00*	13 *92·86*	10 *71·43*	5 *35·71*	4 *28·57*	3 *21·43*	2 *14·29*
Old local administration	81	19 *100·00*	9 *47·37*	5 *26·32*	11 *57·89*	2 *10·53*	2 *10·53*	0 *0·00*
Cours souveraines	363	92 *100·00*	49 *53·26*	28 *30·44*	58 *63·04*	19 *20·65*	17 *18·48*	5 *5·44*
Military	56	19 *100·00*	7 *36·84*	3 *15·78*	9 *47·37*	2 *10·53*	2 *10·53*	0 *0·00*
Church	84	17 *100·00*	9 *52·94*	3 *17·65*	10 *58·82*	3 *17·65*	4 *23·53*	0 *0·00*
Diplomatic service	45	20 *100·00*	14 *70·00*	7 *35·00*	12 *60·00*	6 *30·00*	5 *25·00*	1 *5·00*

Percentages shown in italic.

group's performance. It is clear that there was a tendency for certain groups to relate to institutional involvement in the royal finances rather than to Extraordinary Affairs, and an opposing tendency for other groups. The groups most clearly biassed towards institutional involvement were the Conseil du Roi (93:36) and royal court (71:21), followed by the modern administrative machine (76:46). Below them comes a group more evenly balanced in its relative performances: the diplomatic service (70:60). Below this, the tendency is less towards institutional posts than towards Extraordinary Affairs: the Church (53:59), the cours souveraines (53:63), the old local administration (47:58), and the military (37:47).

Clearly, then, groups like the Conseil du Roi, royal court and modern administrative machine, which were closely linked to the new absolutist state, had a closer institutional involvement with the royal financial administration than had other groups. These other groups, all of which took their origin from a French state older than the Bourbon, were linked more with Extraordinary Affairs than with financial posts. The difference may be the result of any of a number of factors, or of a combination of them. For example, it might be that the older groups with less institutional concern in the finances were composed of persons of relatively high social status who would find it beneath their dignity to identify themselves in an obvious and formal way with the finances. This point is of particular importance with the military. Individual examples of former soldiers like the Duc de Sully and the Maréchaux d'Effiat and de La Meilleraye, who all served as surintendants des finances, might lead to the assumption that the military played a larger role in financial administration than in fact it did. The presence of martial luminaries at the head of affairs was not backed up by the insertion of officers from army or navy in interstices lower in the pyramid of financial administration. Sully, Effiat and La Meilleraye were in a sense foreign bodies, whose presumed military severity and directness would cut through the prevarication and deviousness of professional financiers. It was hoped their appointment would be effective precisely because it was not usual, and because it might frighten the financiers into behaving themselves as upright soldiers would. Perhaps righteousness was a quality of Sully and Effiat, and it would surely have been claimed by La Meilleraye. But it was certainly not part of the survival kit of the average infantry colonel, who, indeed, could show the financiers a thing or two about brazen fraudulence. The fact remains, however, that while the ordinary army officer and the financier were often rogues in similar lines of unofficial business, their paths crossed rarely. In any case, there were questions of social status involved. It was genteel for a scion of the old *noblesse de race* to steal money from the Crown as an army officer running a *passe-volant* racket. It was not genteel to be a *Munitionnaire* passing off mouldy flour and getting paid the rate for flour in good condition. This was a distinction of a kind not unknown to modern society.

So much, then, for the analysis of bald figures. But there is a lot more to the question of relationships between financiers and other groups than this. The first important point to clear up is whether the existence of such relationships between financiers and other groups is unique, or whether other points of contact existed between other groups. In fact it is clear that other contacts were as important as, if not more important than, contacts with the royal finances. Take, for example, the cours souveraines. These were in a sense institutionally schizoid. There were two major groups in the courts—one, a relatively large body of magistrates which treated membership in a cour souveraine as a career in itself; the other, a relatively small body which treated membership in a cour souveraine as merely the beginning of a career in some more effective branch of royal administration. An example of this would be the typical royal *intendant*, who would start as a *conseiller au Parlement*, purchase—or have purchased for him by his father—a post of *maître des requêtes*, and then proceed to the commission of intendant. In the deck there are thirty-seven men who were members of the cours souveraines who also served in the modern administrative machine. This means that just over 10 per cent of the 363 magistrates in the deck formed 37 per cent of the 100 members of the modern administrative machine. Clearly, then, the crossing of boundaries between categories was not an activity confined to men carrying the blight of finance. Such interchanging and combination of categories was common throughout the spectrum of French institutions in the seventeenth century, indicating a flexibility of response from individuals to the needs of governmental action.

Mazarin served France as diplomat, ecclesiastic, local administrator (he was gouverneur of Brouage and La Fère), central administrator, and financial official (he was *surintendant de la maison* of Anne of Austria).[2] Nicolas Fouquet served in as many categories.[3] Nor was this flexibility confined to important people. Etienne Foullé served in a succession of second-rank posts in different categories until he reached his highest point as intendant de justice before becoming intendant des finances in 1649.[4] People moved with insouciance from task to task according to the dictates of greed, ambition and the state's will, whether that will was expressed by monarch, royal favourite, premier ministre, or, occasionally, aristocratic cabal. The financiers fitted into this flexible context. On the other hand, flexibility had its own rules, for there were certain sequences of movement from task to task much more commonly found than others. By examining the careers of individual people, it is possible to establish answers to a number of questions: for example, whether people moved out from the finances into other groups, whether they moved from other groups into the finances, or whether they were members of groups in such a way that it is impossible to assert temporal or functional primacy to their financial or non-financial activity. The answers to these questions are summarised in Figure 4 (see p 200).

It will be recalled that forty-six people straddled the boundary between the modern administrative machine and the finances. Of these, twenty-six were primarily members of the modern administration who turned late in their careers to the finances. One of the best examples of this pattern is provided by the career of Etienne III d'Aligre (1592–1677), who came to be involved in the financial administration as *directeur des finances* from 1648, and who was involved in Extraordinary Affairs in a rather desultory way in the 1650s. Himself the son of a man who served as chancelier de France, Etienne III was a typical member of the *robe d'état*, serving as intendant of Languedoc and Normandy, and as ambassador to Venice before 1648. In 1661, he was appointed member of the *Chambre de Justice* trying the financiers, and of the Conseil Royal des Finances. After the death of Pierre

FIGURE 4: **Patterns of Movement into and out of the Royal Finances**

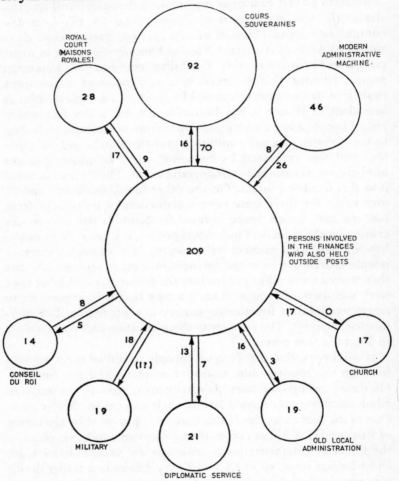

Séguier in 1672, Aligre became chancelier, holding the post until his death. His career, based as it was on descent from a robe d'état parent and on personal membership of the robe d'état for the first thirty-five years or so of his professional life, had its greatest success outside the royal finances. Aligre was a 'financier'

only because the Crown called on him to become one, and because it was in the tradition of men of the robe d'état to serve where the monarchy asked them to serve.[5] He was not alone in this. Nicolas Fouquet was an intendant de justice long before he became surintendant des finances. Eighteen other men who served previously as local intendants were also involved, though in less important ways, in the royal finances. But there were other modern administrative posts that were held by men who later had some involvement in the finances. Not the least important of these posts was that of premier ministre, held by Mazarin himself before he became a Munitionnaire. Three of the four secretaries of state in office during the 1650s had some involvement in the royal finances after they entered their distinguished posts. Michel Le Tellier was of great importance to Mazarin as a financial agent during the Fronde, and occasionally afterwards.[6] Henri Auguste de Loménie de Brienne accepted illegal payments for reformed Billets de l'Epargne.[7] Louis I Phélypeaux de La Vrillière, son of a financier and son-in-law of Particelli d'Emery, was heavily involved with the surintendant in profitable frauds involving the embezzlement of royal funds.[8]

Only eight people were financiers who later came to play roles in the modern administrative machine. Three of these men served as local intendants. They were few compared to the previously mentioned group of intendants. On the other hand, while three secretaries of state turned to finance, three financiers became secretary of state. These were Raymond Phélypeaux d'Herbault, whose career is discussed below; Henri Duplessis-Guénégaud, who began his career in 1638 as trésorier de l'Epargne in succession to his father, and who resigned this office in 1643 to take up that of secretary of state, a post which he held for over twenty years; and François Sublet seigneur des Noyers (1588–1645), whose earliest known post was as trésorier-général de France, who became intendant des finances in 1626, and who served as secretary of state for war from 1636.[9] To be quite fair, it should be pointed out that 26 and 8 add up to only 34, leaving 12 cases somewhere in between the two poles of functional mobility. Frankly, it is very difficult to say whether these twelve started as financiers or not. For example, three men began as commis of secretaries of state. Positions such as these mingled financial responsibilities with formal membership of the modern administrative machine so intimately that it is impossible to assign them to exclusive membership of one category or the other. Nevertheless the indeterminate twelve do not alter the conclusion that must be drawn from the foregoing analysis: it was considerably more common for members of the modern administrative machine to enter the royal finances than it was for financiers to enter the modern administrative machine.

The same calculation can be performed for the other groups. Of the Conseil du Roi, 31 members appeared in the deck, of whom 14 had some kind of involvement in the royal finances. Of these, 8 had established careers outside the finances before they became involved. These included Etienne III d'Aligre, Antoine Le Camus, François Ménardeau-Champré, Abel Servien and Louis Le Tonnelier de Breteuil. Five men were financiers before they became conseillers d'état: Denis Marin, Séraphin de Mauroy, Jacques Bordier, Jean-Baptiste Colbert, and his cousin Charles II Colbert de Terron.[10]

There were twenty-eight members of the royal court who had some financial involvement. Of these, nine are clearly people who were more courtiers than anything else. These include courtiers who became high financial officials, like the Duc de La Vieuville, hereditary *Grand Fauconnier de France*, who became surintendant des finances. Other courtiers turned to the royal finances merely from loyalty to the Crown when the credit that they could provide was all that might stave off disaster. But the opposite tendency, that of career financiers entering the royal court, was much more pronounced. Ten people were clearly financiers before they bought posts in a household. To this group can be added a further seven who held posts at court and at the same time were involved in the royal finances in a serious and professional way. This group of seventeen financiers divides fairly neatly into two. On the one hand are to be found financiers who had made their pile, and now sought some post with an agreeably convolute title that would impress their acquaintance. An example of this was Etienne Chabenas, *Secrétaire du Roi* and commis of Particelli d'Emery. Chabenas purchased the post of *Introducteur des Ambassadeurs et Princes Étrangers auprès du Roi* towards the end of his life.[11] Such financiers who put themselves out to ceremonial grass should be distinguished from those who held posts in the royal court while maintaining their interest in financial affairs. This second group of working financiers tended to buy the post of maître d'hôtel. Eleven men of fairly limited importance held such posts in the Maison du Roi, while one held such a post in the household of Anne of Austria. Jean I Du Vouldy, *Maître d'Hôtel du Roi* and *Secrétaire du Roi maison et couronne de France*, a provincial turned Parisian who was involved in a series of corrupt treaties in the 1630s, was typical of this group.[12]

The cours souveraines present a different picture from the royal court. Of the 92 people who held posts in the cours souveraines and who were also involved in some way in the royal finances, there were 70 who were magistrates before they became involved in finance, and 16 who were financiers before they purchased posts in the cours souveraines. This indicates that not many financiers succeeded in purchasing such posts, and that the general picture is of a fairly large number of magistrates involving themselves in the royal finances. But it is necessary to be more specific than that and to examine particular cours souveraines to see whether some were more liable than others to invasion by financiers.

Of the parlements of France, fifty-six members were involved in the royal finances in some way. Of these only five were financiers first and *parlementaires* second. This little group pales into insignificance compared to the mass of movement in the opposite direction. There were forty-nine magistrates who were involved in finance at a developed stage in their parlementaire careers. And it was not just a question of sheer numbers. The men who became involved were highly important. They included René de Longueil marquis de Maisons, Abel Servien and Nicolas Fouquet, all of whom became surintendants des finances; Etienne III d'Aligre and Nicolas Desmaretz, who became directeurs des finances; Louis Le Tonnelier de Breteuil, Antoine Le Camus, Jacques Le Tillier and François Ménardeau-Champré, who became *contrôleurs-généraux des finances*; Nicolas Jeannin de Castille, who became trésorier de l'Epargne; and so one could go on.[13] These were all parlementaires who came to hold formally constituted financial posts at the highest level. To them may legitimately be added parlementaires who held no formal post but played some role in the finances of the state. The list is headed by two *premiers présidents* of the Parlement of Paris: Nicolas Potier sieur de Novion, who became premier président in 1652, and Guillaume de Lamoignon, who succeeded Potier in 1657. The parlements were, then, by no means unconnected with the royal finances. But the connection was established largely by men who were parlementaires first and financiers second.

The second group of cours souveraines reveals a different story. The chambres des Comptes show significant penetration by career financiers. They are, indeed, the only group of cours souveraines to exhibit a higher number of financiers (12) purchasing office in them, than of members (10) turning to finance. It is worth while to break the figures down into the various grades of office within the chambres. Of six *présidents des Comptes* who had some involvement in finance, only two were career financiers—but they were Claude Cornuel and Jacques Tubeuf.[14] Where they led, a number of lesser financiers followed. Several of them were commis or former commis of surintendants des finances. These included: Jean Coiffier, *premier commis* of two surintendants, Bailleul and Particelli d'Emery; Antoine Guérapin, another of Particelli's commis; and Louis Bruant, premier commis of Fouquet. All of them became *maîtres des Comptes* of the Chambre des Comptes of Paris.[15]

As for the remaining significant cours souveraines, that is to say the cours des Aides and the Grand Conseil, they repeated the pattern established by the parlements. In each case there is to be found only one financier purchasing office, against a combined total of twenty-eight men who, as members of cours des Aides or Grand Conseil, involved themselves in finance.

Contacts between finance and the military were even more one-sided. Of the nineteen people involved in such contacts, only one *may* have been a career financier, and even here there are difficult questions of definition and chronology. The case is of one Nacquart, who appears as a financial agent of Mazarin's in matters relating to the supply of munitions to the army in 1658. He is referred to as *lieutenant-général de l'Amirauté de Dunkerque*. It is not clear whether he was a Munitionnaire with military pretensions or a military man with extracurricular financial interests.

Apart from him, there is nobody who looks remotely like a career financier. On the other hand, there were the four army officers who became surintendants des finances: Sully, Effiat, La Vieuville and La Meilleraye.[16] Other army officers, like the Chevalier Noisy de Maupeou, *capitaine* in the *Régiment des Gardes*, lent money to the state. And many more were cajoled by Mazarin into co-operating with him in the supply of munitions to troops. Even general officers, like Godefroy comte d'Estrades, Lieutenant-général, could not escape such service.[17]

As for the Church, some ecclesiastics held financial posts, though only within the Church itself. Such were the clerics who served their brethren in the highest office with financial duties within the French Church that was held by ecclesiastics, the post of *agent-général du clergé*. Some agents-généraux joined with financiers in comfortable and mostly undetected fraud, as did Bernard Coignet de Marmiesse (d 1680), who was closely allied with Adrien II Hanivel de Manevillette, holder of a post normally held by laymen, that of *receveur-général du clergé*. Other clerics like Gabriel de Boislève, Bishop of Avranches; Hyacinthe Serroni, Bishop of Orange; Guiseppe Zongo Ondedei, Bishop of Fréjus, and Louis Fouquet, Bishop of Agde, had financial links with brothers or friends. But no cleric could be called a career financier, not even Mazarin himself, for all his greed.[18]

The old local administration, or rather that part of it not specifically concerned with the royal finances, was not as barren of career financiers as the Church was. Of the nineteen people who spanned the division between local administration and finance, three could be described as career financiers, and two of this three held posts in the administration of the *Eaux-et-Forêts*. The most important of these was Germain Rolland, an evil old Munitionnaire who survived prosecution in Richelieu's time for failing to meet deadlines, to become *grand maître des Eaux-et-Forêts* in the area of Metz, Toul and Verdun. Another financier who purchased a local post was Jacques Charron, *trésorier de l'Extraordinaire des Guerres* and Jean-Baptiste Colbert's father-in-law. He became gouverneur and *grand bailli et capitaine des chasses* of Blois. But in this case, such posts were clearly baubles designed to dazzle their socially aspiring purchaser, to the financial profit of the Crown.[19] As for those who appear first as local administrators who later involved themselves in the royal finances, many, and indeed all the important ones, have already been either considered by name or else subsumed in the totals given for the other categories in which they held office. Examples here are provided by La Meilleraye, Gouverneur of Brittany, and La Vieuville, Gouverneur of Reims and Mézières and Lieutenant-général of Rethelois.

Diplomacy was a slightly more profitable field for the deployment of a career financier's talents. Of the 21 men spanning the two categories, 13 were not to be described as career financiers. But 7 of the others were. One of these was Jean Camus des Touches, who served as *contrôleur-général de l'Ordinaire des Guerres* (1643-7) and *contrôleur-général de l'Extraordinaire des Guerres* (1647) and, while he retained his financial interests in the fields of general munitions and artillery, went on a number of diplomatic missions in the 1660s. Even those who appear to have been diplomats before they turned to finance were so closely involved in financial matters that it prompts one to call certain categories of diplomat 'financiers'. Residents are particularly liable to this equation. Meules, French Resident at Hamburg, and Brégy, who held a similar post in Poland, spent much of their time wrestling with the largely monetary problem of recruiting mercenary soldiers to serve the French Crown.[20]

The conclusion of this chapter must clearly be this: despite the close integration of the financial world with other spheres of governmental responsibility, it was far more common for men with official posts outside the royal finances to obtain posts or play roles inside those finances than it was for men who began their careers inside the finances to move out—except to bankruptcy, prison, exile or the end of a rope. Certain institutions and areas of service provide exceptions to this statement—notably the chambres des Comptes, royal court and diplomatic service. But they do not amount to much in the context of French governmental institutions as a whole. The limits of the individual financier's mobility were unwritten and largely unformalised. At the same time, they seem to have exerted an iron control. The only mobility the financiers possessed was in the financial administration itself. Only a handful of men, and these were all exceedingly successful financiers, were able to buy posts outside the finances. The posts that they bought were on the whole confined to chambres des Comptes and maisons royales.

On the other hand, the world of the financiers was a source of potential mobility, and of potential social mobility in particu of. This mobility became actual and manifest in the families of financiers. It is therefore to the study of the family that the next chapter is devoted.

Notes to this chapter are on page 256

Chapter 9 THE FAMILY, MARRIAGE
AND SOCIAL MOBILITY

LIKE OTHER early modern European societies, France attributed great importance to the family.[1] This did not mean merely the nuclear family of father, mother and immediate offspring, but involved ranges of relations extending into far realms of cousinage. France was composed in a sense of a network of families each of which meshed in convolute ways with other families. This gave, in theory at least, a kind of geodesic strength to society. And at the same time it gave, to the properly connected, sources of endless pleasure—contemplation of the unique lustre of one's own extended family, and, a corollary, excoriation of the gross pretensions of those whom one happened to dislike. Contemplation might be assisted by material expression of genealogy, as in the extraordinary château constructed in the middle of the sixteenth century for Antoine II de Clermont-Tonnerre at Ancy-le-Franc. In the embrasure of each window, the two sides formed by the thickness of the wall bear a painting, a heraldic representation of a notable alliance entered into by the family. Each painting is different, and there are dozens of them. The other side of the coin, excoriation of supposed inferiors, might occupy a lifetime's bitterness and arrogance. Many must have passed time in such an occupation, though few with the single-mindedness and vitriolic skill of the Duc de Saint-Simon. It was, nevertheless, an art in which even the untalented might, through long practice, achieve a certain competence.

Concern with family and connection was not just a question of snobbery. Evidently it had much to do with the defence of privilege, and ultimately with the protection of the nobility as a congeries of social groups. Equally, the fascination and significance of family and connection were understood not merely by those who were—or defined themselves to be—of the highest nobility. Even the financiers, clambering in haste and in consequence rather inelegantly over the coaming of nobility, expressed their own snobberies about their families, and used those families in the pursuit of affluence and prestige. There was, of course, a difference between the highest nobility and the financiers. The former used marital alliances to preserve things they possessed, like prestige, and to acquire things that were for many of them a diminishing ancestral memory, like solvency. The financiers, on the other hand, were usually concerned to maintain affluence, and to acquire prestige. Financiers' social mobility in this period is of interest largely because of the relatively simple fact that the two social extremes, and many groups between, like families in the *cours souveraines* and modern administrative machine, could satisfy their divergent aspirations by marital fusion. Analysis of the noble side of this reciprocal satisfaction requires a separate study on its own. What follows here is a description of the financial side.

Systematic treatment of families proved to be a complicated matter, as may be inferred from the study of an average family tree. Even to depict the Colbert family (omitting fictitious members of impeachable authenticity) involved a roll of paper one foot wide and twelve feet long, the length being taken up by the collateral fecundity of that extraordinary brood. The problem is smaller for all the other families that were studied, although the Canaye, Fieubet, Fouquet and Béchameil families each take up most of the top of a table of reasonable size. The only possible way to fit the mass of data together was to take each financier and look out from his point of view at the rest of the world. The financier's parents have already been discussed in the chapter on origins (Chapter 5). It remains to look at the financier's siblings; at his marriage or marriages; at his sons, their careers and marriages; and at his daughters, and their marriages and other fates. These matters of immediate family once stated, a comparison can be undertaken of financiers with other groups in society, specifically with magistrates of the cours souveraines and members of the modern administrative machine. But such analysis and comparison, confined to two generations, cannot convey the full role of financiers in French society. It was decided, therefore, after the foregoing analyses had been performed, to supplement them by taking one successful family over a number of generations, recounting in detail the particular offices held by its members. Only thus can be observed the importance of the financier in, and the complexity of his relations with, the high society of early modern France.

Through the resistant tangle of interlocking family trees, one thread may be followed. In the declension from financiers and siblings to wives, to children and so on, there is broadly speaking a change from links with the matrix of finance to links with groups functionally unconnected to finance, that is to say, a change from professional concerns to matters of social prestige. To put it another way, at first financiers used marital and genetic links to reinforce their business enterprises. These enterprises once established, reinforced and made to produce over a period of time, it was possible to turn upward for an ascent to some social stratosphere. The process may be observed in schematic form in Figure 5 (see p 211).

At an early stage in the development of the individual financier's fortunes, finance dominated family relationships. The most obvious fact about financial families is that financiers' siblings tended to be involved either directly or indirectly in the royal finances. The brothers of a financier tended themselves to be financiers. The careers are known of fifty-three brothers of men in the Primary Elite. Of these 53, 28 (53 per cent) were financiers; 9 (17 per cent) were, rather remarkably, members at a relatively elevated level of the hierarchy of the Church. The categories of local administration, central administration and army officers each had 4 brothers, each group representing 8 per cent of the whole. The cours souveraines, with 3 brothers, had 6 per cent. Many of the brother financiers ran family partnerships over long periods, as did Pierre and Nicolas Monnerot, Rolland Gruin du Boucher and Charles Gruin des Bordes, Claude and Guillaume Cornuel, and Pierre and Claude Girardin. But these are examples of only the most obvious kind of partnership, that between brothers both of whom were financiers in their own right.[2] Among the twenty-five non-financier brothers of financiers in the

Primary Elite were men who acted in concert with their financial brothers in financial affairs. Nicolas Fouquet overdid things, perhaps, in that four of his five brothers—including two bishops and an archbishop—were involved with him in some rather questionable dealings, but he was by no means alone in such use of a family.[3] Claude de Boislève was involved in business matters with his two brothers, one Gabriel, Bishop of Avranches; the other Henri, a local administrator of some importance in Anjou.

FIGURE 5: **The Trend away from Finance towards Social Prestige**

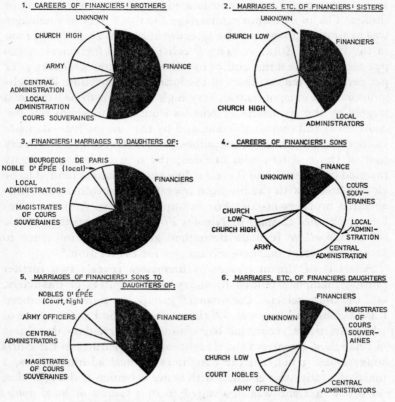

1. CAREERS OF FINANCIERS' BROTHERS
UNKNOWN
CHURCH HIGH
ARMY
CENTRAL ADMINISTRATION
LOCAL ADMINISTRATION
COURS SOUVERAINES
FINANCE

2. MARRIAGES, ETC. OF FINANCIERS' SISTERS
UNKNOWN
CHURCH LOW
FINANCIERS
CHURCH HIGH
LOCAL ADMINISTRATORS

3. FINANCIERS' MARRIAGES TO DAUGHTERS OF:
BOURGEOIS DE PARIS
NOBLE D'ÉPÉE (local)
LOCAL ADMINISTRATORS
MAGISTRATES OF COURS SOUVERAINES
FINANCIERS

4. CAREERS OF FINANCIERS' SONS
FINANCE
UNKNOWN
COURS SOUVERAINES
CHURCH LOW
CHURCH HIGH
ARMY
LOCAL ADMINISTRATION
CENTRAL ADMINISTRATION

5. MARRIAGES OF FINANCIERS' SONS TO DAUGHTERS OF:
NOBLES D'ÉPÉE (Court, high)
ARMY OFFICERS
CENTRAL ADMINISTRATORS
MAGISTRATES OF COURS SOUVERAINES
FINANCIERS

6. MARRIAGES, ETC. OF FINANCIERS' DAUGHTERS
FINANCIERS
MAGISTRATES OF COURS SOUVERAINES
UNKNOWN
CHURCH LOW
COURT NOBLES
ARMY OFFICERS
CENTRAL ADMINISTRATORS

THE QUANTITATIVE DATA ON WHICH THIS FIGURE IS BASED DERIVE FROM ANALYSIS OF THE PRIMARY ELITE.

The occasional financier did better still, by severing formal connections with the financial world but leaving a brother behind to carry out orders and, if necessary, pay the price of legal proceedings. Such was the displeasing case of Henri du Plessis-Guénégaud, who became secretary of state in 1643, selling the family post of *trésorier de l'Epargne* to his much younger brother Claude, a sad and incompetent fellow who was fined, ruined and exiled in 1667.* Henri, having remained sagaciously in the financial background, escaped virtually scot-free.[4]

Relationships with sisters did not exhibit this heavy financial bias, if only because it was not usual—though it was not completely unknown—for women to engage in financial operations. But a sister could have importance in the financier's scheme of things. The most common marriage for the sisters of financiers was to another financier. The fates are known of 25 sisters of men in the Primary Elite: 11 (41 per cent) married financiers; 7 (26 per cent) became nuns, and 5 (19 per cent) became *abbesses*; 3 (11 per cent) married members of the local administration. The religious avocation is, of course, very high here. It is to be explained largely by the six sisters of Nicolas Fouquet, of whom five became nuns and one an abbesse, and by the four of Jean-Baptiste Colbert's sisters who became abbesses.[5] At all events, one can say that of those sisters who married, the overwhelming majority married financiers. And it is clear that these alliances tended to be closely linked with the financial operations of brothers and prospective brothers-in-law. For example, Jacques Amproux Delorme, *Premier Commis* of Nicolas Fouquet, was brother-in-law of the *Gabelleur* Jean de Beringhen and used his influence to secure important business advantages for his relation.[6]

Analysis of the marriages of financiers reveals two further points: financiers tended to marry the daughters of financiers, and the more selected the financial group, the more pronounced this marital tendency was. Of the 22 men of the Primary Elite of whose marriages record has been found, 15 married the daughters of financiers, 2 married the daughters of magistrates in the cours souveraines, 3 married the daughters of local administrators, 1 married a lady who claimed with some vehemence though, alas, no proof that she was descended from a family of local *nobles*

* See above, p 160.

d'épée, while another married the daughter of a surgeon. The most prestigious marriages were the two to the daughters of magistrates, but these were made by men who, though they appear in the Primary Elite, were members of the *robe d'état* before they became involved in the royal finances. Neither can be considered as a career financier. It is legitimate to extract them from the discussion, concentrating on the remaining twenty names. The resultant group is composed of some of the most distinguished financiers of the age. Of those financiers who married financiers' daughters, reference might be made to Michel Particelli d'Emery, who married Marie, daughter of the financier Nicolas Le Camus, in 1616; and to Jean-Baptiste Colbert, who married Marie, daughter of Jacques Charron de Ménars, *Trésorier de l'Extraordinaire des Guerres*.[7] This pattern of marriage was shared by others like Paul Ardier, François Catelan, Etienne Chabenas, Nicolas Monnerot, and eight other members of the Primary Elite. Clearly, even highly important financiers like these did not tend to marry out of the familial groups established by those involved in the royal finances. Marriage, indeed, was for these financiers largely a cementing of previously existing business ties.

Just as in the previous chapter it was seen that financiers did not on the whole escape from the world of the finances into more respectable employment, so here it is apparent that such men married the daughters of their financial colleagues. Social mobility in terms of career and marriage options does not seem to have been readily available to financiers. They did, however, experience such options through the lives of their children.

For a start, it is apparent from analysis of the careers followed by the sons of financiers that they did not tend to follow in their fathers' footsteps. Even in the least selected variable (any financial involvement whatsoever), which includes some very lowly and minor financiers, there is a clear tendency among the 258 sons of 128 fathers to follow careers in the cours souveraines and the central administration, categories which here individually rate more highly than the finances. Other careers were not ignored. The sum of those sons involved in the army and the Church (17 per cent) is roughly equal to the total of sons entering the finances. Moreover, the sum of all the known non-financial

careers comes to 65 per cent, which completely swamps the
financier sons of financiers. In the progression towards more
highly selected financial groups, the trend of sons away from the
finances becomes more pronounced still, until in the Tertiary
Elite it appears that only 7 per cent of the sons of financiers
entered the finances. At the same time, the balance among non-
financial careers changes. The record of those sons entering the
Church is difficult to interpret, but it would appear that there was
a progressive decline in the proportion. The proportion of sons
entering the cours souveraines shows more or less the same pattern. The proportion of sons entering the central administration
shows an increase, but only a slight one. The contrast of all these
groups with the large proportional increase of those sons entering
upon martial careers is sharp, and at first sight unexpected. It
would seem to indicate that the more successful a financier was,
the more concerned he was to provide his sons with modes of
gaining rapid acceptance into the nobility in the only way in
which this might be unequivocally achieved—by real or assumed
bravery on the field of battle.

Once more, such a bald summary can be supplemented by an
examination of the role played by the Primary Elite, 37 of whose
members are known to have had 82 sons following a total of 58
known careers. One thing that is fairly obvious is that the specific
nature and success of a father's career tended to influence what
career his son or sons would adopt. In the Primary Elite there are
ten sons of financiers who became in their turn financiers. They
included François Jacquier sieur de la Burelle, *Commissaire-
général des Vivres*, and his brother Jean vidame de Vieilmaisons,
the sons of Claude Jacquier, who had ended his career as con-
troller of military food supply in Champagne.[8] The common
tendency of this group is that the fathers of its members were
relatively new men who had insufficient prestige or pretensions to
hope to push their sons into callings more honourable than their
own. The sons who appear as financiers were to become fathers
of children who would enter much more prestigious careers.

A second group is composed of sixteen financiers' sons who
became magistrates of the cours souveraines and did not move on
to more prestigious employment in the central administration.
These included Denis Languet, *Conseiller* of the Parlement of

Rouen (1646), and later *Procureur-général* of the Parlement of Dijon, who was the son of Guillaume Languet.[9] Another example is provided by Pierre III Gargan, Conseiller of the Parlement of Metz, son of Pierre II Gargan, Intendant des Finances.[10] Common tendencies in this group are that the fathers were wealthy but lacking in prestige—ie they were *fermiers-généraux* or had spent most of their careers as *Munitionnaires*. The sons ascended to high positions only in second-rate cours souveraines like the *Cour des Aides* of Paris or the then relatively new Parlement of Metz. Those sons in this group who chose posts in the Parlement of Paris, as for example did Charles, son of Thomas III Bonneau, had to be content with posts as mere conseillers.

Four sons of financiers became members of the local administration. The group is too small to exhibit common characteristics, but it is worth pointing out that two of its members, who were both sons of Thomas III Bonneau, became respectively *procureur du roi* and conseiller of the *Châtelet* of Paris. The Châtelet was a *prévôté*, a local judicial institution in a sense, but in this case of far greater importance than most provincial cours souveraines, for its administrative competence extended almost as far as that of the Parlement of Paris. The point is, however, that, like their brother in the Parlement of Paris, the two Bonneau brothers who entered the Châtelet had to be content with minor positions.[11]

Thirteen sons of financiers became members of the central administration. Some, as a matter of fact, can only be presumed to have been central administrators. It is known simply that they acquired posts of *maître des requêtes*, which on the whole implies membership of the central administration. Others have left more complete data, like Louis II, son of Louis I Béchameil, one of Colbert's most trusted and corrupt agents. Louis II served as intendant of Tours (1680–9) and of other places, and was royal *commissaire* in a number of special investigations thereafter.[12] Other financiers' sons served in different categories closely related to the central administration. One such was Pierre, son of Claude Girardin, who became French ambassador to Constantinople in 1685.[13] The characteristic common to these thirteen sons is this: their fathers tended to be owners of more considerable positions than the fathers of those men who followed on in the finances or who acquired posts in cours souveraines or the legal side of local administration.

Thirteen sons of financiers entered the army—but with widely differing results. Arnoul Garnier was third son of Mathieu I Garnier, *Trésorier des Parties Casuelles* in the 1630s. Arnoul became Seigneur de Salins, and then acquired a post of *enseigne* in the royal *Gardes du Corps*. He was not to hold the post for long, for, as the Garnier genealogy cryptically points out, he was 'obligé de quitter, n'étant pas gentilhomme'.[14] But this is the only example I have found of pressures working against the sons of financiers in so crude and obvious a way. It is true, of course, that some financiers' sons did not advance very far, like Hugues-François, second son of François Jacquier, who acquired a commission in the Dragoons before he became *Chevalier de l'Ordre de Saint-Lazare* in 1670.[15] Thereafter he lived a life of relentless obscurity until his death in 1744. But other sons of financiers rose to posts of some eminence, as did Charles-Léon, second son of Guillaume Cornuel, who became *Inspecteur-général de Cavalerie* in 1704.[16] The best example of the military involvement of the sons of financiers is the family of Jean-Baptiste Colbert. Three of his sons entered the army, and all three died in battle or as a result of wounds received in action.[17] One of the reasons given by the noblesse d'épée for their exemption from the taxes paid by unprivileged *roturiers* was that nobles paid a tax of blood. If willingness to pay such a tax indicated anything, then the Colbert clan had really arrived—but to such an extent that its own extinction was portended.

The common characteristics of this group of sons is that their fathers were all relatively distinguished, either by the size of their fortune or by their move into positions of administrative importance. The sons of small or recently established men could not hope to make much of a showing in the military. On the other hand, it is important to point out that France was not so caste-ridden that men from non-noble backgrounds could make no showing at all. The group of sons under discussion shows that there was significant openness of entry even into this apparently most closed of circles.

The last and perhaps most difficult sector into which the sons of financiers might break was the higher levels of the Church.

Four sons of men in the Primary Elite achieved high status in the Church. Two are worthy of mention, for they stand at opposite poles of the ecclesiastical world. One was the son of Etienne Pavillon, holder of the somewhat wordily named post of *receveur des restes des officiers comptables de la Chambre des Comptes de Paris*. Etienne's second son, Nicolas, became Bishop of Alet—before the Crown and the ecclesiastical establishment discovered that he was a resolute Jansenist. But by then it was too late, and it was impossible to move him from his mountain fastness in the Pyrenees until he eventually died.[18] His career was very unlike that of the erastian son of another financier. Jacques-Nicolas, son of Jean-Baptiste Colbert, was given the abbacy of Bec and became Prior of La Charité-sur-Loire, an enormously wealthy benefice, before he was twenty-five years old. In 1680 he became Coadjutor of the Archbishop of Rouen, François Rouxel de Médavy. In 1682 he took the Archbishop's place at the *Assemblée du Clergé*, where he assumed a loyal monarchical position on the Four Articles. In 1691 Rouxel de Médavy died, and Jacques-Nicolas succeeded him.[19] But these are extreme examples, which should not be treated as typical of the involvement of the sons of financiers in the Church.

This analysis of the careers of the sons of men in the Primary Elite shows clearly how far financiers' sons might remove themselves from the occupations that had made their families' fortunes. But the mobility of financiers' sons was a qualified phenomenon. It applied to career, which was a part, but certainly by no means the whole, of the complex of factors which made up a man's social position. The point is that the marriage options available to financiers' sons were far more limited than the choice of careers that those sons might take.

Examination of the deck as a whole reveals that sons of financiers tended to marry the daughters of other financiers, or of magistrates of the cours souveraines. Daughters of men in central administration came a very distant third. There are 16 known marriages of sons of members of the Primary Elite: 6 were to daughters of financiers; 6 to daughters of magistrates in cours souveraines; 1 to the daughter of a central administrator; 1 to the daughter of an army officer; and 2 to the daughters of high court nobles d'épée. These examples, though few, are nevertheless

instructive. The most obvious pattern, that of financiers' sons who
became financiers in their turn and married financiers' daughters,
needs no explanation. But there is a second kind of marriage
which is much more significant. This is of the son of a financier
who leaves his father's calling and adopts a socially more acceptable one, yet who marries the daughter of a financier. Two
examples here are provided by the children of Thomas III Bonneau: Thomas IV, Procureur du Roi au Châtelet, married Jac-
queline, daughter of Denis Marin, Intendant des Finances, while
Etienne Bonneau, *Avocat-général* of the Cour des Aides, and
later *Président* of the Parlement of Metz, married Anne, daughter
of Cléophas Deshalus, Secrétaire du Roi.[20] Both these marriages
seem to have been related to the Bonneau family's financial concerns. It is permissible to conjecture that while a son might be
encouraged to pursue a career outside the finances, he might
nevertheless be drawn back into that world by his father's or his
family's concern to weld business ties with the bond of children's
marriages.

On the other hand, the pattern revealed by the Primary Elite
indicates that it could be as common for the sons of financiers to
marry the daughters of magistrates of cours souveraines as the
daughters of other financiers. An example of this is Théophile,
son of the financier François Catelan, who married Geneviève,
daughter of Jacques Le Coigneux, Président of the Parlement of
Paris.[21] The Hervart and Béchameil families provide further
examples of this phenomenon. It should be pointed out that it
was only very big financiers who could expect to marry their sons
off into instant respectability in this way. But even here, success
was strictly qualified, for the families into which the sons of these
financiers married were relatively low down in the pecking order
of the *noblesse de robe*. It was one thing to marry into a new robe
family, itself but recently emerged from relative obscurity, like
the Le Ragois into which Barthélemy Hervart's son Anne married
in 1686. It was quite another to break into the exalted circles
inhabited by older robe families like the Molé or the Harlay.[22]

The tale of the rest of these marriages is soon done, for the sons
of financiers were few who ascended above the level of cours
souveraines in their, or their parents', search for suitable
alliances. Technically, one son married the daughter of a central

administrator, but the latter was a very minor figure who, in any case, had started off as a household servant. In another case, the son of a financier married an army officer's daughter. But here again, when the case is examined, its significance is seen to be limited. Nicolas II Doublet seigneur de Persan, Secrétaire du Roi and Fermier-général, had three sons, of whom the eldest married Anne, daughter of the Arnoul Garnier to whom reference was made above.[23] Clearly the marriage was important to the Doublet not because Arnoul Garnier had for a short period tried to serve in a regiment far above his social station, but because he was the wealthy son of an important financier. His example can hardly be said to disprove the contention that it was rare indeed for financiers' sons to marry the daughters of army officers. There is only one family whose sons were able, despite their financial origins, to reach up for the hands of daughters of the noblesse d'épée. This was the family of Jean-Baptiste Colbert. Colbert's eldest son, Jean-Baptiste II marquis de Seignelay, married first an Alègre, and second a Matignon. Colbert's fourth son, Louis comte de Linières, married Marie-Louise, daughter of Louis du Bouchet marquis de Sourches.[24] But, once again, these few exalted examples should not lead one to ignore the fact that for the financiers at large sons tended to marry the daughters of other financiers. Of the fifty-three sons of men who appear in the variable entitled 'Any financial involvement whatsoever', twenty-five, or almost half, married the daughters of other financiers. It is important to state this rather obvious point, because the social pattern created by the marriages of the daughters of financiers was quite different from that of the girls' brothers.

Analysis of the marriages made for financiers' daughters, together with the pitifully few additional socially acceptable options for women in seventeenth-century French society, reveals that only a small proportion of these girls married financiers. Most financiers' daughters married out of the finances. Take, for example, the 60 daughters of men in the Primary Elite. Of these daughters, 5 married financiers; 14 married magistrates of cours souveraines; 12 married members of the central administration; 4 married army officers; and 6 married court nobles; 2 daughters became nuns. The fates of 17 girls remain unknown, but it should be pointed out that this gap derives largely from the fact that out of the 11 daughters of Guillaume Cornuel the fate of only 1 is known.[25] Subtract this one family from the group, and the category of unknown fates becomes quite small.

The five daughters of financiers who married financiers all came from newly prominent families. For example, Anne Ardier, who married Gaspard I de Fieubet, Trésorier de l'Epargne, was the daughter of Paul Ardier, Trésorier des Parties Casuelles and later Trésorier de l'Epargne. Ardier, successful though he was, seems to have been preceded by no notable financial forebear.[26] One might have expected that these daughters who married financiers would differ substantially from the fourteen girls who married magistrates of the cours souveraines. But this is not the case. Not merely were the girls similar in origin, but some of them were sisters. For example, Suzanne Ardier, who married Jean Dyel, *Premier Président* of the Cour des Aides of Paris, was sister of the Anne Ardier mentioned above. Similarly, amongst the daughters of Pierre II Gargan is to be found a mixture of different types of husband. Two daughters married members of the cours souveraines, while two others married men with a financial past.[27] On the whole, the relatively new financiers whose daughters married magistrates of the cour souveraines were happy enough to be able to secure such sons-in-law, though few financiers could ever have been as happy as François Berthelot on 9 October 1680, for on that day his youngest daughter Anne married André III Potier seigneur de Novion, marquis de Grignon. At that time Potier, a mere twenty-one years old, was only Conseiller of the Parlement of Paris. But he belonged to a great *parlementaire* family and his advance to the highest positions could be confidently expected. In the event he became Maître des Requêtes (1687), Président of the Parlement, and *Commandeur des Ordres du Roi*. His socially aspiring wife did not, however, see his final triumph, for she died in 1697 and her widower did not become Premier Président of the Parlement of Paris until 1723.[28]

Not all financiers felt that the summit of their ambitions was reached when their daughters contracted such alliances. Indeed, members of the cours souveraines seem to have been almost more ready to marry the daughters of financiers than some financiers really liked, as can be deduced from the case of Marie, daughter of the important financier Claude Cornuel. Her first

husband was Louis de Machault seigneur de la Marche, Conseiller of the Cour des Aides. He died in 1634, and Marie chose
to marry again, this time 'contre la volonté de son père' as the
Cornuel genealogy has it, Jean Collon, Conseiller of the Parlement of Paris. It would seem that Collon was simply not good
enough for the daughter of a financier as rich and well-established
as Cornuel. Whereas at an earlier stage of his career Cornuel
might have accepted a mere conseiller of the Cour des Aides, by
1635 his affairs had burgeoned to the extent that, as Intendant
des Finances and Président of the *Chambre des Comptes* of Paris,
he might hope that his daughter would acquire greater prestige
from her second marriage.[29]

At all events, the daughters of financiers are certainly to be
found in more elevated positions. Twelve daughters of financiers
married members of the central administration, men like Louis
Chauvelin, Maître des Requêtes and Intendant of Franche-
Comté (1675–83) and of Amiens (1684), who married Claude,
daughter of Thomas III Bonneau.[30] But even in this category
there is often more than meets the eye. For example, Claude de
Boislève, the Munitionnaire who became Intendant des Finances,
looks like a new man who prospered so remarkably that he was
able to secure a marriage alliance between his daughter Louise
and Jacques-Honoré Barentin, Conseiller of the Parlement of
Rouen (1647) and later of that of Paris, Maître des Requêtes,
Intendant of Poitiers (1665–9) and of Limoges (1665–7), and
Président of the *Grand Conseil*. Yet if the Boislève and Barentin
families are examined, it becomes easy to see that the match was
not quite as surprising as it might seem. Boislève was a financier,
but not a man from the lower depths. One of his brothers was a
bishop, while another was an important officer in the local administration of Anjou. On the other hand, Jacques-Honoré
Barentin, for all the pure essence of robe d'état conveyed by his
curriculum vitae, was the grandson of Honoré Barentin sieur de
Charonne, Trésorier des Parties Casuelles under Henri IV.[31]

Some financiers' daughters married men from families which
served at levels in the central administration higher than that of
mere intendant. One of the daughters of François Bossuet
married Armand-Léon Le Bouthillier comte de Chavigny, whose
grandfather Claude had been *surintendant des finances* during the

last decade or so of Richelieu's ministry, and whose father Léon had been secretary of state during the later years of the reign of Louis XIII and the early years of that of Louis XIV.[32] Nicolas Ladvocat, Secrétaire du Roi and *Maître à la Chambre des Comptes*, married off his daughter Catherine to Simon Arnauld marquis de Pomponne in 1660. Pomponne had already served as *intendant de l'Armée* in Italy, in the Paris area and in Catalonia in the period 1644–51. In the latter year he was given a post of full *conseiller d'état*. Although his career suffered somewhat through friendship with Nicolas Fouquet, in 1671 he became Secretary of State for Foreign Affairs.[33] Nor was a Secretary of State the highest official whom a financier's daughter might aspire to marry, as is shown by the marriage of Madeleine, daughter of Louis I Béchameil, to Nicolas Desmaretz, who was to become *Contrôleur-général des Finances* in 1708. This post had long since ceased to be merely a financial one, and was in fact the nearest thing that Louis XIV permitted to the office of *premier ministre*.[34]

Marriage of financiers' daughters to army officers was possible, though not very common. François Jacquier's daughter Marie-Antoinette married one in 1680. He was Joseph d'Espinay Saint-Luc marquis de Lignery, *Gouverneur* and *Lieutenant-général* of Péronne, Montdidier and Roye. He rose to the rank of *maréchal des Camps et des Armées*, *commandant la Maison du Roi*, before he was killed at the battle of Neerwinden in August 1693. Other girls married even higher, like Marie-Elisabeth, daughter of François Berthelot. Her husband was Charles-Auguste de Goyon comte de Matignon et de Gacé, who became *Maréchal de France* in 1708.[35]

Distinguishing between a high-ranking army officer and a court noble is often an otiose proceeding. Obviously Goyon de Matignon was a court noble as well as a soldier. It would have been quite proper to have added the two categories together in the present discussion. On the other hand, the seven men who are called here court nobles and who married financiers' daughters were discovered in non-military contexts, which is why they are considered separately here. It was possible for a really big financier to marry off his daughter at this exalted level. Guillaume Cornuel, for example, managed to snare the Marquis de Guerchy into marriage with his daughter Geneviève.[36] But nobody could equal Jean-Baptiste Colbert's record. His three daughters all married dukes: in 1667, Jeanne-Marie-Thérèse married the Duc de Chevreuse; in 1671, Henriette married the Duc de Beauvilliers; and in 1679, Marie-Anne married the Duc de Mortemart.[37] It may well have been Colbert's daughters rather than his administration that prompted Saint-Simon to complain of a regime of vile bourgeoisie. But Colbert's success should certainly not be taken as typical of the world of the financiers. It was, rather, the extreme upward limit of social mobility.

There is one last point to be made about daughters. Only two girls entered religious communities. These were the two daughters of Jean Doublet, *Receveur des Décimes* of Troyes and fermier-général (of what the document does not make clear) in 1643. But what this lack of professionally pious ladies really means can emerge only from taking a broader approach than has been adopted so far.[38]

The preceding section on career- and marriage-patterns of financiers, their sons and daughters needs to be set in context by a study of all kinds of other groups in French society. This study has not yet been done and remains merely a project. But it is nevertheless possible to give some indication of what such a study might show by discussing some of the groups that have been discerned impinging on, or in some way affecting, the world of the financiers. One group which is of some relevance here is the cours souveraines. Some 363 members of the cours souveraines appear in the deck. A second group is the modern administrative machine, a band 100 strong. The data that have been collected for both these groups according to the familial categories discussed already in this chapter in relation to financiers can be used in comparison with the Primary Elite (see Figure 6, pp 224-5).

In the marriages contracted by the three groups, the financial bias of the deck manifests itself in the large percentages of men marrying the daughters of financiers. As one might have expected, members of the Primary Elite were the most prone to marry such ladies, though members of the modern administrative machine were almost as ready as the financiers were to contract such marriages. The existence of a limit on the personal upward mobility of the financiers is confirmed by the small number of such men who married into the cours souveraines, and the fact that no

FIGURE 6: Comparison of Familial Patterns of Primary Elite, Cours Souveraines, and Modern Administrative Machine

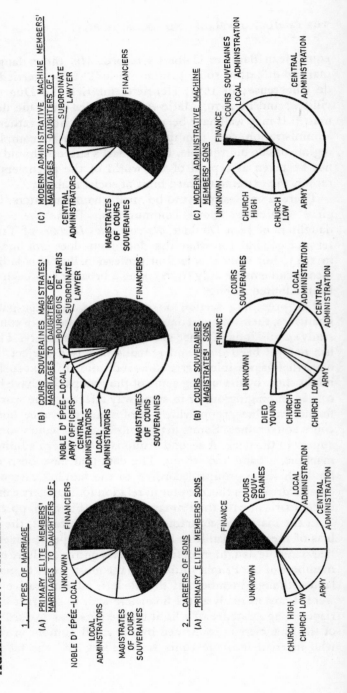

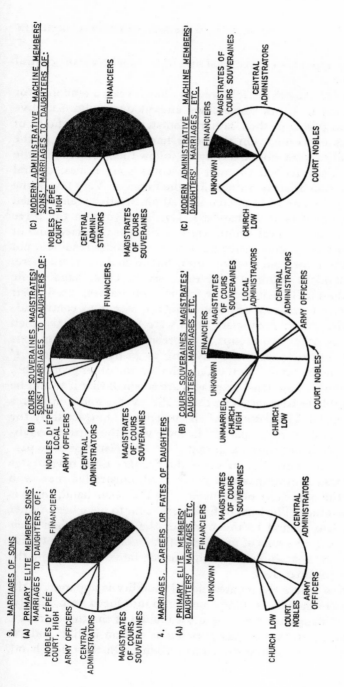

3. MARRIAGES OF SONS

(A) PRIMARY ELITE MEMBERS' SONS'
MARRIAGES TO DAUGHTERS OF:

NOBLES D'ÉPÉE COURT, HIGH
ARMY OFFICERS
CENTRAL ADMINISTRATORS
FINANCIERS
MAGISTRATES OF COURS SOUVERAINES

(B) COURS SOUVERAINES MAGISTRATES'
SONS' MARRIAGES TO DAUGHTERS OF:

NOBLES D'ÉPÉE LOCAL
ARMY OFFICERS
CENTRAL ADMINISTRATORS
FINANCIERS
MAGISTRATES OF COURS SOUVERAINES

(C) MODERN ADMINISTRATIVE MACHINE MEMBERS'
SONS' MARRIAGES TO DAUGHTERS OF:

NOBLES D'ÉPÉE COURT, HIGH
CENTRAL ADMINISTRATORS
FINANCIERS
MAGISTRATES OF COURS SOUVERAINES

4. MARRIAGES, CAREERS OR FATES OF DAUGHTERS

(A) PRIMARY ELITE MEMBERS'
DAUGHTERS' MARRIAGES, ETC.

CHURCH LOW
COURT NOBLES
ARMY OFFICERS
UNKNOWN
MAGISTRATES OF COURS SOUVERAINES'
CENTRAL ADMINISTRATORS
FINANCIERS

(B) COURS SOUVERAINES MAGISTRATES'
DAUGHTERS' MARRIAGES, ETC.

UNMARRIED
CHURCH HIGH
CHURCH LOW
COURT NOBLES
UNKNOWN
MAGISTRATES OF COURS SOUVERAINES
LOCAL ADMINISTRATORS
CENTRAL ADMINISTRATORS
ARMY OFFICERS
FINANCIERS

(C) MODERN ADMINISTRATIVE MACHINE MEMBERS'
DAUGHTERS' MARRIAGES, ETC.

CHURCH LOW
UNKNOWN
FINANCIERS
MAGISTRATES OF COURS SOUVERAINES
CENTRAL ADMINISTRATORS
COURT NOBLES

H

financiers appear to have married the daughters of central administrators.

Analysis of the careers followed by sons reveals a tendency for sons of men in cours souveraines and modern administrative machine to follow in their fathers' footsteps, as far as choice of career was concerned. On the other hand, sons of men in the Primary Elite were more likely *not* to follow their fathers into the finances. They tended to enter the cours souveraines, central administration or army, rather than the finances. Very few of the sons of magistrates or of the modern administrative men deigned to become professional financiers. Hardly anyone in the three categories entered local administration. Sons of financiers and of magistrates in the cours souveraines showed some readiness not only to enter the cours souveraines, but to make careers there. Sons of modern administrative men, on the other hand, while they undoubtedly entered the cours souveraines, used their magistracies merely as way-stages on the ascent to central administrative office. Financiers' sons were far more martial than those of the other two groups, if the relative percentages of sons entering military careers are anything to go by. But financiers' sons did much less well in the Church than the other groups did.

The numbers for sons' marriages are so small that it would be unreasonable to base much on them. However, some conjectures may be made. The patterns of the marriages contracted by the sons of the three groups parallel in some ways the patterns established by their progenitors, in that there are relatively large percentages of the sons of members of the Primary Elite, magistrates of the cours souveraines and modern administrative men who married the daughters of financiers. On the other hand, there is some difference. The sons of financiers seem to have been rather less maritally bound to the world of the financiers than their fathers were. The sons of members of the modern administrative machine show a similar though smaller move away from the daughters of financiers.

The area where the greatest social mobility is apparent is the marriages of daughters. One point leaps into focus immediately: financiers' daughters were the most mobile of the three groups. They started from the least prestigious station in life, and yet were able to marry into the court nobility. On the other hand, comparison with the success of the other groups puts this success into perspective. Though one-sixth of the financiers' daughters married nobles d'épée of some kind, this performance was less successful than that of the two-fifths of the daughters of members of the modern administrative machine who performed the same feat. The really significant difference comes, however, with the role of the daughters of the three groups in the religious orders of the Church. The daughter of a member of the Primary Elite was six-and-a-half times less likely to enter the cloister than was the daughter of a modern administrative man and over ten times less likely than was the daughter of a magistrate of a cour souveraine.

There is no obvious reason why this should have been so. The usual reason given for the entry of some otherwise nubile female into a convent is that there was not enough money to pay for her dowry. But this is improbable, for entry to a convent cost a lot of money, and was certainly not a cheap way out. A family had to guarantee to support a daughter who became a nun, and if she lived to a ripe old age this involved a protracted charge on the family's income. Furthermore, a girl entering a convent had to take with her supplies of linen and tableware and other domestic impedimenta which were specified in the notarised agreement between family and convent that had to be signed before the girl could enter.[39] Another reason commonly advanced is that there were not enough socially acceptable husbands to go round. This may indeed have been the reason why some girls entered the religious life. But there are a number of other possible explanations.

To enter the cloister was socially acceptable—until some study of the membership of French convents in the seventeenth century is carried out, it will not be known exactly how acceptable such entry was, but it clearly *was* acceptable.

Another explanation lies is this bipartite argument. First, there was a veritable *ruée vers le cloître* in the seventeenth century, which can be seen as one of the more obvious manifestations of the French Catholic Reformation. Second, marriage for many women was simply a death sentence. They were often forced to keep bearing as rapidly as their systems could perform until they died. For example, Guillaume Cornuel, Trésorier de l'Extraordinaire des Guerres, married twice. His second wife, Anne

Bigot, had eleven children. The dates of birth of eight of them were as follows: 1628, 1629, 1630, 1632, 1633, 1634, 1636, and 1642. The dates of birth of three others are not known—perhaps they fitted into the idle period of Anne Bigot's life between 1636 and 1642.[40] Women of less courage than Anne Bigot and more freedom of action might well have pondered the tranquillity and probable longevity—if relative lack of excitement—of convent life. The point is that this kind of option seems to have been available only to daughters of families which no longer felt the need to struggle upwards in French society. Entering a convent was accepted socially, but there it ended. There would be no legitimate grandchildren for a man whose daughter took such a step. Financiers simply could not afford to let their daughters retire from the world. The girls had to work like everybody else in the family to further its collective rise.

The picture that can be derived from the analyses conducted up to now in this chapter might have seemed constricted to men in seventeenth-century France, for the polite society of the time was in its own eyes naturally interested in, and in our eyes obsessed with, the length of each person's genealogy and the illustriousness of ancestors, descendants and even distant kinsmen. One of the basic elements of such a concern was the age of one's family. Anyone who was anyone strove to show how ancient their family was, tracing their descent back to people like Priam of Troy or even to the first Adam. Obviously the bulk of these genealogical assertions were the purest bunkum. But one would have thought that memories would have extended back over perhaps two centuries, and that even the grandchildren of *arrivistes* would have been generally disdained by polite society. And yet it is obvious that some new and particularly successful families came to be accepted with great speed. Evidently the chronology of acceptance had some parallels with medieval customary law, in which something that had existed for ten years was defined as age-old, while forty years rendered things immemorial. The passage of three generations, indeed a short period of time in a society that claimed to be so conscious of prescription and tradition, would often sanctify the way in which a family's fortunes were first established.

At the same time, there was not merely rapid sanctification but

also a surprising diversity of employment and function undertaken and carried out by relatively restricted numbers of people
related to one another by blood. The importance of a family
clearly has to be measured not merely as a function of the height
to which individual members might ascend, but also as a function
of the numbers of sons, brothers, cousins, and in-laws who held
posts of importance in the various branches of royal administration, the army, and the Church. Numerological analysis of so
complex a phenomenon would itself be so complicated that the
meaning of a verbal representation of it could be descried only
with the greatest difficulty. It seems better, therefore, to describe
briefly one characteristic successful dynasty to show what a
family whose origins were financial might look like.

The family of Phélypeaux d'Herbault was founded by Raymond Phélypeaux seigneur d'Herbault, de la Vrillière et du
Verger, who was born in 1560 and died in 1629. He became
Secrétaire de la Chambre du Roi in 1590, Trésorier des Parties
Casuelles in 1591 and Trésorier de l'Epargne in 1599. In 1621,
he became Secretary of State, a post he was to hold for the rest of
his life. He had three sons, Balthazar, Louis I and Antoine, each
of whom inherited one of their father's fiefs. Balthazar seigneur
d'Herbault became Conseiller of the Parlement of Paris in 1618.
He subsequently became Trésorier de l'Epargne. He married the
daughter of a maître des requêtes, and by her had two sons:
François, Conseiller au Parlement (it is not clear which, but it
was probably that of Paris); and Balthazar, Abbé of Bourgmoyen
and of Saint-Laurent (near Cosne, on the upper Loire). The
second son of Raymond, Louis I, became Seigneur de la Vrillière. Born in 1599, he was *breveté* Conseiller d'Etat in 1620 and
became Secretary of State after his father's death in 1629. He
married Marie, daughter of Michel I Particelli d'Emery. In 1643
he became *Prévôt et Maître des Cérémonies des Ordres du Roi*. He
died in 1681, having had three sons: Louis II, who succeeded his
father as Secretary of State in 1654, resigning in 1669; Balthazar;
and Michel, who became successively Conseiller au Parlement,
Abbé of Nieul, Saint-Lô and l'Absie, Bishop of Uzès in 1664, and
Archbishop of Bourges in 1676. Michel died in 1694. The third
son of Raymond, the founder, was Antoine seigneur du Verger.
Not much is known of his early career, but it is clear that he

became *Intendant de Justice* in Bourbonnais, that he became Conseiller d'Etat, and that he died in 1665. He had two sons: Raymond Balthazar, who became successively *Lieutenant-général des Armées du Roi, Conseiller d'Etat d'Epée, Envoyé extraordinaire* to Cologne, Ambassador to Turin and other courts and *Gouverneur-général des isles d'Amérique*; and, finally, Jacques Antoine, who became Bishop of Lodève in 1690 and died in 1732.[41]

The 11 male Phélypeaux of these three generations held between them: 4 important posts in the financial administration, 7 in the modern administrative machine, 3 in the cours souveraines, 7 in the Church, 2 in the diplomatic service, and 1 each in the royal court, military, and old local administration. This kind of pattern was repeated over and over again by different families, such as the Ardier, Béchameil, Bellinzani, Berryer, Berthelot, Bullion, Colbert, Cornuel, Fieubet, Garnier, Girardin, Languet, Machault, Marin, and Maupeou, to mention only the most obvious.

Looking at the whole complex of variables which in some sense bear on the problem of social mobility, that is to say, adding to the questions of kinship and family discussed in this chapter other factors discussed earlier, like success or failure in the finances, expenditure on offices, land, houses, building, dowries, and so on, the following conclusion emerges: the financiers in the mass showed a rapid upward movement which was of relatively restricted size. The key limitations are the inability of most financiers to rise above the title of sieur or seigneur, to purchase worthwhile posts outside the royal finances or to marry women other than financiers' daughters. The only people involved in the finances who showed significant personal mobility were those who combined financial with other roles, like magistracies in the cours souveraines or, much better, posts in the modern administrative machine. And, as has been shown in Chapter 8, those men were few and far between who *began* as financiers and *then* moved out into other functional categories.

What disturbed people about the financiers was the speed, not the size of their social leap. People deduced from the speed of the movement that its size was large, but this was not the case. The important large-scale social movement connected with the finances was in fact long-term, involving two, or better still three, generations. And here it is apparent that social motion was a complex affair in which numerous functional categories other than the royal finances played their part. Nevertheless, the finances provided the kinetic energy for a short upward leap by the particular financier, and the potential energy for much larger upward climbing by his sons, daughters and grandchildren.

The source of both kinetic and potential energy was money, of course. But, as has been sufficiently shown, money could operate only in certain patterns laid down unconsciously perhaps, but none the less effectively, by society itself. In any case, all this movement cannot be taken to imply that French society in the seventeenth century was in the process of some major transformation. What has been observed is largely a series of similar phenomena repeated in a fairly substantial number of cases, showing how some particularly favoured persons and families and a short series of particularly favoured groups might rise into a number of social categories and institutional bodies possessed of prestige and acceptability greater than that to which those persons, families and groups could have laid claim at the beginning of their individual and collective careers.

The fact that such people became part of these higher (for want of a better word) bodies means not that some kind of social revolution was under way, but rather that the higher echelons of French society were prepared to accept new faces and new blood. At the upper levels at least, French society was not a society that was dying, or rather it was a society dying in the way that an organism dies from the moment of its birth. That is to say, it was able to compensate for the ordinary attrition of life, in which elements or cells of the organism die, by replacing them with new ones. French society, far from being potentially revolutionary, possessed a certain instinct for survival in that it would accept particularly vigorous and aggressive people and families into the ruling circle, thus ensuring that such people would not turn to activities deleterious to its survival, and at the same time availing itself of their services in a positive direction.

Notes to this chapter are on pages 257–8

Conclusion

By 1661, the royal finances had been almost entirely subverted by the search for short-term credit. The process of subversion had two distinct elements. The first and more obvious was the inversion of chains of command within specific important institutions. The clerks of *Surintendance*, *Epargne* and *Contrôle-général* came to have more power than their nominal masters during the 1650s. But this was not all, for there was a second element which was less obvious but more important than the first. This second element is complex, but it can be reduced to a single formula: the legal function of institutions shrank in importance in comparison with Extraordinary Affairs. The Ordinary Machine became little more than a front behind which the financiers carried on their affairs with studied indifference towards the damage that they did to the government and contempt for the suffering of the tax-paying elements of the population.

By 1661, the government was sunk in debt. Its income was largely devoted to servicing that debt, partly by paying wages to venal officers, partly by meeting in a halting way obligations to purchasers of *Rentes sur l'Hôtel de Ville*, partly by paying interest on outstanding loans; but also, and perhaps largely, by paying out exorbitant sums to men who as state officials often enough wrote out the documents by which, in their private capacity as financiers, they received their illegal profits. And though the government might be unable to make ends meet, even though the war with Spain had ended two years before in 1659, the overall level of taxation in 1661 was 200 per cent higher than it had been in 1610. As a result of this increase, insolvent tax-payers died in thousands each winter in the prisons into which they had been thrown to encourage them to pay what *Traitants* said they owed.

Colbert tried to reverse this situation. He set up the *Chambre de Justice* to punish the financiers, and created a new *Conseil Royal des Finances* to direct the financial machine, together with new accounting systems to ensure that proper standards were maintained. The Surintendance des Finances and the Epargne disappeared, and were replaced by the new Contrôle-général and the *Trésor-royal*. But it is evident that his efforts were a failure. The new institutions were able to supply the needs of the monarchy only so long as the king did not involve France in war. Once war broke out, even Colbert was forced to resort to extraordinary expedients, and to avail himself of the services of the financiers who operated such expedients. By a strange irony, the reforming *Contrôleur-général* was driven to employ some of the very men whom he had once tried to destroy, in particular François Jacquier, *Commissaire-général des Vivres*. Jacquier, released from prison in 1664, went on until his death in 1684 supplying the royal armies with food, clothing, equipment and ammunition, just as he had done throughout the ministry of Mazarin.[1]

It is no reflection on Colbert's intelligence and ability to say that he did not fully understand the size and nature of the problems presented by the royal finances. His mind tended to focus on institutional questions, and he seems to have believed that the new bodies that he created would be able to provide the money that the Crown needed without doing too much violence to the country at large. Even on this level, there was no chance of his succeeding, because of the way in which those who ran the finances were recruited, and because of the way in which power operated within the financial system.

The men who staffed financial institutions owed loyalty neither to those institutions, nor to the state. Their prime concern was to make their own fortunes as rapidly as possible. To encompass this necessarily meant undermining the formal purpose of institutions as completely as possible. To improve the standard of administrative conduct would have involved destroying the system of venality of offices, dismissing the incumbent office holders, and replacing them with properly trained civil servants. For economic reasons (the Crown could never have bought back all the financial offices), political reasons (mass dismissals of tens of thousands of officials would probably have brought about a minor civil war), and educational reasons (there were far too few trained people for the posts to be filled), fundamental moves essential for effective reform could not be made.

Moreover, Colbert was personally trapped by the existing system in a curious but complete way. He attained prominence by means of his skills as a financier, skills which were noticed by Mazarin, who eventually bequeathed Colbert to Louis XIV. Even before Mazarin's death, Colbert gained a measure of power by creating a clientèle many of whose most important members were financiers. To maintain power after 1661 he had to keep up relationships with financiers like Béchaméil, Bellinzani and Berryer. Had he tried to implement his aim of reorganising the royal finances, he would have had to sever these links, and in doing so destroy a large part of the basis of his power. Without this power, he would have been unable to countenance an administrative reorganisation. As a result, he was to remain perched uncomfortably between the horns of this dilemma until death solved all his terrestrial difficulties in 1683.[2]

The fundamental problem of the royal finances lay beyond the institutional and fiscal matters that Colbert saw so clearly. On one level, there was the question of the French monarchy itself. There was a paradox at the heart of the administrative history of the *ancien régime*. On one hand, the government built up new administrative structures that were supposed to be immune to corruption. The most visible example of this is the institution of *intendants*, who were *commissaires*, not *officiers*, and who could therefore be dismissed by the Crown at the slightest hint of corruption or recalcitrance, or even, an unusual ground in most administrative systems, incompetence. But while monarchs and their advisers were creating new agencies to promote more efficient administration, they were at the same time formalising and systematising methods of financing that led to even greater corruption than had existed before. The monarchy was simultaneously building two mutually hostile systems. On the one hand there was the admirable modern administrative machine which was created largely in the sixteenth and seventeenth centuries and which in the eighteenth century was to be the envy of the civilised world. And, on the other hand, there was the deplorable financial system of the state, though system implies a kind of rational organisation which was in this instance not readily to be discerned.

Nevertheless, though the modern administration of the absolutist state and the new financial arrangements might appear to stand at opposite ends of the spectrum of administrative efficiency, they were united in the purpose they served—to allow the monarchy to wage the wars which were its most serious and pleasant occupation. The personal links between the men who ran the two systems, indeed the qualified interchangeability of personnel of the two systems, point towards a conclusion: the financial habits of the French monarchy were not an avoidable aberration of the absolutist government but an integral part of it. The financiers were part of an ongoing system of supply which, inefficient and corrupt though it was, had to be allowed to continue to exist. The Crown had to have the continual transfusions of money that the system provided. It seemed that, were those transfusions to be even momentarily interrupted, the state would die. There could be no question of calling a halt to everything, and building a new, efficient, incorruptible system which would, after an interval, take over the task of supplying the state. There might be some piecemeal reform. But, though this was to take place at a slowly increasing pace in the eighteenth century, its effects were not to be felt substantially until the Revolution.

These institutional matters were not the only problems posed by the financiers. Indeed, to seventeenth-century observers, financiers were less of a threat to government than they were to society. The seventeenth century was curiously incapable of understanding what can be seen in retrospect as a fairly normal kind of social movement, which had been proceeding, in the financiers' case, at least as early as the fifteenth century. The movement may be formalised quite simply from the point of view of the upper ranks of society as a process of continuous renewal.

Demographic studies have revealed how short the history of the average family tends to be; how soon, in particular, a noble line will die out through default of heirs male. This process has gone on throughout French history. The original Frankish aristocracy of birth died out very rapidly right at the beginning of

the feudal period, its demise accelerated by the violence of the
age. In periods of relative peace both internal and external the
rate of disappearance would tend to fall; but it is not to be
doubted that the centuries from 1300 to 1700 were sufficiently
lethal for the process to continue apace. Subsistence crises would
evidently tend to influence the noble less than the average
peasant. But there were enough mortal factors present to maintain
a fairly high rate of failure of noble lines. These ranged from
various kinds of plague to war. Conflict, first with England, then
with the Hapsburg dynasty, and, during the interludes of the late
sixteenth and mid-seventeenth centuries, civil war of Frenchman
with Frenchman killed off large numbers of the nobility in arms.
This process was still going on in Louis XIV's reign. Noble
genealogies of the period in which two or even three sons were
killed in action or died of wounds are depressingly common.
Many of these men were junior officers who died before they had
had time to get married let alone beget children. As if this were
not enough to limit the fecundity of noble families, very large
numbers of the sons of the nobility who did not enter the army
went into the Church. For these reasons there was a continuous
rarefaction of the atmosphere at the apex of society. It is not surprising that men rushed in to fill this partial vacuum.

What is surprising is the hostility that was felt by society at
large towards such social movement in the seventeenth century.
Much of it can no doubt be related to the various kinds of crisis
about which so much has been written in the last sixteen years.[3]
French society in the seventeenth century felt cold winds blowing. Though it was the peasants who suffered first and worst,
since the vast majority had no savings to tide them over even the
most short-term difficulty, the effect of agrarian crisis was inevitably felt in sectors other than that of primary agricultural
production. Obviously food supply in towns was affected by
rural dearth. But the effects of difficulties in production would
also strike those who depended for their income on the appropriation of part of the surplus value produced by peasants. Those
affected would be all those in receipt of seigneurial dues and
profitable feudal incidents. Nor should one forget those members
of the hierarchy of the Church drawing profit from the tithe. But
the state, too, would be affected, and all those officers both

military and administrative whose wages were paid by the state.

Plainly these effects would not have been uniform. Languedoc, for example, experienced its crisis much later than the area around Beauvais. Equally, different social groups would have been affected differently. On the other hand, very large sectors of the population (though unable, as most people in the grip of a crisis are, to evaluate the precise nature of their suffering), experienced fear and anguish, and even the most calm would have produced some reaction to a more or less cruel fate. There was a closing of the ranks among groups that felt themselves threatened. Amongst long established groups proud of a certain stability in membership, there was even some hysteria about persons who moved around socially, and who appeared to weaken the precarious equilibrium which seemed to be all that prevented social collapse.[4]

Certainly there are signs of this sort of reaction amongst the articulate. Loyseau, at the beginning of the century, made much of the idea of hierarchy, claiming that everyone in France from the king down to the humblest peasant had his place in society, a place that had been ordained by God and which, therefore, no man should seek to change. Later on, Bossuet stressed in highly emotional terms the need for total subordination to the royal will, and the equation of political with divine authority.[5] In terms of symbol, a similar reaction may be seen. The earthy atmosphere of the court of Henri IV, which in many respects resembled an amiably drunken and anarchic zoo, gave way eventually to the formalism of the court of Louis XIV, which expressed the great king's fear that without rigid control of every aspect of each social organism, and of the person down to the slightest gradation of remark or facial expression, society might collapse into anarchy. All this meant that social movement would be much frowned on. But did it mean that the rate of upward social motion would in fact slacken?

Probably in the aggregate there was some slackening. During the general crisis, money would inevitably be harder to mobilise. This would make it harder for people in general to rise. But it would appear that the financiers were not affected by general economic and social conditions to anything like the extent that

other people were. It is not hard to see why. Kings insisted on
fighting wars, whatever economic conditions happened to exist.
They depended on financiers to mobilise the funds needed for
troops and their supply. Moreover, it became more and more
difficult to levy taxes by ordinary methods, since, as a result of
the general crisis, the peasants found it more and more difficult
to pay the taxes at which they were optimistically assessed. And
then, of course, there were local revolts against the taxation
system, which reduced yields still further. Inevitably the Crown
came to depend more and more heavily on the financiers to
provide what the ordinary system could no longer supply. The
more difficult the mobilisation of funds was, and the more desperate the Crown became, the more it had to pay to the financiers to secure their services. The net result was that the general
crisis of the seventeenth century was ultimately profitable to the
financiers. The size of the sums that they could extract from the
Crown rose in proportion to the Crown's desperation, which was
in turn conditioned partly by wars, but also by the economic
condition of the country.

All this has a bearing on the position of financiers in society.
There came into existence groups of successful financiers with
large amounts of money waiting to be invested in ways that
would provide prestige both for themselves and for their descendants. At the same time, society was particularly hostile to
social movement in general, and to the financiers because of the
way they made their money. Inevitably there was confrontation,
not merely between financier and angry peasant, but between
financiers and other groups in polite society. The second type of
confrontation had its effect on the social mobility of financiers.
They could move up in the finances, but very few of them, and
these only highly successful men who had the ear of some important minister (as Bruant had that of Fouquet), were able to
purchase prestigious posts outside the finances. Financiers'
money had to go into other things, particularly the careers of
sons and the marriages of daughters. Society's hostility to the
financier did not extend with anything like the same force to his
children. Money, if there were enough of it, soon acquired respectability, so long as those who owned it did not go on making
money in socially unacceptable ways. Since financiers' money

went mostly into forms of property, its taint was lost with surprising speed. While financiers were on the whole possessors of nobility only by virtue of purchase of office—a nobility which was generally accepted to be a low order—the children of financiers were permitted to move into social and functional categories which were closed to their fathers, and to become, in time, respected members of the various branches of the nobility.

Despite the amount of money that financiers made, and the great houses that they built, and despite the success of their children, the place of financiers in French society was very insecure. Financiers were always liable to raids by the state, and to the violence of members of all kinds of social groups. This insecurity is rather difficult to explain. The answer lies partly in the conspicuousness of what financiers did. For example, it was demonstrated that financiers were often the first members of their families to purchase land which gave them a foothold on the ladder that would eventually confer on their families identity as landed nobles. When plain Jean Hérault became Monsieur de Gourville, it was clear that something had happened. Yet this is not the whole answer, for people in different functional groups were doing similar things, and nobody seemed to mind very much. Members of the *cours souveraines* acquired land in much the same way as the financiers did, though with less exuberance. On the question of acquisition of technical nobility, there was little to choose between financiers and magistrates. Loyseau, in discussing such nobility, mentions the role of posts of *secrétaire du roi* and *conseiller au Parlement* as though they were comparable.[6] Further, the financiers were by no means as successfully acquisitive in the land market as high members of the modern administrative machine.

The rest of the answer lies in what might be called the psychology of organisation. Organised groups were very important in early modern France. Institutions like *parlements* and *chambres des comptes* were important not merely as institutions but also as clubs dedicated to the maintenance of special liberties or privileges. The significance of such matters can best be seen in the extraordinary history of the Parlement of Paris in the eighteenth century, when that body, in exacting its revenge for centuries of what it conceived to be mistreatment at the hands of Valois and

Bourbon kings, played a major role in weakening the monarchy to the extent that a not particularly serious financial crisis could precipitate revolution. The financiers, on the other hand, for all their purchase of posts like those of secrétaire du roi, never succeeded in creating the sense of community and the powers of mutual protection achieved by cours souveraines. The financiers had no group identity. Their dearest wish was to make money as quickly as possible, acquire the appurtenances of nobility, and turn their backs forever on the institutional nexus in which their fortunes had been made. They were, as a result, divided into small competing groups, each attempting to corner the pickings to be made and, as a consequence, showing very little concern for the health or even lives of their fellows. In such a context as this, there could be no consciousness of pride of group amongst financiers, merely a frightening instability based on internal division and conflict. This meant that the financiers, for all their money, were collectively weak. They were fair game for other groups organised for collective action, like that taken against financiers by the cours souveraines during the Fronde.

This lack of group identity was reflected in the way individual financiers conducted themselves. Their patterns of behaviour did not form a coherent, integrated, easily recognised life-style comparable to that of members of the military nobility or that of those men who served throughout their careers as magistrates of Parisian cours souveraines. Financiers invited comparison with a series of other groups both functional and social. In institutional conduct, the financiers related most closely to the modern administrative machine—and, as has been pointed out, possessed members in common with the latter group. In attitudes to life outside the making of money and the conduct of institutions, the most successful financiers frankly aped an element of the nobility. But their imitation was not of the *gentilshommes campagnards* to whom, one would assume, the most elevated professional financiers, as recent and minor nobles, would be most naturally assimilated, but of the high nobility at Court. This was to cause the financiers a great deal of trouble, both from nobles anxious to defend their social status and privileges, and from society at large.

Some financiers believed themselves the equal of the high

nobility and entered into competition with them. There was the case of Bartet, who insulted the Duc de Candale in a comprehensive way in 1655, saying that the duke, shorn of his long hair and lace, would be no more than 'un squelette ou un atome'. The duke retaliated by having Bartet's head shaved, and his lace *rabat*, *canons* and *manchettes* forcibly removed. Bartet complained repeatedly to Mazarin but, as Voltaire was to find seventy years later after he had been beaten up by the servants of the Chevalier de Rohan, the monarchy would not punish nobles for chastising impertinent members of the lower orders.[7]

Other financiers were able to compete with the high nobility in fields less demanding than the trading of complicated insults and ritualised violence, the successful undertaking of which depended on feudal tradition and long years of self-discipline. Gambling was such a less demanding field. The passion for wagering was so strong that social distinctions tended to be overlooked. A subsidiary factor here may have been some feeling amongst the well-connected that gambling would be a legitimate way of sharing financiers' ill-gotten wealth with those who needed and, in any case, deserved it. At all events, several of the richer and more presentable financiers commonly rubbed shoulders round the gaming table with high nobles. One financier, Gourville, attained the supreme honour of an invitation to gamble with the king and his ladies.[8]

Such a bending of traditional barriers was reinforced by the marriage patterns of financiers' daughters and by other things. It all led to more grandiose imitation of the nobility in ways that society found less forgivable—in particular, that building of châteaux and *hôtels* which was discussed above. Nor was it just a question of the fact of building. Financiers went to enormous expense in decorating their constructions, as did Charles Gruin des Bordes in his house on the quai d'Anjou. The best example of all is Nicolas Fouquet's château at Vaux-le-Vicomte. Fouquet was not by origin or training a financier; but he became thoroughly assimilated to the extravagance of those from whom he borrowed. He went even further, adding a lack of measure that was beyond the most extravagant of financiers, like Henri du Plessis-Guénégaud, Jacques Bordier and Nicolas Monnerot. Fouquet's special quality was expressed in his device: *Quo non ascendet*. It was also to be seen at Vaux. Here it was not just a question of Le Vau's magnificent building. It is necessary to consider too the fêtes given by the *surintendant*.[9] These were of such opulence that they helped to convince Louis XIV that the surintendant and the financiers were destroying the moral fibre of the country, and should therefore be punished severely.

The effortless clichés in which Louis XIV naturally thought reflected a body of opinion in the country that was hostile to financiers. They were considered criminal not merely because they stole money from Crown and people, but also because they failed to observe the canons of social fixity in which the seventeenth century had so strong and fearful a belief. Small wonder was it that, on the one hand, society should behave with contemptuous indifference punctuated by outbursts of archaic violence, and, on the other hand, the financiers should treat society as their oyster to be plundered and exploited at will.

Their failure to fit in does not mean that the financiers were a portent of a new age that was to dawn in the nineteenth century. In a certain sense financiers were a phenomenon of change, in that they helped to provide new recruits for superior functional and social groups. But as an economic force they derived nothing from commercial and industrial prerevolutions like those that were coming into being in the United Provinces and England. The capital which the financiers invested in the royal finances was largely produced from the illegal exploitation of the lower levels of financial administration (like the collection of the *Taille*) and reinvested at higher levels (like loans to the state). The financiers were therefore in this context largely a parasitic growth. Unproductive themselves, they lived almost entirely on the labour of others.

Parasitic though they might be, however, they were a natural and almost predictable outgrowth of the *ancien régime*. Though groups that felt themselves to be both morally and socially superior to financiers spent a good deal of time denigrating them, it is important to stress two things. First, such groups basically tolerated financiers. The Crown needed them for the credit they could provide; and nobles, administrators and magistrates needed them for the dowries that came with financiers' daughters, and for the way in which financiers' descendants filled essential posts in the administrative and social governance of France. Second, if the financiers were parasites, it is difficult to see, from the point of view of peasants and artisans, whether this quality distinguished them markedly from other superior groups in French society during the period of the *ancien régime*.

Notes to this chapter are on pages 258–9

Notes

Abbreviations

AE   Archives du Ministère des Affaires Etrangères
AN   Archives Nationales
BN   Bibliothèque Nationale
MCAN   Minutier Central des Archives Notariales

INTRODUCTION (pages 7–23)

1 Bourgoin, J. *La chasse aux larrons* (Paris 1618), see copy in BN Thoisy 397, 8r ff; F. Véron Duverger de Forbonnais, *Recherches et considérations sur les finances de France depuis 1595 jusqu'à 1721* (2 vols Bâle 1758), 1: 172

2 La Bruyère, J. de. *Les caractères* (ed R. Garapon. Paris 1962), ii, 181, 184–5, 186

3 Buisseret, D. *Sully* (1968), 80–2

4 Ranum, O. A. *Richelieu and the Councillors of Louis XIII* (Oxford 1963), 120–80

5 Forbonnais, 1: 12–15, 119, 241, 290

6 Moreau de Beaumont, J. L. *Mémoires concernant les impositions et droits en Europe et en France* (4 vols Paris 1768–9)

7 Mousnier, R. *La vénalité des offices sous Henri IV et Louis XIII* (Rouen 1945); Esmonin, E. *La taille en Normandie au temps de Colbert (1661–1683)* (Paris 1913)

8 Doucet, R. *Les institutions de la France au XVIe siècle* (2 vols Paris 1948); Zeller, G. *Les institutions du XVIe siècle* (Paris 1948); Marion, M. *Dictionnaire des institutions de la France aux XVIIe et XVIIIe siècles* (Paris 1923); Bosher, J. F. *The Single Duty Project* (1964); Bosher, *French Finances 1770–1795* (Cambridge 1970)

9 Marion, 143

10 *Encyclopédie méthodique. Finances* (3 vols Paris 1784), 2: 203

11 Ford, F. L. *Robe and Sword* (Cambridge, Mass 1953)

12 Pagès, G. *La monarchie d'ancien régime en France* (Paris 1932), 182–215; Rosenberg, H. *Bureaucracy, Aristocracy and Autocracy: the Prussian experience* (Cambridge, Mass 1958), 1–20

13 Loirette, F. 'L'administration royale en Béarn de l'union à l'in-

tendance (1620–1682): Essai sur le rattachement à la France d'une province frontière au XVIIe siècle', *XVIIe siècle*, no 65 (1964), 66–108; Tilly, C. 'Food Supply and Public Order in Modern Europe' (unpublished paper, to appear in *The Building of States in Western Europe*), 23–4

14 Roupnel, G. *La ville et la campagne au XVIIe siècle. Etudes sur les populations du pays dijonnais* (Paris 1955); Bloch, M. *Les caractères originaux de l'histoire rurale française* (2 vols Paris 1931–56); Goubert, P. *Beauvais et le Beauvaisis au XVIIe siècle* (Paris 1960); Le Roy Ladurie, E. *Les paysans de Languedoc* (Paris 1966)

Chapter 1 THE ORDINARY FINANCIAL MACHINE (pages 27–43)

1 See, for example, Martinière, Pinson de la (ed), *Etat de la France* (Paris 1650)

2 Chéruel, P. A. *Mémoires sur la vie publique et privée de Fouquet* (2 vols Paris 1862), 1: 236–7; Lair, J. A. *Nicolas Fouquet, procureur-général, surintendant des finances, ministre d'état de Louis XIV* (2 vols Paris 1890), 1: 316; Martin, G.-L. and Bezançon, M. *Histoire du crédit en France sous le règne de Louis XIV*, vol 1, 'Le crédit public' (Paris 1913), 4–5, 7; Viollet, P. *Le roi et ses ministres pendant les trois derniers siècles de la monarchie* (Paris 1912), 216; Chéruel, *Dictionnaire historique des institutions, moeurs et coutumes de la France* (7th edition, 2 vols Paris 1899), 1: 375

3 Mousnier, 'Le conseil du roi de la mort de Henri IV jusqu'au gouvernement personnel de Louis XIV', *Etudes d'histoire moderne et contemporaine*, 1 (1947), 29–67; Martin, *Crédit public*, 7, 29–30; Choisy, F. T. de, *Mémoires pour servir à l'histoire de Louis XIV* in Petitot and Monmerqué, *Collection de mémoires relatifs à l'histoire de France*, 63: 155–277 (cited hereafter as: Choisy, *Mémoires*), 223–4

4 Viollet, *Le roi et ses ministres*, 215–16; Lair, *Fouquet*, 1: 315

5 Moreau de Beaumont, *Mémoires concernant les impositions* (2nd edition 5 vols Paris 1787–9), 4: 341–691; Chéruel, *Dictionnaire des institutions*, 1: 52–3, 119; 2: 962, 1041, 1050; Forbonnais, 1: 304; BN Thoisy 397, 208r–223v, 385r–386r; Clément, P. (ed), *Lettres, instructions et mémoires de Colbert* (7 vols Paris 1861–82), 6: 103–11

6 Esmonin, *La taille*, 1–7; Moreau de Beaumont, 2: 1–13; Stourm, R. *Les cours des finances. Le budget, son histoire et son mécanisme* (Paris 1899), 31–7; Forbonnais, 1: 10; Lair, *Fouquet*, 1: 309–10

7 Moreau de Beaumont, 2: viii, 18; Esmonin, *La taille*, 27; Forbonnais, 1: 12, 258; Chéruel, *Dictionnaire des institutions*, 2: 1199; Lavisse, E. (ed), *Histoire de France depuis les origines jusqu'à la Révolution* (9 vols Paris 1900–11), 7 (i): 188–9

8 Forbonnais, 1: 11; Moreau de Beaumont, 2: 13–15, 114–16; BN Thoisy 160, 200r; Feillet, A. *La misère au temps de la Fronde et Saint Vincent de Paul* (Paris 1862), passim; Jacquart, J. 'La Fronde des

princes dans la région parisienne et ses conséquences matérielles',
Revue d'histoire moderne et contemporaine, 7 (1960), 257–90

9 Esmonin, *La taille*, 22; Chéruel, *Dictionnaire des institutions*, 1:
376, 378; Moreau de Beaumont, 2: 19–28, 70–114, 190–285; Charmeil, J.-P. *Les trésoriers de France à l'époque de la Fronde* (Paris 1964),
150–8; Marion, *Dictionnaire des institutions*, 257

10 Esmonin, *La taille*, 501; Forbonnais, 1: 273, 291–302

11 Milne, P. *L'impôt des aides sous l'ancien régime (1360–1791)* (Paris
1908), 1–140; Forbonnais, 1: 10, 266, 290; Moreau de Beaumont
(2nd edition), 3: 226–56; Chéruel, *Dictionnaire des institutions*, 2:
568–9; Lair, *Fouquet*, 1: 311, 356–7, 418; AN AP 61, *Dossier* 6

12 Matthews, G. T. *The Royal General Farms in Eighteenth Century
France* (New York 1958), 88–9, 92–5; Beaulieu, E. P. *Les gabelles
sous Louis XIV* (Paris 1903), 20, 49–59

13 Matthews, 99–100; Moreau de Beaumont (2nd edition), 3: 76–7

14 Matthews, 91, 95, 103–4, 108; Beaulieu, 17; Moreau de Beaumont
(2nd edition), 3: 83, 84, 90; Forbonnais, 1: 259, 290

15 Lavisse, 7 (i): 201–2; Forbonnais, 1: 164–6, 281, 290; Moreau de
Beaumont (2nd edition), 3: 347–413; Charléty, S. 'Le régime
douanier de Lyon au XVIIe siècle', *Revue d'histoire de Lyon*, 1
(1902), 487–509

16 Matthews, 38–43, 45, 46; Moreau de Beaumont (2nd edition), 3:
79–82; Beaulieu, 11–15; Milne, 107; Forbonnais, 1: 113–18; BN 500
Colbert 235, 223v; Thoisy 396, 184r

17 Forbonnais, 1: 273, 290

18 Forbonnais, 1: 137, 180; Martin, *Crédit public*, 96, 97, 165; Lair,
Fouquet, 1: 464

19 Martin, *Crédit public*, 25; Cans, A. *L'organisation financière du
clergé de France* (Paris 1909), 145–53; Forbonnais, 1: 180, 209, 251,
268; Blet, P. *Le clergé de France et la monarchie* (2 vols Rome 1959),
2: 83–108; Dent, C. A. 'The French Church and the Monarchy in
the reign of Louis XIV: An Administrative Study' (London University PhD thesis, 1967)

20 Moreau de Beaumont, 2: 188–90; Forbonnais, 1: 192, 290–1, 304
bis, 308–10

21 André, L. *Michel Le Tellier et l'organisation de l'armée monarchique*
(Paris 1906), 303; Doucet, *Institutions*, 2: 609, 645; Martin, *Crédit
public*, 7

22 Audouin, F. *Histoire de l'administration de la guerre* (4 vols Paris
1811), 3: 165–6

23 Forbonnais, 1: 267, 269; Bailly, A. *Histoire financière de la France
depuis les origines de la monarchie jusqu'à la fin de 1786* (2 vols Paris
1830), 1: 409; Joubleau, F. *Etudes sur Colbert ou exposition du
système d'économie politique suivi en France de 1661 à 1683* (2 vols
Paris 1856), 1: 11–14; Clément, P. *Histoire de la vie et de l'administration de Colbert* (Paris 1846), 127

Chapter 2 THE EXTRAORDINARY FINANCIAL MACHINE: RENTES AND TREATIES (pages 44–64)

1 For the early part of this section, I have been much indebted to Schnapper, B. *Les rentes au XVIe siècle* (Paris 1957)
2 Schnapper, 46, 65–6
3 BN Thoisy 157, 253v, 254v
4 Martin, *Crédit public*, 26; Schnapper, 45
5 Martin, *Crédit public*, 23–5; Schnapper, 111, 152–6; Forbonnais, 1: 272; Cans, *Organisation financière du clergé*, 154
6 BN MSS français 16533, 235r–v; 17335, 70r; AN AP 62, *Dossier 24, pièce 2*; Schnapper, 155
7 Schnapper, 156; Martin, *Crédit public*, 26; Forbonnais, 1: 214–15, 220, 221–2, 229, 234–5, 248, 254, 265, 267, 268; Milne, *Aides*, 126; Martin, *Le surintendant Fouquet et les opérations du crédit public* (Paris 1914), 14
8 Cauwès, P. L. 'Les commencements du crédit public en France. Les rentes sur l'Hôtel de Ville au XVIe siècle', *Revue d'économie politique*, 10 (1896), 454 ff, cited by Schnapper, 156; Forbonnais, 1: 273
9 Martin, *Crédit public*, 26, 30; Lair, *Fouquet*, 1: 501–4, 556–7
10 BN MS français 16533, 383r
11 Forbonnais, 1: 254–5; Normand, C. *La bourgeoisie française au XVIIe siècle (1604–1661)* (Paris 1908), 168; Mousnier, 'Comment les français du XVIIe siècle voyaient la constitution', *XVIIe siècle*, nos 25–6 (1955), 23 ff; BN MS français 16533, 491r
12 Forbonnais, 1: 327–8; BN MS français 17335, 70r
13 Schnapper, 156–7; MCAN Etude 51, 548, Docts of 26 April 1659
14 Forbonnais, 1: 222–3, 246; Lecestre, L. (ed), *Mémoires des Gourville* (2 vols Paris 1894), 1: xiii–xiv; BN 500 Colbert 228, 139r
15 Martin, *Crédit public*, 30, 85–7; Forbonnais, 1: 306; BN Thoisy 397, 355r, 381r
16 This section draws on the study of a number of treaties of the 1650s. Discussion of specific treaties occurs in the documents of the Ormesson Archive, and in those of BN Thoisy 147–152

   The word 'treaty' is used here as a translation for the French word *Traité*. It is not a very good translation, but it seemed better to use it in preference to the French word, which might be understandably confused with the customs dues or *Traites* discussed in the previous chapter. As for the choice of 'treaty', it seemed better to use this word rather than, for example, 'contract', which existed in its own right in seventeenth-century France, and was not the same thing as a *Traité*. To be precise, a *Traité* was a specific kind of *Contrat*—of what kind, the following section will show
17 BN Thoisy 149, 15r–23r; 397, 151r–v, 381r; 500 Colbert 235, 233r–v; AN AP 61, Doct 3
18 BN Thoisy 160, 89r–91v, particularly 89v

19 Mousnier, *Vénalité*, 1–19, 199–216, 506–14; Doucet, *Institutions*, 1: 410–11; Lair, *Fouquet*, 2: 34–7; MCAN Etude 51, 544, Doct of 11 December 1657

20 Mousnier, *Vénalité*, 397–8; Forbonnais, 1: 329

21 BN Thoisy 160, 49r; Forbonnais, 1: 260, 329; Mousnier, *Vénalité*, 366–9; Lair, *Fouquet*, 1: 403–5

22 Mousnier, *Vénalité*, 133, 134, 143; Martin, *Crédit public*, 203–4; Ranum, *Richelieu and the Councillors*, 138–9

23 Mousnier, *Vénalité*, 135–42; Forbonnais, 1: 183–7, 266; Robin, P. *La compagnie des secrétaires du roi* (Paris 1933), 23–7; BN MS français 18218, 5v; AN AP 61, Doct 11, 1r

24 Mousnier, *Vénalité*, 365–6; Beaulieu, 54–5; AN AP 60, Doct 10, 5r; AP 62, Doct 13, 2v, 4v; Doct 17, 3r; AP 73, *Dossier 2, pièce* b; BN *Imprimés* F 47009 (*pièce 23 : Déclaration du roi* of 24 December 1657); Thoisy 151, 321r–324v; 397, 170r–v

25 Mousnier, *Vénalité*, 394; BN MS français 18219

26 Forbonnais, 1: 266, 290; BN MSS français 18218, 3r–5v; 18228, 1r, 2v, 5r–v; AN AP 62, *Dossier 24, pièces* 3, 7

27 AN AP 70, *Dossier 6, pièce* 6; BN Clairambault 766, 511, 518

28 Forbonnais, 1: 236; Martin, *Crédit public*, 20; BN MS français 4222, 290r; Thoisy 160, 207r, 208r; Lecestre, *Mémoires de Gourville*, 1: xiv, 141–5

29 AN AP 62, *Dossier 24, pièces* 7, 11; BN Thoisy 160, 30r–35r, 63r; Chéruel, *Dictionnaire des institutions*, 1: 700–1

30 BN Thoisy 148, 4r–7v

31 BN MS français 18228 (Treaties for 1655, no 5)

32 AN AP 61, Doct 6, 1r, 2r

33 BN MS français 18218, 45r; 500 Colbert 235, 245r; Thoisy 151, 213r; 157, 17r, 23r, 25r, 157r, 171r–188r; Lair, *Fouquet*, 1: 446; AN AP 61, Doct 1, 12v–13r; AP 62, Doct 1, 2r; Ormesson, O. Lefebvre d'. *Journal* (ed P. A. Chéruel. 2 vols Paris 1860–1), 2: 11

34 See BN MS français 18228

Chapter 3 THE EXTRAORDINARY FINANCIAL MACHINE: SHORT-TERM LOANS AND FRAUD (pages 65–91)

1 British Museum 5423 e 16 (*Arrêt de la Chambre de Justice*, 29 December 1662); AN AP 74, *Dossier 2, pièce* e

2 Sully's role is too well known to need elaboration. Effiat, on the other hand, has been left in a historical limbo, which is rather unfair. He was appointed to the Surintendance in 1626, and died in office in 1632. He brought considerable ability and application to the problems confronting him. His analysis of the weaknesses of the Crown's financial position, made in a report to the *Assemblée des Notables* of 1626, is highly intelligent. It is quoted fully in Forbonnais, 1: 188–203

3 Forbonnais, 1: 173
4 Saint-Simon, *Mémoires* (ed A. de Boislisle, L. Lecestre, J. de
   Boislisle. 43 vols 2nd impression. Paris 1923–8), 13: 311; BN MSS
   français 14018, 169r–170r; 18220, passim; Boislisle, A.
   de *La chambre des comptes de Paris—pièces justificatives pour servir à
   l'histoire des premiers présidents, 1506–1791* (Nogent-le-Rotrou 1873),
   lv; Martin, *Crédit public*, 14–30; Forbonnais, 1: 255
5 Kerviler, R. *Répertoire général de bio-bibliographie bretonne. Livre I:
   Les bretons* (17 vols Rennes 1886–1908), 14: 276–304; Saint-Simon,
   29: 141–6; Chéruel, *Mémoires sur . . . Fouquet*, 1: 2–3, 5, 6, 7–8, 28,
   138–43, 144 ff, 218–19
6 Lair, *Fouquet*, 1: 338–9; Chéruel, *Mémoires sur . . . Fouquet*, 1: 223–
   35, 263; BN 500 Colbert 194, 289r–290v
7 Lair, *Fouquet*, 1: 440
8 AN AP 71, *Dossier 9*
9 BN MS français 16533, 15r–17r
10 BN 500 Colbert 235, 22v–25v
11 Lair, *Fouquet*, 1: 479; 2: 23–4, 52
12 BN Thoisy 156, 51v. Copies of the documents setting out the terms
   of loans and payments of interest are contained in BN MSS français
   18221–18227
13 Eg, BN MS français 18228 (Treaties of 1655, no 16)
14 See BN MS français 18228, 12r (1655), 43v (1657), 56v (1658), 67r–
   72r (1659). The total given for 1655 does not mention the level of
   Remise. For 1656, no attempt at adding up the total of loans appears
   to have been made. The existence of three blank sides after the last
   loan mentioned implies that the list for 1656 may not be complete.
   Nevertheless it seemed worth while to add up the total after *Remise*
   of the loans actually mentioned. The figure given in brackets as the
   final total for 1656 is the result
15 BN 500 Colbert 235, 312r ff; Thoisy 397, 382v; AN AP 61, Doct 3,
   32v, Doct 4, 51v–53v; AP 62, Doct 1, 25v; AP 74, *Dossier 4, pièce* h;
   Ormesson, *Journal*, 2: 295, 780; Lair, *Fouquet*, 1: 354–5; Funck-
   Brentano, F. *Les lettres de cachet à Paris. Etude suivie d'une liste des
   prisonniers de la Bastille (1659–1789)* (Paris 1903), 20
16 Chéruel, *Mémoires sur . . . Fouquet*, 1: 330
17 AN AP 61, Doct 1, especially 7r, Doct 4, 11r ff, 18v; AP 70, *Dossier 5*,
   Docts 1, 2, 3; Lair, *Fouquet*, 1: 425
18 AN AP 61, Doct 4, 19r–20v, 26r–27v; Chéruel, *Mémoires sur . . .
   Fouquet*, 2: 356–7
19 BN MS français 14018, 289r; Clément, *Lettres . . . de Colbert*, 7: 167;
   Lecestre, *Mémoires de Gourville*, 1: 145; Lair, *Fouquet*, 1: 425–7;
   Chéruel, *Mémoires sur . . . Fouquet*, 1: 384–6; 2: 162–3
20 AN AP 61, Doct 4, 40r, 56v–57v, 66r–v, Doct 6, 11r ff
21 Chéruel, *Mémoires sur . . . Fouquet*, 2: 67–70
22 Chéruel, *Mémoires sur . . . Fouquet*, 2: 73–6
23 Hartung, F. and Mousnier, R. 'Quelques problèmes concernant la

monarchie absolue'. *Comitato internazionale di scienze storiche. X congresso, 1955. Relazioni*, 4, 3–55, see especially pp 44–5

24 BN MS français 7625, 504r–v
25 BN MSS français 7625, 505r–v, 525r–v, 527r–v; 18423, 92r–389r; Thoisy 156, 2r–22r
26 Forbonnais, 1 : 267; Martin, *Le surintendant Fouquet*, 30–1, 39–45
27 Saint-Simon, 11 : 209–10; AN AP 60, Doct 5, iv, 2v–3r; AP 62, Doct 1, 10v; BN MSS français 10229, 514r–515r; 14018, 215v, 248r; Thoisy 156, 547r–554r, 561r; Lair, *Fouquet*, 1 : 336
28 Saint-Simon, 10 : 108; BN MS français 18423, 106v; Thoisy 397, 382v; AN AP 62, Doct 1, 9r–v
29 BN Thoisy 157, 12r; 500 Colbert 235, 51r–52r; 236, 40v, 235r; Saint-Simon, 22 : 226
30 BN MS français 18423, 104r, 148r–159r, 160v, 187r
31 BN Thoisy 156, 50v, 51r, 51v
32 Martin, *Crédit public*, 86; BN MSS français 7625, 506r–v; 18423, 386v; AN AP 61, Doct 3, 7r–8r, 23v–24r; AP 62, Doct 18, passim
33 BN Thoisy 156, 52r–53v
34 Boislisle, *Chambre des Comptes*, 465; BN 500 Colbert 236, 41r–v; Bailly, *Histoire financière*, 1 : 419
35 Martin, *Crédit public*, 9
36 Forbonnais, 1 : 266–7
37 AN AP 74, *Dossier 3, pièce 6*
38 AN AP 60 Doct 5, 6r
39 AN AP 61, Doct 4, passim
40 BN Thoisy 397, 381r–383r; AN AP 61, Doct 3

Chapter 4 ACCOUNTING (pages 92–109)

1 BN MS français 4222, 196r–v
2 Forbonnais, 1 : 187–203
3 The organisation of the Contrôle-général was constantly changing. Sometimes there was one contrôleur-général on his own, sometimes there were two. At times the post was left vacant, as in the years before 1643, a period during which the functions of the post were combined with those of the intendants des finances. See: Griselle, E. (ed), *Formulaire de lettres de François Ier à Louis XIV et Etat de la France dressé en 1642* (Paris 1919), 240; Marion, *Dictionnaire des institutions*, 143; Chéruel, *Dictionnaire des institutions*, 1 : 227–8
4 BN MS français 4222, 197r–v
5 Martin, *Crédit public*, 16, 18
6 BN MS français 14018, 169r–170r; MS français na 9735, 275v; Chéruel, *Mémoires sur . . . Fouquet*, 1 : 28, 149; Chéruel, *Histoire de France sous le ministère de Mazarin* (3 vols Paris 1882), 2 : 26; Lecestre, *Mémoires de Gourville*, 1 : 141; BN Thoisy 160, 49r
7 BN MS français na 9735, 277r; MS français 14018, 226v–227r
8 Depping, G. 'Un banquier protestant en France au XVIIe siècle.

Barthélemy Hervart', *Revue historique*, 10 (1879), 285–338; 11 (1879), 63–80; Martin, *Le surintendant Fouquet*, 3–5, 13

9 AN AP 61, Doct 4, 62v

10 Lair, *Fouquet*, 1: 348; Chéruel, *Mémoires sur* ... *Fouquet*, 2: 13–19, 361; Chéruel, *Ministère de Mazarin*, 3: 275–6; Ormesson, *Journal*, 2: 94–5

11 AN AP 61, Doct 3, 28r–v, Doct 4, 3r, 6v, 62v–63r, Doct 28, 1r–v; AP 62, Doct 1, 10r–12v, 50r, 52v–53r, 54r; BN MS français 18423, 385r; Thoisy 157, 129v; 500 Colbert 233, 371 ff; MS français na 9735, 276r; Lair, *Fouquet*, 2: 15; Clément, *Lettres* ... *de Colbert*, 2: cxcvi–cxcix, cc

12 Charmeil, J.-P. *Les trésoriers de France à l'époque de la Fronde* (Paris 1964), 256–7; Martin, *Crédit public*, 10; BN MS français 4222, 207r, 250r

13 Charmeil, 257–60; Chéruel, *Mémoires sur* ... *Fouquet*, 1: 286–7; BN MS français na 9735, 361r, 386r, 387v, 392r–v

14 BN Thoisy 397, 307r

15 Boislisle, *Chambre des Comptes*, xxi–xxii; Chéruel, *Dictionnaire des institutions*, 1: 429

16 Boislisle, xxv

17 Boislisle, 465

18 Boislisle, xxii–xxiii, li–lv, 391; BN MS français 14018, 272v; Thoisy 157, 200r; 397, 298 *bis* r. For a more systematic discussion of the penetration of the Chambre des Comptes by financiers, see below, p 204

19 Boislisle, xxxii

20 BN Thoisy 396, 296r–309v

21 Boislisle, xxxi

22 Forbonnais, 1: 73, 175–6; BN Thoisy 397, 97r–v

23 BN Thoisy 397, 172r–175r

24 AN 4999

25 Various copies of the edict remain, eg BN Thoisy 397, 241r ff; Clairambault 766, 1 ff

26 Chéruel, *Mémoires sur* ... *Fouquet*, 2: 271–440; Lair, *Fouquet*, 2: 64–432; Mongrédien, G. *L'affaire Fouquet* (Paris 1956); BN 500 Colbert 228–237

27 BN Thoisy 397, 287r, 291r–294v, 385r, 472r–473r, 565r–618r

28 Chéruel, *Mémoires sur* ... *Fouquet*, 2: 274–5, 356–8, 371, 436; Lair, *Fouquet*, 2: 239, 241; BN 500 Colbert 237, 151r ff

29 BN Thoisy 397, 660r–665r; Clairambault 766, 499–523; 500 Colbert 233–4

30 British Museum 5423 e 16 (unpaginated): *Arrêt de la Chambre de Justice portant défenses aux Commissaires du Châtelet et à tous autres d'aller dans les maisons des marchands et négotiants s'il ne leur est particulièrement ordonné* ... 29 December 1662

Chapter 5 ORIGINS (pages 113–31)

1   Clément, *Lettres . . . de Colbert*, 1: 73; Chéruel, P. A. and d'Avenel,
    G. (eds). *Lettres de Mazarin* (9 vols Paris 1872–1906), 1: xi–xii, 581;
    2: 943; 4: 760; Martin, *Le surintendant Fouquet*, 11; Saint-Simon,
    13: 311; Schnapper, *Rentes*, 156–7
2   Roupnel, G. *La ville et la campagne*, discusses this point at length
3   Esmonin, E. *Etudes sur la France des XVIIe et XVIIIe siècles* (Paris
    1964), 394; BN PO 861, Entry 19320, 194r–199v; Charmeil, 258,
    413; AN AP 62, Doct 21; Clément, *Lettres . . . de Colbert*, 1: 100
4   Eg Normand, C. *La bourgeoisie française au XVIIe siècle* (Paris 1908)
5   Chéruel, *Mémoires sur . . . Fouquet*, 2: 387
6   Moreau, C. (ed), *Choix de Mazarinades* (2 vols Paris 1853), 1: 113–
    39: 'Catalogue des partisans, ensemble leur généalogie et extraction,
    vie, moeurs et fortune', 26 January 1649 (cited hereafter as *Catalogue
    des partisans*), 114
7   BN 500 Colbert 236, 36r; Thoisy 152, 29r; MCAN Etude 51, 521,
    Doct of 31 March 1648
8   MCAN Etude 51, 544, Doct of 8 October 1657; BN Thoisy 152,
    107r
9   Labatut, J.-P. 'Situation sociale du quartier du Marais pendant la
    Fronde parlementaire 1648–9', *XVIIe siècle*, no 38 (1958), 55–81,
    especially 56–7
10 MCAN Etude 51, 280, passim; 522, Doct of 31 August 1648
11 Charmeil, 258
12 Montagné, P. *Larousse gastronomique* (Eng trans by N. Froud and
    C. Turgeon, 1961), 984–5
13 Charmeil, 259
14 Lecestre, *Mémoires de Gourville*, 1: i–iii
15 BN Thoisy 157, 113r; Clairambault 766, 557
16 BN Thoisy 150, 76r
17 BN PO 861, Entry 19320, 195v
18 Charmeil, 37, 459; BN MS français 14018, 249v
19 Lecestre, *Mémoires de Gourville*, 1: ix–xi
20 Clément, *Lettres . . . de Colbert*, 1: 467–86

Chapter 6 SUCCESS AND FAILURE (pages 132–63)

1   BN PO 861, Entry 19320, 198r; Charmeil, 258; AN AP 62, Doct 1,
    51v–54r
2   AN AP 62, Doct 17
3   Lecestre, *Mémoires de Gourville*, 1: 195
4   AN AP 61, Doct 4, 3r–v; Doct 13, 7v; BN 500 Colbert 235, 112v–
    114r
5   Charmeil, 45, 131; Chéruel, *Lettres de Mazarin*, 3: 459
6   Martin, *Le surintendant Fouquet*, 7

7   Charmeil, 257
8   Lecestre, *Mémoires de Gourville*, 1: ci
9   Charmeil, 411; *Catalogue des partisans*, 134
10 AN AP 62, Doct 21, 2r
11 BN Thoisy 397, 313r; Martin, *Le surintendant Fouquet*, 7
12 BN Thoisy 147, 134r, 253r, 257r; *Catalogue des Partisans*, 131–2
13 Chéruel, *Lettres de Mazarin*, 3: 936; 6: 570; 8: 753; Clément, *Lettres . . . de Colbert*, 1: 463
14 BN MS français 14018, 289r; AN AP 70, *Dossier* 6, *pièce* 6
15 BN PO 312, Entry 6844, 99r; De La Chenaye des Bois, F. A. A. and Badier, *Dictionnaire de la noblesse* (3rd edition 19 vols Paris 1863–76), 11: col 6
16 Lecestre, *Mémoires de Gourville*, 1: iii–xi; BN Thoisy 397, 306v
17 *Dictionnaire de la noblesse*, 11: cols 6–7; BN Thoisy 151, 391r
18 BN PO 861, Entry 19320, 194v–196r
19 Chéruel, *Lettres de Mazarin*, 7: 506
20 BN Thoisy 157, 116r–120r
21 AE France 176, 21r–133r; BN Imprimés série in 4to F23703, *pièces* 2, 40, 85, 91; Dent, C. A. *The French Church and the Monarchy*, 258–9
22 BN Thoisy 397, 338r
23 AN AP 60, Doct 10, 3r–4r, 17r–18r; Lair, *Fouquet*, 1: 360–1; BN 500 Colbert 235, 238r–244r
24 BN Clairambault 766, 499–523
25 BN Thoisy 397, 170r–v
26 Betcherman, L.-R. 'Balthazar Gerbier—a Renaissance man in early Stuart England' (University of Toronto PhD dissertation 1968), 12–34, 195–7, 205–21, 246, 264
27 Martin, *Le surintendant Fouquet*, 22; Chéruel, *Lettres de Mazarin*, 6: 678
28 Matthews, *General Farms*, 46
29 Chéruel, *Lettres de Mazarin*, 1: 581; 9: 817
30 Martin, *Le surintendant Fouquet*, 3–5
31 BN Clairambault 766, 513
32 Clément, *Lettres . . . de Colbert*, 1: 369, 370; BN MS français 7718, 1022–31
33 BN Clairambault 766, 499–518
34 Funck-Brentano, *Lettres de cachet*, 21–4
35 Chéruel, *Mémoires sur . . . Fouquet*, 2: 441–63
36 Funck-Brentano, 22; Charmeil, 136
37 BN Thoisy 157, 113r–188r; Cosnac, D. de, *Mémoires*, 2: 29
38 BN Thoisy 157, 14r–16r
39 Chéruel, *Mémoires sur . . . Fouquet*, 2: 334

Chapter 7   THE USES OF MONEY (pages 164–90)

1   Chéruel, *Mémoires sur . . . Fouquet*, 1: 286–7
2   MCAN Etude 51, 544, two Docts of 11 December 1657
3   Lair, *Fouquet*, 1: 315
4   Lecestre, *Mémoires de Gourville*, 1: 146
5   Clément, *Lettres . . . de Colbert*, 1: 345–6
6   Floquet, *Etudes sur la vie de Bossuet*, 1: 156–7
7   MCAN Etude 51, 548, Doct of 3 January 1659; BN PO 861, Entry 19320, 148r
8   BN MSS français 7620, 36r; 18423, 406r; MCAN Etude 51, 554, Doct of 13 March 1662; Mousnier, *Lettres et mémoires adressés au chancelier Séguier* (2 vols Paris 1964), 1: 171–2; 2: 1033–4; Saint-Germain, J. *La Reynie et la police au grand siècle* (Paris 1962), 19
9   BN PO 861, Entry 19320, 148r; MS français 18423, 407r
10 Clément, *Lettres . . . de Colbert*, 1: 520–30
11 BN PO 861, Entry 19320, 148r; 500 Colbert 235, 271v; Thoisy 160, 72r
12 Clément, *Lettres . . . de Colbert*, 2 (i): 56; BN 500 Colbert 235, 271v
13 Topographical information on Paris in the seventeenth century was drawn from numerous sources, in particular the following works: Friedmann, A. *Paris, ses rues ses paroisses du moyen âge à la révolution* (Paris 1959), see especially pp 231, 308, and map 'Les paroisses de Paris d'après les rôles de la taille vers 1292'; Christ, Y. and others. *Le Marais* (Paris 1964); Hillairet, J. *Dictionnaire historique des rues de Paris* (2 vols Paris, 1963); Blunt, A. *Art and Architecture in France 1500–1800* (1953); Hillairet, *La rue de Richelieu* (Paris 1966)
14 MCAN Etude 51, 544, Doct of 7 September 1657
15 MCAN Etude 51, 505, Doct of 8 July 1640; 522, Doct of 31 August 1648
16 MCAN Etude 51, 504, Doct of 10 January 1640
17 BN Clairambault 766, 402
18 BN PO 35, Entry 742, 8r
19 MCAN Etude 51, 544, Doct of 11 December 1657
20 BN PO 861, Entry 19320, 27r
21 BN PO 1281, Entry 28835, 13r
22 MCAN Etude 51, 548, Doct of 28 January 1659
23 Blunt, 164
24 BN PO 35, Entry 742, 8r
25 Hillairet, *Rue de Richelieu*, 146–50
26 BN PO 35, Entry 742, 22r
27 BN PO 312, Entry 6844, 8r; 500 Colbert 235, 261r; MCAN Etude 51, 521, Doct of 31 March 1648; 544, Doct of 14 November 1657; Chéruel, *Lettres de Mazarin*, 7: 14–15
28 BN PO 35, Entry 742, 8r–9v
29 MCAN Etude 51, 522, Doct of 20 May 1648

30 BN PO 861, Entry 19320, 148r; Thoisy 397, 312r–v

31 Bitton, D. *The French Nobility in Crisis 1560–1640* (Stanford 1969), 92–117

32 Loyseau, C. *Cinq livres du droit des offices* (Paris, 1613), 131, para 20

33 Lecestre, *Mémoires de Gourville*, 1: xv–xvi, 149, 152–3, 195–6

34 BN MS français 14018, 249r, 317v–318r; PO 35, Entry 742, 7r; MCAN Etude 51, 521, Doct of 31 March 1648; 544, Doct of 7 September 1657; 548, Doct of 14 April 1659; AE France 894, 23r–28r; Lair, *Fouquet*, 1: 425; *Dictionnaire de la noblesse*, 8: col 53; Chéruel, *Lettres de Mazarin*, 3: 921; 7: 14–15, 506; 9: 71

35 AE France 894, 23r–28r: *Lettres patentes* confirming the elevation of the barony of Mayence to a *marquisat*, and the resulting *marquisat* to a *duché et pairie*, January 1655

36 MCAN Etude 51, 521, Doct of 31 March 1648

37 BN PO 861, Entry 19320, 148r; MCAN Etude 51, 279, Doct 50 (18 April 1641), 82 (15 July 1638)

38 Labatut, J.-P. 'Aspects de la fortune de Bullion', *XVIIe siècle*, no 60 (1963), 11–39

39 Kerviler, *Bio-bibliographie bretonne*, 14: 278; BN 500 Colbert 235, 16v, 247r; Thoisy 400, 413v; MCAN Etude 51, 544, Doct of 25 September 1657; 548, Docts of 28 February and 14 April 1659; Chéruel, *Mémoires sur . . . Fouquet*, 1: 394; 2: 220–1

40 BN MS français 14018, 147v–148r; Clairambault 766, 401

41 Chéruel, *Lettres de Mazarin*, 1: 520–30; Clément, *Lettres . . . de Colbert*, 1: 335, 349, 363

42 Furetière, A. *Le roman bourgeois* (ed F. Tulov. Paris 1919), 33–4

43 BN PO 312, Entry 6844, 40r–v, 42r–v

44 BN PO 35, Entry 742, 7r–38r

45 See, in particular, works by Blunt and Christ cited above, and Hautecoeur, L. *Histoire de l'architecture classique en France* (7 vols Paris 1943–57)

46 Christ, 195, 235, 243–4, 265–6; Babelon, J.-P. *Demeures parisiennes sous Henri IV et Louis XIII* (Paris 1965), 272; Blunt, 118–19, 203, 211

47 Christ, 249–51; Blunt, 53, 150, 155, 164, and plate 107A

48 Babelon, 277

49 Hautecoeur, 1: 91; Blunt, 6

50 Blunt, 159–61; *Catalogue des Partisans*, 115; Chéruel, *Mémoires sur . . . Fouquet*, 1: 380–2; 2: 6–7, 178–83, 222–7

51 MCAN Etude 51, 279, Doct 50; Blunt, 149–50, 210 (note 54), 268, 285 (note 44); Hautecoeur, 1: 508–9

52 Buisseret, *Sully*, especially 187–9; Hautecoeur, 1: 531–7, 578–9

Chapter 8 RELATIONSHIPS BETWEEN THE FINANCIERS AND THE WORLD AT LARGE (pages 191–207)

1 Chéruel, *Lettres de Mazarin*, 2: 888; 3: 150
2 Chéruel, *Lettres de Mazarin*, 1: xii–xviii; 4: 206; 5: 594, 637, 701
3 Kerviler, *Bio-bibliographie bretonne*, 14: 282; Chéruel, *Mémoires sur . . . Fouquet*, 1: 5, 7–8, 235
4 Charmeil, 259; BN MS français 14018, 194r
5 Saint-Simon, 22: 252–5; Chéruel, *Mémoires sur . . . Fouquet*, 1: 182, 230; 2: 391; Clément, *Lettres . . . de Colbert*, 1: 98
6 Chéruel, *Lettres de Mazarin*, 4: 712
7 AN AP 61, Doct 6, 4r
8 Lair, *Fouquet*, 1: 331
9 *Dictionnaire de la noblesse*, 15: col 782; Saint-Simon, 10: 108; BN MS français 18423, 115v; Clément, *Lettres . . . de Colbert*, 1: 56; Chéruel, *Lettres de Mazarin*, 1: 849
10 BN MS français 14018, 147v, 169r–170r; PO 419, Entry 9373, 31r; Chéruel, *Lettres de Mazarin*, 9: 747; Saint-Simon, 2: 284–5; 6: 38; Clément, *Lettres . . . de Colbert*, 1: 60; 2 (i), 241–2; MCAN Etude 51, 548, Doct of 26 April 1659; Clément, *Histoire de Colbert et de son administration* (2nd edition 2 vols Paris 1874), 1: 152–3
11 Charmeil, 37
12 MCAN Etude 51, 554, Doct of 30 January 1662
13 Saint-Simon, 1: 151; 6: 38; 29: 141–6; BN MS français 14018, 147v–148r, 169r–170r, 215v, 217v, 248r, 306r; MS français na 9735, 275v; Kerviler, *Bio-bibliographie bretonne*, 14: 282; Chéruel, *Mémoires sur Fouquet*, 1: 5–6, 235; Chéruel, *Lettres de Mazarin*, 5: 7; MCAN Etude 51, 544, Doct of 18 September 1657
14 BN PO 861, Entry 19320, 27r; MS français 14018, 272v
15 Charmeil, 35, 45, 131; BN Thoisy 397, 298 *bis* r
16 Chéruel, *Lettres de Mazarin*, 3: 150, 880; 8: 743, 753; Clément, *Lettres . . . de Colbert*, 1: 37–8, 463; 2 (i): 227; Saint-Simon, 19: 343–4
17 BN MSS français 14018, 145r–v; 16533, 15v; Mousnier, *Lettres et mémoires*, 2: 1210; Lecestre, *Mémoires de Gourville*, 1: 169; Chéruel, *Mémoires sur . . . Fouquet*, 1: 485; Chéruel, *Lettres de Mazarin*, 1: 132–3, 157, 924–5; 5: 601; 7: 609
18 Kerviler, *Bio-bibliographie bretonne*, 14: 280–1; BN MS français 10484; *Dictionnaire de la noblesse*, 15: col 783; Chéruel, *Lettres de Mazarin*, 2: 1065; 4: 587, 740; 5: 65, 514, 535, 540, 541; 7: 666, 683; 9: 922; Chéruel, *Ministère de Mazarin*, 2: 28–9; Clément, *Lettres . . . de Colbert*, 1: 212; MCAN Etude 51, 544, Doct of 30 September 1657
19 AE France 820, 46r–79r; BN Thoisy 147, 191r; 157, 124v; 500 Colbert 235, 241r; Clément, *Lettres . . . de Colbert*, 1: 272
20 BN MSS français 7718, 857–64; 14018, 148r–v; Thoisy 396, 214r; Chéruel, *Lettres de Mazarin*, 2: 697, 734; 4: 604

Chapter 9 THE FAMILY, MARRIAGE AND SOCIAL
MOBILITY (pages 208–31)

1 A considerable amount has been done in recent years in historical
demography, particularly on the family. The names of Pierre Goubert, Louis Henry, T. H. Hollingsworth, Lawrence Stone and E. A.
Wrigley spring immediately to mind. The following chapter depends
to a large extent on things that they, and people like Peter Laslett and
Philippe Ariès, have written and said. A brief selection of the works
of these writers would include: Goubert, P. *Beauvais et le Beauvaisis
au XVIIIe siècle* (Paris 1960); Henry, L. *Manuel de démographie
historique* (Geneva/Paris 1967); Hollingsworth, T. H. *Historical
Demography* (New York 1969); Stone, L. *The Crisis of the Aristocracy
1557–1641* (Oxford 1965); Wrigley, E. A. *Population and History*
(New York 1969); Laslett, P. *The World we have lost* (London 1965);
Ariès, P. *L'enfant et la vie familiale sous l'ancien régime* (Paris 1960.
English translation by R. Baldick under the title *Centuries of Childhood*, 1962)

On the other hand, it is important to be clear that the present
chapter makes no attempt to discuss the family with the precision
that those closely interested in historical demography have achieved,
nor does it seek to answer many of the questions that concern such
people. The size of families (that is to say the number of children
born and the number that survived infancy), the frequency of preg-
nancies, the patterns of rearing of children, the limitation of conception, the length of marriage, these and many other related topics are
beyond the scope of the present inquiry, which is concerned with
different problems

2 BN Thoisy 157, 126v–127r; 500 Colbert 235, 238r–244r, 257v;
Catalogue des partisans, 113

3 BN MS français 7620, 257r, 265v; 500 Colbert 235, 21v

4 BN MS français 18423, 106r–v, 115v; Thoisy 156, 38r, 55r; 397,
301v, 303r–v; *Catalogue des partisans*, 134; Saint-Simon, 18: 246

5 Kerviler, *Bio-bibliographie bretonne*, 14: 278; Clément, *Lettres . . . de
Colbert*, 1: 478

6 BN 500 Colbert 235, 230r–v

7 Esmonin, *Etudes sur la France*, 394; Clément, *Lettres . . . de Colbert*,
1: 246

8 *Dictionnaire de la noblesse*, 9: cols 6–9

9 BN MS français 18423, 406r

10 BN PO 1281, Entry 28835, 74r

11 BN PO 408, Entry 9101, 107r

12 BN MS français 14018, 342r–343r; Clément, *Lettres . . . de Colbert*,
2 (i): cclxxix

13 BN PO 1331, Entry 30128, 17r

14 BN PO 1284, Entry 28897, 15r

I

15 *Dictionnaire de la noblesse*, 9: cols 7–8
16 BN PO 861, Entry 19320, 198r
17 Clément, *Lettres . . . de Colbert*, 1: 478
18 Dejean, E. *Un prélat indépendant au XVIIe siècle—Nicolas Pavillon* (Paris 1909), 1; MCAN Etude 51, 530, Doct of 7 September 1652
19 Dent, C. A. *The French Church and the Monarchy*, 508–9
20 BN PO 408, Entry 9101, 107r
21 Charmeil, 136
22 BN MS français 14018, 328v
23 BN PO 1019, Entry 23322, 38r
24 Clément, *Lettres . . . de Colbert*, 1: 478
25 BN PO 861, Entry 19320, 198r–v
26 BN PO 87, Entry 1803, 38r
27 BN PO 1281, Entry 28835, 74r
28 *Dictionnaire de la noblesse*, 3: col 36
29 BN PO 861, Entry 19320, 197v
30 BN PO 408, Entry 9101, 107r
31 BN Thoisy 396, 296r–297v; 397, 97v, 301v, 303r–v, 315r; Lecestre, *Mémoires de Gourville*, 1: 180
32 Floquet, 2: 138
33 Saint-Simon, 5: 332–54
34 BN MS français 7655, 82v–83r
35 *Dictionnaire de la noblesse*, 3: col 36; 11: col 8
36 BN PO 861, Entry 19320, 198r–v
37 Clément, *Lettres . . . de Colbert*, 1: 478
38 BN PO 1019, Entry 23322, 39r
39 See MCAN Etude 51, 554, Docts of 30 January and 4 February 1662
40 BN PO 861, Entry 19320, 198r–v
41 *Dictionnaire de la noblesse*, 15: col 782–7

CONCLUSION (pages 232–43)

1 *Dictionnaire de la noblesse*, 11: cols 6–9; Ormesson, *Journal*, 2: 73
2 Clément, *Lettres . . . de Colbert*, 1: 369, 370; 2: 771 ff; BN MS français 14018, 342v
3 The most compendious secondary source for this field is Aston, T. (ed), *Crisis in Europe 1540–1640* (1965). See also: Lublinskaya, A. D. *French Absolutism: the crucial phase, 1620–1629* (Cambridge 1968); Stone, *Crisis of the Aristocracy*; Bitton, *French Nobility in Crisis*; Goubert, *Beauvais et le Beauvaisis*; Goubert, *Louis XIV et vingt millions de français* (Paris 1966); Le Roy Ladurie, *Paysans de Languedoc*
4 See AE France 188, 144r–153r. This is a series of very violent protestations made by a group of members of the exclusively noble *Ordre du Saint-Esprit* in 1657 against a number of supposed usurpations of their privileges by financial administrators
5 Loyseau, *Cinq livres du droit des offices*; Loyseau, *Traité des ordres et*

simples dignités (Paris 1613); Bossuet, J. B. 'Sermon sur la providence', *Oeuvres choisies* (5 vols Paris 1903–4), 5: 309–20, especially pp 313, 318

6   Loyseau, *Cinq livres*, 131; Bitton, 111
7   Conrart, *Mémoires*, 265–6; AE France 894, 171r–178r, 196r–207r
8   Lecestre, *Mémoires de Gourville*, 1: 176
9   Lair, *Fouquet*, 1: 480 ff, 519–35; Cheruel, *Mémoires sur . . . Fouquet*, 1: 178–83, 222–7; Blunt, 159–61

Bibliography

ARCHIVE MATERIAL

A   ARCHIVES NATIONALES

1. GENERAL SERIES

P 4999	*Chambre de Justice.* 1654
V² 14	*Secrétaires du Roi*
V² 31	*Titres généraux des Secrétaires du Roi* (1387–1695)
V² 32–3	*Lettres de Provision d'office*
X² B 1228	*Parlement de Paris: Interrogatoires des financiers Martin Tabouret, Andre Canto, Jean Lombard et Germain Chalanges.* 1648–9
Z¹ᵃ 473	*Etats généraux des officiers de la Maison du Roi 1643–1657*
Z¹ᵃ 883	*Taxes de la Chambre de Justice* [case of Toussaint Levesque, 23–4 November 1666]

2. PRIVATE ARCHIVES (ARCHIVES PRIVEES)

AN 156 mi AP 60–74 (Fonds d'Ormesson)

AP 60

Dossier 1: *Premier interrogatoire de M Fouquet, 4 mars 1662 et jours suivants,* 147 folios

Dossier 2: *Second interrogatoire de . . . Fouquet, 7 juin 1662 . . .,* 44 folios

Dossier 3: *Troisième interrogatoire de . . . Fouquet avec les confrontations qui lui ont été faites 21 juin 1662 . . .,* 48 folios

Dossier 4: *Information pour le procureur-général du Roi, demandeur et accusateur, contre messire Nicolas Fouquet, deffendeur et accusé, 17 juin 1662 . . .,* 36 folios

Dossier 5: *Interrogatoire de M Jeanin de Castille . . . 1 avril 1662 . . .,* 21 folios

Dossier 8: *Interrogatoires des sieurs Maridor et Deslandes, ensemble leurs confrontations avec M Fouquet 8 juin 1662,* 10 folios

Dossier 10: *Dépositions et Déclarations de Béringhen, Mallet, Châtelain, les sieurs Rambouillet, Benoît, Apoil et Doublet 9 février 1662, 28 mai, 6 juin, 16 juillet, 3 septembre 1663,* 24 folios

Dossier 12: *Information faite à Belle-Isle et Concarneau par le sieur Ayrault, Lieutenant criminel à Angers, 14 février 1663* . . . 17 folios
Dossier 14: *Confrontation faite à M Fouquet des témoins contre lui ouis à Belle-Isle, 30 avril 1663* . . . 13 folios

AP 61

Dossier 1: *Grosse du procès-verbal de consommation des traités de 1657, 9 août 1662 et jours suivants,* 56 folios
Dossier 3: *Procès-verbal de la consommation du traité passé en 1657 avec le sieur Jacquier pour plusieurs affaires de finance, 12 mai 1662,* 38 folios
Dossier 4: *Procès-verbal d'examen des billets expédiés par les Trésoriers de l'Epargne pour les ordonnances de remises d'intérêts pour prêts en l'année 1657, 18 août 1662,* 74 folios
Dossier 5: *Déclaration du 12 septembre 1662 par Jacques Morin,* 2 folios
Dossier 6: *Procès-verbal de la consommation du traité de l'aliénation de la moitié des octrois des villes, 29 avril 1662,* 5 folios
Dossier 7: *Déclaration du 11 octobre 1662 par Pierre Dalibert,* 3 folios
Dossier 8: *Déclaration du 7 octobre 1662 par Jean Doublet,* 2 folios
Dossier 9: *Déclaration du 2 août 1662 par Charles Séjourné,* 3 folios
Dossier 10: *Déclaration du 19 août 1662 par Louis Betault,* 4 folios
Dossier 11: *Interrogatoire de Pierre Dalibert, 21 août 1662,* 5 folios
Dossier 12: *Déclaration du 25 août 1662 par Jean Faverolles,* 2 folios
Dossier 13: *Déclaration du 11 septembre 1662 par Jean Frarin,* 8 folios
Dossier 14: *Déclaration du 4 octobre par Pierre Pidou,* 3 folios
Dossier 15: *Déclaration du 5 octobre 1662 par Gilles Hochereau,* 1 folio
Dossier 16: *Déclaration du 11 octobre 1662 par François Bousselin,* 1 folio
Dossier 17: *Déclaration du 11 octobre 1662 par Pierre Baron,* 2 folios
Dossier 18: *Déclaration du 12 octobre 1662 par Pierre Dalibert,* 2 folios
Dossier 19: *Déclaration du 19 décembre 1662 par Benjamin Pouget,* 2 folios
Dossier 20: *Déclaration du 19 décembre 1662 par Daniel Chartier,* 1 folio
Dossier 21: *Déclaration du 29 décembre 1662 par Rolland Gruin du Bouchet,* 1 folio
Dossier 22: *Déclaration du 29 décembre 1662 par Eustache Le Couturier,* 2 folios
Dossier 23: *Déclaration du 29 décembre 1662 par Samuel Guichon,* 2 folios
Dossier 24: *Déclaration du 30 décembre 1662 par Simon Le Noir,* 2 folios
Dossier 26: *Déclaration du 30 décembre 1662 par Jacques Sableau,* 1 folio
Dossier 28: *Déclaration du 30 décembre 1662 par Guillaume Languet,* 1 folio
Dossier 29: *Déclaration du 30 décembre 1662 par Martin Tabouret,* 1 folio
Dossier 30: *Déclaration du 30 décembre 1662 par Balthazar Rouveau,* 4 folios

AP 62

Dossier 1: *Procès-verbal de la consommation du traité passé par* . . . *Fouquet au mois d'octobre 1657 pour l'aliénation des 12 deniers pour livres sur les Tailles, 23 octobre 1662* . . ., 80 folios

Dossier 2: *Procès-verbal du traité de la revente du domaine de Bretagne en 1658, 16 octobre 1662* . . ., 17 folios

Dossier 3: *Déclaration du 17 octobre 1662 par Simon Lefebvre*, 13 folios

Dossier 11: *Déposition faite le 9 août 1662* . . . *par* . . . *César Collin, receveur des Tailles en l'élection d'Amiens*, 3 folios

Dossier 12: *Déposition faite le 11 août 1662 par* . . . *Collin*, 3 folios

Dossier 13: *Procès-verbal des Augmentations de gages des Secrétaires du Roi en 1658, 3 octobre 1662*, 8 folios

Dossier 14: *Procès-verbal de divers traités de finances supposés, 6 octobre 1662*, 43 folios

Dossier 15: *Procès-verbal de la consommation de plusieurs parties de rentes assignées sur les Cinq Grosses Fermes [en 1658], 10 octobre 1662*, 33 folios

Dossier 17: *Procès-verbal concernant le traité passé en 1658 avec les sieurs Monnerot, Jacquier et Hochereau pour le recouvrement de plusieurs taxes sur les officiers de greniers à sel, élections et autres, 30 octobre 1662*, 38 folios

Dossier 17 (*bis*): *Interrogatoire de Gilles Hochereau, 9 novembre 1662*, 14 folios

Dossier 18: *Procès-verbal de la consommation de diverses ordonnances pour billets réformés en 1658, 8 novembre 1662*, 146 folios

Dossier 19: *Interrogatoire de* . . . *Guillaume Audibert, commis au greffe du Conseil des Finances, 10 novembre 1662*, 18 folios

Dossier 20: *Interrogatoire de* . . . *Barthélemy Paris, commis au greffe du Conseil des Finances, 10 novembre 1662*, 27 folios

Dossier 21: *Interrogatoire de* . . . *Jean Rouvière, ancien commis de M Catelan, secrétaire du Conseil, commis de M Colbert, Intendant des Finances, 14 novembre 1662*, 13 folios

Dossier 22: *Interrogatoire de* . . . *Vincent le Nérat, secrétaire du Roi, ancien commis de M Catelan, 16 novembre 1662*, 7 folios

Dossier 24: *Déclarations* by Dominique Conbarré [Cambacarrès], Pierre Perrault, Pierre Bezard, Simon Lefebvre, Jean Gobin, Pierre Baron, Jean de Brie, Charles Gruin des Bordes, Jean Corné de la Vallée, Guillaume de Brisacier, Anne de Chambré, François Félix, Jacques Charpentier, Claude Coquille, la veuve de François Morice, Maucquereau, Bellassier, Pierre Dalibert, Adrien Bance, Vincent Duval, les héritiers de Georges Pelissari, Roland Gruin du Bouchet, and the *Secrétaires du Roi des différents collèges*

Dossier 26: *Interrogatoire de* . . . *François Jacquier* . . . *détenu au Fort L'Evêque, 4 janvier 1663*, 15 folios

Dossier 27: *Interrogatoire de* . . . *Nicolas Monnerot, Trésorier des Parties Casuelles*

AP 70

Dossier 1: *Documents sur les accusations contre Claude de Guénégaud* (nd)

Dossier 2: *Pièces imprimées au sujet des accusations contre le même*

Dossier 5: *Documents concernant les poursuites entamées par la Chambre de Justice contre Jacques Amproux sieur de Lorme* [Delorme]
Dossier 6: *Pièces diverses de procédure de la Chambre de Justice.* [NB *Concussions et fraudes commises dans les Cours des Monnaies*]

AP 71
Dossier 9: *Extraits de 38 comptes rendus à M Fouquet par M Bruant contenant les différentes sommes de deniers reçues et payées par les ordres ou pour le service du sieur Fouquet.* 12 folios

AP 73
Dossier 2: (a) *Interrogatoire de . . . Jean Corné de la Vallée, 2 août 1662,* 2 folios
    (b) *Interrogatoire de . . . Gruin du Bouchet, 21 août 1662,* 10 folios
    (c) *Interrogatoire de . . . Léon de Briou, 9 septembre 1662,* 2 folios
    (d) *Interrogatoire de Etienne Maugeais, 9 septembre 1662,* 3 folios
    (e) *Interrogatoire de . . . Claude Bavot, 25 septembre 1662,* 2 folios
Dossier 3: *Déclarations par Etienne Maugeais, Jacques Morin, Charles Séjourné, la veuve de Mons. Hiérosme de Nouveau, et autres*
Dossier 4: *Copies de documents produits par le procureur-général et par M Fouquet*

AP 74
Dossier 3: *Extraits par Olivier d'Ormesson des pièces produites par Fouquet, 13 pièces.* cf *pièce 3 (Extrait de l'état de menu de comptant du quartier d'octobre 1656)* and *pièce 6*
Dossier 4: *Copies de lettres:*
    (a) *de la main de M le cardinal de Mazarin à M Fouquet [A la Fère, 31 août 1655; A Compiègne, 11 mars 1655; A la Fère, 24 juillet 1656; 28 août 1660],*
    (b) *de Mazarin à Bernard, 26 février 1660,*
    (c) *de Bernard à Lespine, 18 mars 1660*
Dossier 5: *Etat de la recette et de la dépense du Royaume, 31 décembre 1648*

B ARCHIVES DU MINISTERE DES AFFAIRES ETRANGERES

Série: Mémoires et documents—FRANCE
167 *Officiers de la Couronne et de la Maison du Roi*
176 *Surintendants des Finances, Conseil du Roi, Secrétaires du Roi,* etc
187 *Ordres de Chevalerie*
188 *Ordre du Saint-Esprit*
189 *Ordre du Saint-Esprit*
203 *Cours Souveraines,* etc

819	State correspondence, 1635–6
820	„ „ , 1636
837	„ „ , 1640
894	„ „ , 1655
912	„ „ , 1661–2

C BRITISH MUSEUM

5423 e 16 *Arrêt de la Chambre de Justice, 29 décembre 1662*

D BIBLIOTHEQUE NATIONALE

1 *Collection Joly de Fleury*
2503 Trial of Fouquet
2 *Collection Moreau*
779 Trial of Fouquet
3 *Fonds Clairambault*
    443 Documents attacking Fouquet
    766 Documents on the *Chambres de Justice* of 1661 and 1716
  1081 cf fol 196—bullying by Fouquet's brothers
  1207 Documents on Fouquet's family
4 *Fonds Cinq Cents Colbert*
  (cited as 500 Colbert)
    194 *Réglements . . . du Conseil du Roi*
  228–37 [*Journal de la Chambre de Justice*]
  257–60 *Etats et évaluation par généralités de tous les officers . . . 1665*
5 *Fonds des manuscrits français*
  (cited as MS/MSS français)
  4222 *Règlements au fait des finances*
  4616 *Généalogies de quelques familles bourgeoises de Paris*
  7607 *Recueil de pièces secrètes communiquées à Fouquet pour servir à se défendre*
 7620–5 [Documents relating to the *Chambre de Justice* of 1661]
  7627 [Documents relating to the *Chambre de Justice* of 1661]
  7628 *Registres de la Chambre de Justice*
  7650 *Procès-verbal contenant les interrogatoires des prisonniers détenus dans les prisons de Paris . . . 1660*
  7655 *Dictionnaire des Bienfaits du Roi*
  7686 *Tissues envoyées des généralités du royaume à nosseigneurs les députés du royaume, assemblés en la Chambre du Trésor à Paris, commençant en l'année 1648. Recueillies et assemblées par Simon Fournival commis-général de nosdits seigneurs (1647–53)*
  7707 *Autorité et jurisdiction de la Chambre des Comptes et autres choses concernantes icelle registrées aux Mémoriaux. cf fols 52r ff: Officers reçus céans étants du corps de la Chambre, 1500–1648*
  7708 *Extraits des Mémoriaux de la Chambre des Comptes, registres D, G, H, I et E*

7716 *Correcteurs des comptes, suivant l'ordre de leurs réceptions, à commencer en 1410 jusques à présent [1756].* cf also fol 25r: *Clercs des Comptes depuis Auditeurs des Comptes par Edit de 1511, suivant l'ordre de leurs réceptions à commencer en 1296 jusqu'à présent [1756]*

7718 *Edits, déclarations, privilèges, lettres d'anoblissement et autres, registrés à la Cour des Aides, 1635–1716*

7719–23 *Extrait des registres de la Cour des Aides,* etc 1360–1779. cf in particular 7723: *Tableau Chronologique de tous les officiers de la Cour des Aides de Paris depuis son établissement*

10228–9 *Recueil de plusieurs pièces curieuses touchant les affaires du temps concernant M Fouquet et autres (1660–4)*

14018 [*Maîtres des Requêtes (1575–1722)*]

16226 *Conseil des Finances,* etc

16533 [Documents relating to (a) Creditors of Fouquet, (b) *Baux des Fermes,* (c) *Gabelles de France,* (d) *Rentes*]

17335 [Documents relating to *Rentes sur l'Hôtel de Ville* and *Gabelles*]

18158 [Documents relating to the *Conseil du Roi*]

18219 [*Alphabet des Traitants, 1631–53*]

18220 [*Alphabet de ceux sous les noms desquels l'on a fait des prêts au roi . . .; Etat par extrait de tous les prêts faits au Conseil du Roi, 1640–8*]

18221–7 Treaties and Loans, 1653–9

18228 *Etat sommaire des traités et prêts qui ont été faits au Conseil du Roi pour chaque année (1655–9)*

18239 *Secrétaires du Roi*

18423 [Documents on the *Chambre de Justice* including material relating to (a) Activities of agents of the *Chambre* in the provinces, (b) the trial of *Claude de Guénégaud, Trésorier de Epargne,* (c) criminal proceedings against the heirs of Guillaume Languet]

22437 Includes documents on the Guise in the late sixteenth century

23945 *Etat au vrai des recettes et dépenses . . . de la maison de la reine-mère du roi, faites par M Etienne Jeannot de Bartillat . . . durant l'année 1653*

6 *MSS français, nouvelles acquisitions*
   (cited as MSS français na)

na 9735 Documents on financial institutions

7 *Mélanges de Colbert*

107 *bis* Lettres to Colbert about Fouquet. [Undated but presumably of early 1662] eg fol 1157r: *Créatures de Fouquet dans la marine*

8 *Pièces originales*

35, Entry 742 D'Alibert
87, Entry 1803 Ardier
270, Entry 5906 Bellinzani
312, Entry 6844 Berthelot
408, Entry 9101 Bonneau à Tours et à Paris

419, Entry 9373   Bordier
426, Entry 9623   Bossuet
585, Entry 13546   Canaye
618, Entry 14522   Catelan
850, Entry 19041   Coquille à Paris
861, Entry 19320   Cornuel
1019, Entry 23321   Doublet
1019, Entry 23322   Doublet
1194, Entry 26976   Forcoal
1281, Entry 28835   Gargan
1284, Entry 28894   Garnier à Paris
1284, Entry 28897   Garnier de Salins
1284, Entry 28898   Garnier de Mauricet
1268, Entry 28504   Galland
1331, Entry 30128   Girardin
1998, Entry 45862   Monnerot

9 *Fonds Thoisy* [BN Réserve]
147–52   Tax-farms, war-contracting and financiers
156   Trial of the *Trésoriers de l'Epargne*, and others
157   Various *Chambres de Justice* 1606/7–1661/5, etc
158–9   Trial of Fouquet
160   Venality of officers, *Droit annuel, Taille*, etc
396   Organisation of tax-farms, *Correction des Comptes*
397   Bourgoin [*La Chasse aux Larrons*; *Le Pressoir des Eponges du Roi*], *Chambres de Justice* of 1648, 1661, etc, *Défenses* of Boislève, Catelan, provincial affairs of the *Chambre de Justice* of 1661–5, etc etc
400–3   Trial of Fouquet
404   War-contractors and provincial affairs of *Chambre de Justice* of 1661–5

10 *Imprimés*
Série in 4to F 23703, *Arrêts du Grand Conseil*

E MINUTIER CENTRAL DES ARCHIVES NOTARIALES

Etude 51
279   (*Liasse Cornuel*)
280   (*Dernière liasse des Gabelles, 1655–8*)
504   (1640)
505   (1640)
521   (1648)
522   (1648)
522 *bis* (1649)
523   (1649)
530   (1652)
544   (1657)
548   (1659)

549   (1659)
554   (1662)

CONTEMPORARY JOURNALS, MEMOIRS, LETTERS, ETC

Bossuet, J. B. *Oeuvres choisies.* (5 vols Paris 1903–4)

Bourgoin, Jean. *La chasse aux larrons, ou avant-coureur de l'histoire de la chambre de justice. Des livres du bien public; et autres oeuvres faites pour la recherche des financiers et de leurs fauteurs.* (Paris 1618)

——. *Le pressoir des éponges du roi, ou épître liminaire de l'histoire de la chambre de justice établie l'an 1607, pour la recherche des abus, malversations et péculats commis ès finances de sa majesté.* (Paris 1623)

Callières, Jacques de. *La fortune des gens de qualité, et les gentilshommes particuliers. Enseignant l'art de vivre à la cour, suivant les maximes de la politique et de la morale.* (Paris 1664)

Caquets de l'Accouchée (Les), 1623 (ed Marpon et Flammarion. Paris 1890)

Chéruel, P. A. and Avenel, G. d' (eds). *Lettres de Mazarin.* (9 vols Paris 1872–1906)

Choisy, F. T. de. *Mémoires pour servir à l'histoire de Louis XIV.* Ed Petitot and Monmerqué, *Collection de mémoires relatifs à l'histoire de France,* 63: 155–277. (Paris 1828)

Clément, P. (ed). *Lettres instructions et mémoires de Colbert.* (7 vols Paris 1861–82)

Etat de la France, 1650. Ed Pinson de la Marinière [Martinière]. (Paris 1650)

Fouquet, Nicolas. *Défenses.*
    The *Défenses* appeared in two collected editions:
    (i) 15 vols *sans lieu* (Amsterdam), 1665–8
    (ii) 16 vols Paris 1696
    For further bibliographical details, cf Kerviler, *Biobibliographie Bretonne,* 14: 283

Furetière, A. *Le roman bourgeois* 1666. (ed F. Tulov. Paris 1919)

Lecestre, L. (ed). *Mémoires de Gourville.* (2 vols Paris 1894)

Loyseau, C. *Cinq livres du droit des offices.* (Paris 1613)

——. *Traité des ordres et simples dignités.* (Paris 1613)

Moreau, C. *Choix de Mazarinades.* (2 vols Paris 1853)

Nouveau style des finances (Le). (Paris 1629)

Ormesson, Olivier Lefebvre d'. *Journal.* (ed Chéruel. 2 vols Paris 1860–1)

Saint-Simon, *Mémoires.* (ed A. de Boislisle, L. Lecestre, J. de Boislisle. 43 vols 2nd impression, Paris 1923–8)

SECONDARY WORKS

André, L. *Michel Le Tellier et l'organisation de l'armée monarchique.* (Paris 1906)

Antoine, M., Buffet, H.-F., Clémencet, S., Ferry, F. de, Langlois, M.,

Lanhers, Y., Laurent, J.-P., Meurgey de Tupigny, J. *Guide des recherches dans les fonds judiciaires de l'ancien régime.* (Paris 1958)

Ariès, P. *L'enfant et la vie familiale sous l'ancien régime.* (Paris 1960). See also English translation of the above by R. Baldick under the title *Centuries of Childhood.* (1962)

Aston, T. (ed) *Crisis in Europe 1540–1640.* (1965)

Audouin, F. *Histoire de l'administration de la guerre.* (4 vols Paris 1811)

Avenel, G. d'. *Richelieu et la monarchie absolue.* (4 vols Paris 1884–90)

——. *La fortune privée à travers sept siècles.* (Paris 1895)

Babelon, J.-P. *Demeures parisiennes sous Henri IV et Louis XIII.* (Paris 1965)

Badalo-Dulong, Claude. *Banquier du Roi; Barthélemy Hervart (1606–1667).* (Paris 1951)

Bailly, Antoine. *Histoire financière de la France depuis les origines de la monarchie jusqu'à la fin de 1786.* (2 vols Paris 1830)

Beaulieu, E. P. *Les gabelles sous Louis XIV.* (Paris 1903)

Behrens, C. B. A. *The Ancien Regime.* (1967)

Betcherman, Lita-Rose. 'Balthazar Gerbier—a Renaissance man in early Stuart England.' (Unpublished PhD dissertation, 1968. Toronto University Library)

Bitton, D. *The French Nobility in Crisis 1540–1640.* (Stanford 1969)

Blet, Pierre. *Le clergé de France et la monarchie. Etude sur les assemblées générales du clergé de 1615 à 1666.* (2 vols Rome 1959) [*Analecta Gregoriana,* 106, 107]

Bloch, M. *Les caractères originaux de l'histoire rurale française.* (2 vols Paris 1931–56)

Bluche, F. *L'origine des magistrats du Parlement de Paris au XVIIIe siècle.* (Paris 1956)

——. 'L'origine sociale des secrétaires d'état de Louis XIV.' *XVIIe siècle,* nos 42–3 (1959)

——. *Les magistrats du parlement de Paris au XVIIIe siècle (1715–1771).* (Paris 1960)

Blunt, A. *Art and Architecture in France 1500–1800.* (1953)

Boislisle, A. de. *La chambre des comptes de Paris—pièces justificatives pour servir à l'histoire des premiers présidents, 1506–1791.* (Nogent-le-Rotrou 1873)

Boislisle, Jean de. *Mémoriaux du Conseil de 1661.* (3 vols Paris 1905–7)

Bonnaffée, E. *Les amateurs de l'ancienne France. Le surintendant Fouquet.* (Paris/London 1882)

Bosher, J. F. *The Single Duty Project.* (1964)

——. *French Finances 1770–1795: From Business to Bureaucracy.* (Cambridge 1970)

Bottineau, Y. 'La cour de Louis XIV à Fontainebleau.' *XVIIe siècle,* no 24 (1954)

Boulenger, M. *Mazarin, soutien de l'état.* (Paris 1929)

Bourgeois, E. and André, L. *Les sources de l'histoire de France,* part 3, vols 11–18: 'Le dix-septième siècle (1610–1715).' (Paris 1913–35)

Bouvier, J. and Germain-Martin, H. *Finances et financiers de l'ancien régime.* (Paris 1964)

Bresson, J. *Histoire financière de la France depuis l'origine de la monarchie jusqu'à 1828.* (2 vols Paris 1857)

Buisseret, D. *Sully.* (1968)

Cans, Albert, *L'organisation financière du clergé de France.* (Paris 1909)

Cauwès, Paul Louis. 'Les commencements du crédit public en France. Les rentes sur l'Hôtel de Ville au XVIe siècle.' *Revue d'économie politique,* 10 (1896)

Charléty, S. 'Le régime douanier de Lyon au dix-septième siècle.' *Revue d'histoire de Lyon,* 1 (1902)

Charmeil, J.-P. *Les trésoriers de France à l'époque de la Fronde.* (Paris 1964)

Châtelain, U. V. *Le surintendant Fouquet, protecteur des lettres, des arts et des sciences.* (Paris 1905)

Chauleur, A. 'Le rôle des traitants dans l'administration financière de la France de 1643 à 1653.' *XVIIe siècle,* no 65 (1964)

Chérot, H. [Review of Lair's book on Fouquet.] *Revue des questions historiques,* 49 (1891)

Chéruel, P. A. *Mémoires sur la vie publique et privée de Fouquet, surintendant des finances, d'après ses lettres et des pièces inédites conservées à la Bibliothèque Impériale.* (2 vols Paris 1862)

——. *Saint-Simon considéré comme historien de Louis XIV.* (Paris 1865)

——. *Histoire de France pendant la minorité de Louis XIV.* (4 vols Paris 1879–80).

——. *Histoire de France sous le ministère de Mazarin.* (3 vols Paris 1882)

——. *Dictionnaire historique des institutions, moeurs et coutumes de la France.* (7th edition. 2 vols Paris 1899)

Christ, Y. and others. *Le Marais.* (Paris, 1964)

Clamageran, J. J. *Histoire de l'impôt en France.* (3 vols Paris 1867–76)

Clément, P. *Histoire de la vie et de l'administration de Colbert, contrôleur-général des finances . . . précédée d'une étude historique sur Nicolas Fouquet, surintendant des finances, suivie de pièces justificatives, lettres et documents inédits.* (Paris 1846)

——. *Histoire de Colbert et de son administration.* (2nd edition. 2 vols Paris 1874)

Cobban, A. B. 'The Vocabulary of Social History'. *Political Science Quarterly,* 71 (1956)

——. *A History of Modern France.* (2nd edition. 3 vols 1965)

Dareste de la Chavanne, A. E. C. *Histoire de l'administration en France et des progrès du pouvoir royal depuis le règne de Philippe-Auguste jusqu'à la mort de Louis XIV.* (2 vols Paris 1848)

De La Chenaye des Bois, F. A. A., and Badier. *Dictionnaire de la noblesse.* (3rd edition. 19 vols Paris 1863–76)

Delort, J. *Histoire de la détention des philosophes et des gens de lettres à la Bastille et à Vincennes, précédée de celle de Fouquet, de Pellisson et de Lauzun.* (3 vols Paris 1829)

Dent, C. A. 'The French Church and the Monarchy in the Reign of

Louis XIV.' (Unpublished PhD dissertation, 1967. London University Library)

Dent, J. 'The Financial Administration of the French Monarchy 1653–61.' Unpublished PhD dissertation, 1965. London University Library)

———. 'An Aspect of the Crisis of the Seventeenth Century: the Collapse of the Financial Administration of the French Monarchy (1653–61).' *Economic History Review* (2nd series), 20 (1967)

———. 'The role of Clientèles in the financial elite of France under Cardinal Mazarin.' (To appear in a volume of essays in memory of Prof A. B. Cobban)

Depping, G. 'Un banquier protestant en France au XVIIe siècle. Barthélemy Hervart.' *Revue historique*, 10 and 11 (1879)

Dickson, P. G. M. *The Financial Revolution in England: a Study in the Development of Public Credit 1688–1756.* (1967)

Diderot D. and Alembert, J. le R. d' (eds). *Encyclopédie ou dictionnaire raisonné des sciences, des arts et des métiers, par une société de gens de lettres.* (17 vols Paris 1751–65)

Doolin, P. R. *The Fronde.* (Cambridge, Mass 1935)

Doucet, R. *Finances municipales et crédit public à Lyon au XVIe siècle.* (Paris 1937)

———. *Les institutions de la France au XVIe siècle.* (2 vols Paris 1948)

Dupont-Ferrier, E. M. J. G. *Nouvelles études sur les institutions financières à la fin du moyen âge.* (Paris 1933)

Eccles, W. J. *The Canadian Frontier.* (New York 1969)

Encyclopédie méthodique, Finances. (3 vols Paris 1784)

Eon de Beaumont, C. G. L. A. A. T. d'. *Essai historique sur les différentes situations de la France par rapport aux finances sous le règne de Louis XIV et la régence du duc d'Orléans.* (Amsterdam 1753)

Esmonin, E. *La taille en Normandie au temps de Colbert (1661–1673).* (Paris 1913)

———. *Etudes sur la France des XVIIe et XVIIIe siècles.* (Paris 1964)

Fage, R. *Etats de la vicomté de Turenne.* (2 vols Paris 1894)

Feillet, A. *La misère au temps de la Fronde et Saint Vincent-de-Paul ou un chapitre de l'histoire du paupérisme en France.* (Paris 1862)

Ferrière, C. de. *Corps et compilation de tous les commentateurs anciens et modernes sur la coutume de Paris.* (4 vols Paris 1714)

Floquet, A. *Etudes sur la vie de Bossuet (1627–1670).* (3 vols Paris 1855)

Forbonnais, F. V. D. de. *Recherches et considérations sur les finances de France depuis 1595 jusqu'à 1721.* (2 vols Bâle 1758)

Ford, F. L. *Robe and Sword.* (Cambridge, Mass 1953)

———. *Strasbourg in Transition.* (New York 1966)

Friedmann, A. *Paris, ses rues, ses paroisses du moyen âge à la révolution.* (Paris 1959)

Funck-Brentano, F. *Les lettres de cachet à Paris. Etude suivie d'une liste des prisonniers de la Bastille (1659–1789).* (Paris 1903)

Gioffre, D. *Gênes et les foires de change de Lyon à Besançon.* (Paris 1960)

Goubert, P. *Beauvais et le Beauvaisis au XVIIe siècle.* (Paris 1960)
———. *Louis XIV et vingt millions de français.* (Paris 1966)
Griselle, E. *Formulaire de lettres de François Ier à Louis XIV et Etat de la France dressé en 1642.* (Paris 1919)
Hatton, R. *Europe in the Age of Louis XIV.* (1969)
Hautecoeur, L. *Histoire de l'architecture classique en France.* (7 vols Paris 1943–57)
Henry, L. *Manuel de démographie historique.* (Geneva/Paris 1967)
Hexter, J. H. *Reappraisals in History.* (London, 1961)
Hillairet, J. *Dictionnaire historique des rues de Paris.* (2 vols Paris 1963)
———. *La rue de Richelieu.* (Paris 1966)
Hollingsworth, T. H. *Historical Demography.* (New York 1969)
Huyard, E. *L'affaire Fouquet.* (Paris 1937)
Jacquart, J. 'La Fronde des Princes dans la région parisienne et ses conséquences matérielles.' *Revue d'histoire moderne et contemporaine,* 7 (1960)
Joubleau, F. *Etudes sur Colbert ou exposition du système d'économie politique suivi en France de 1661 à 1683.* (2 vols Paris 1856)
Jougla de Morénas, H. *Grand armorial de France; Catalogue des armoiries des familles nobles de France.* (6 vols Paris 1934–49)
Kerviler, R. *Répertoire général de bio-bibliographie bretonne; Livre I, Les Bretons.* (17 vols Rennes 1886–1908). cf 14: 276–304 on the Fouquet family
Kossmann, E. H. *La Fronde.* (Leiden 1954)
Labatut, J.-P. 'Situation sociale du quartier du Marais pendant la Fronde parlementaire 1648–9.' *XVIIe siècle,* no 38 (1958)
———. 'Aspects de la fortune de Bullion.' *XVIIe siècle,* no 60 (1963)
Lair, J. A. *Nicolas Fouquet, procureur-général, surintendant des finances, ministre d'état de Louis XIV.* (2 vols Paris 1890)
La Roncière, C. de. *Le vrai crime du surintendant Fouquet.* (Paris 1914)
Laslett, P. *The World we have lost.* (1965)
Lavisse, E. (ed). *Histoire de France depuis les origines jusqu'à la Révolution.* (9 vols Paris 1900–11)
Le Roy Ladurie, E. *Les paysans de Languedoc.* (Paris 1966)
Loirette, F. 'L'administration royale en Béarn de l'union à l'intendance (1620–1682): Essai sur le rattachement à la France d'une province frontière', *XVIIe siècle,* no 65 (1964)
Lublinskaya, A. D. *French Absolutism: the crucial phase, 1620–1629.* (Cambridge 1968)
Mallet, J. R. *Comptes rendus de l'administration des finances du royaume de France pendant les onze dernières années de Henri IV, le règne de Louis XIII, et soixante-cinq années de celui de Louis XIV.* (London/Paris 1789)
Marion, M. *Dictionnaire des institutions de la France aux XVIIe et XVIIIe siècles.* (Paris 1923)
Martin, G.-L. *Le surintendant Fouquet et les opérations du crédit public.* (Paris 1914)

Martin, G.-L. and Bezançon, M. *Histoire du crédit en France sous le règne de Louis XIV.* vol 1, 'Le crédit public'. (Paris 1913)

Matthews, G. T. *The Royal General Farms in Eighteenth Century France.* (New York 1958)

Méthivier, H. *Le siècle de Louis XIV.* (Paris 1962)

———. *Le siècle de Louis XIII.* (Paris 1964)

Meuvret, J. 'Circulation monétaire et utilisation économique de la monnaie dans la France du XVIe siècle et du XVIIe siècle.' *Etudes d'histoire moderne et contemporaine,* 1 (1947)

———. 'Comment les français du XVIIe siècle voyaient l'impôt.' *XVIIe siècle,* nos 25–6 (1955)

Michaud, H. *La grande chancellerie et les écritures royales au seizième siècle (1515–1589).* (Paris 1967)

Milne, P. *L'impôt des aides sous l'ancien régime (1360–1791).* (Paris 1908)

Mongrédien, G. *L'affaire Fouquet.* (Paris 1956)

Moore, B. *Social Origins of Dictatorship and Democracy: Lord and Peasant in the Making of the Modern World.* (Boston 1967)

Moote, A. L. 'The Parlementary Fronde and Seventeenth Century Robe Solidarity.' *French Historical Studies,* 2 (1962)

———. *The Revolt of the Judges: the Parlement of Paris and the Fronde 1643–1652.* (Princeton 1971)

Moreau de Beaumont, J. L. *Mémoires concernant les impositions et droits en Europe et en France.* (2 pts in 4 vols Paris 1768–9) [2nd edition, augmented. 5 vols Paris 1787–9]

Mousnier, R. *La vénalité des offices sous Henri IV et Louis XIII.* (Rouen 1945)

———. 'Le conseil du roi de la mort de Henri IV au gouvernement personnel de Louis XIV.' *Etudes d'histoire moderne et contemporaine,* 1 (1947)

———. *Les XVIe et XVIIe siècles. Les progrès de la civilisation européenne et le déclin de l'orient (1492–1715).* (Paris 1954)

———. 'Comment les français du XVIIe siècle voyaient la constitution.' *XVIIe siècle,* nos 25–6 (1955)

———. 'Recherches sur les soulèvements populaires avant la Fronde.' *Revue d'histoire moderne et contemporaine,* 5 (1958)

———. 'Recherches sur les syndicats d'officiers pendant la Fronde. Trésoriers-généraux de France et élus dans la révolution.' *XVIIe siècle,* nos 42–3 (1959)

———. 'L'évolution des institutions monarchiques en France et ses relations avec l'état social.' *XVIIe siècle,* nos 58–9 (1963)

———. *Lettres et mémoires adressés au Chancelier Séguier (1633–1649).* (2 vols Paris 1964)

———, *Fureurs paysannes: les paysans dans les révoltes du XVIIe siècle.* (Paris 1967)

———, *La plume, la faucille et le marteau: institutions et société en France du moyen âge à la Révolution.* (Paris 1970)

Mousnier, R. et Hartung, F. 'Quelques problèmes concernant la monarchie absolue.' *Comitato Internazionale di scienze storiche, X congresso, 1955, Relazioni,* 4

Mousnier, R., Labatut, J.-P., and Durand, Y. *Problèmes de stratification sociale—Deux cahiers de la noblesse 1649–1651.* (Paris 1965)

Normand, C. *La bourgeoisie française au XVIIe siècle; la vie publique, les idées et les actions politiques (1604–1661).* (Paris 1908)

O'Connell, D. P. *Richelieu.* (1968)

Pagès, G. *La monarchie d'ancien régime en France.* (Paris 1932)

——. 'Essai sur l'évolution des institutions administratives en France du commencement du XVIe siècle à la fin du XVIIe siècle.' *Revue d'histoire moderne,* 7 (1932)

Peignot, E. G. *Documents authentiques et détails curieux sur les dépenses de Louis XIV.* (Paris 1827)

Pfnor, R. and France, A. *Le château de Vaux-le-Vicomte dessiné et gravé.* (Paris 1888)

Porchnev, B. *Les soulèvements populaires en France de 1623 à 1648.* (Paris 1963) (French translation of the original Russian edition of 1948. See also German translation as *Die Volkaufstände in Frankreich vor der Fronde 1623–1648.* Leipzig 1954)

Rabb, T. K. *Enterprise and Empire: Merchant and Gentry Investment in the Expansion of England, 1575–1630.* (Cambridge, Mass 1967)

Ranum, O. A. *Richelieu and the Councillors of Louis XIII.* (Oxford 1963)

Ravaisson-Mollien, F. *Archives de la Bastille. Documents inédits recueillis et publiés par . . .* (17 vols Paris 1886, etc)

Rebillon, A. *Les états de Bretagne de 1661 à 1789. Leur organisation, l'évolution de leurs pouvoirs, leur administration financière.* (Paris/Rennes 1932)

Rich, E. E. and Wilson, C. H. (eds). *The Cambridge Economic History of Europe,* vol 4, 'The Economy of expanding Europe in the sixteenth and seventeenth centuries'. (Cambridge 1967)

Richer, A. *Les vies des surintendants des finances et contrôleurs-généraux.* (3 vols Paris 1790)

Robin, P. *La compagnie des secrétaires du roi.* (Paris 1933)

Rosenberg, H. *Bureaucracy, Aristocracy and Autocracy: the Prussian experience.* (Cambridge, Mass 1958)

Rothkrug, L. *Opposition to Louis XIV: the Political and Social Origins of the French Enlightenment.* (Princeton 1965)

Roupnel, G. *La ville et la campagne au XVIIe siècle. Etudes sur les populations du pays dijonnais.* (Paris 1955)

Rousset, C. *Histoire de Louvois et de son administration politique et militaire.* (4 vols Paris 1862–4)

Schnapper, B. *Les rentes au XVIe siècle.* (Paris 1957)

Shennan, J. H. *The Parlement of Paris.* (1968)

Steinberg, S. H. *The Thirty Years War.* (1966)

Stone, L. *The Crisis of the Aristocracy 1558–1641.* (Oxford 1965)

Stourm, R. *Les cours des finances. Le budget, son histoire et son mécanisme.* (Paris 1899)

Sutherland, N. M. *The French Secretaries of State in the Age of Catherine de Medici*. (London 1962)

Tapié, V. L. 'Les XVIe et XVIIe siècles de Roland Mousnier.' *XVIIe siècle*, no 23 (1954)

Taylor, G. V. 'Types of capitalism in eighteenth-century France.' *English Historical Review*, 79 (1964)

——. 'Noncapitalist wealth and the origins of the French Revolution.' *American Historical Review*, 72 (1967)

Tilly, C. *The Vendée*. (Cambridge, Mass 1964)

——. 'Food Supply and Public Order in Modern Europe' (to appear in *The Building of States in Western Europe*)

Vilar-Berrogain, G. *Guide des recherches dans les fonds d'enregistrement sous l'ancien régime*. (Paris 1958)

Viollet, P. *Le roi et ses ministres pendant les trois derniers siècles de la monarchie*. (Paris 1912)

Vührer, A. *Histoire de la dette publique en France*. (2 vols Paris 1886)

Vuitry, A. *Etudes sur le régime financier de la France*. (3 vols Paris 1878)

——. *Le désordre des finances et les excès de spéculation à la fin du règne de Louis XIV et au commencement du règne de Louis XV*. (Paris 1885)

Wallace-Hadrill, J. M. and McManners, J. (eds). *France: government and society*. (1957)

Wilson, C. H. *England's Apprenticeship 1603–1763*. (1965)

——. *Anglo-Dutch Commerce and Finance in the eighteenth century*. (Cambridge 1966)

Wolf, J. B. 'The formation of a king.' *French Historical Studies*, 1 (1958)

——. *Louis XIV*. (New York 1968)

Wrigley, E. A. *Population and History*. (New York 1969)

Zeller, G. *Les institutions du XVIe siècle*. (Paris 1948)

Acknowledgements

It would be impossible for me to record here the names of all those people and institutions whose assistance I have had in the writing of this book. At the top of any list, however, must come the late Professor A. B. Cobban, who was first a patient and helpful supervisor of my graduate work, and later a source of advice and encouragement. I have been much indebted to Professor Charles Tilly for his counsel on ways of handling the more complicated aspects of the second part of the book. I am grateful to M l'Ambassadeur de France Wladimir d'Ormesson for permission to consult documents from the archives of his family, and to Maître Etienne Tonnellier for permission to consult documents in Etude 51 of the notaries of Paris. I have had help from friends at the Institute of Historical Research, at University College London, and at the Universities of Toronto and Chicago; and particularly from John Bosher, Natalie Z. Davis, William J. Eccles, Richard M. Saunders and N. M. Sutherland. The librarians and archivists of the following institutions have been of great help: in Paris, the Archives du ministère des affaires étrangères, Archives nationales, Bibliothèque nationale and Minutier central des archives notariales; in London, the British Museum, Institute of Historical Research, University College London and University of London; and, in North America, the Sigmund Samuel Library, Toronto, and the Newberry Library, Chicago. I should like to thank the following people and institutions for financial help in my research: the Master and Fellows of Peterhouse, Cambridge; the trustees of the Nathan Scholarship of the British Institute in Paris; the trustees of the Central Research Fund of the University of London; the University of

275

Toronto; the Canada Council. Most of all, my thanks go to my wife, Cynthia Ann, an acute and knowledgeable critic.

                                                                J.D.

Index

Figures in bold denote main references

QUEEN MARY
COLLEGE
LIBRARY